LINDA STRADLING

PRODUCTION
MANAGEMENT
FOR TV AND
FILM

THE PROFESSIONAL'S GUIDE

methuen | drama

Methuen Drama

1 3 5 7 9 10 8 6 4 2

Copyright © Linda Stradling 2010

Linda Stradling has asserted her right under the Copyright, Designs and Patents Act, 1988 to be identified as the author of this work.

Methuen Drama
A & C Black Publishers Limited
36 Soho Square
London W1D 3QY
www.methuendrama.com

A CIP catalogue record for this book is available from the British Library.

ISBN: 978 1 408 12180 1

Printed and bound by Martins the Printers, Berwick-upon-Tweed

Contents

⌨ The Methuen Drama website, www.methuendrama.com, contains accompanying material, which can be viewed by clicking on the Extras tab on the book page.

Acknowledgements

I am very much indebted to a number of people in the television industry whom I have had the good fortune to work with during my career, and whose experience and knowledge I have plundered shamelessly.

My sincere thanks go to:

Julie Clark for all her hard work during a busy summer writing the brilliant chapter on drama, from which I learned masses!

Ness Tovell for a huge contribution to the chapter on setting up shoots.

Ngoki Ubaka and **Helen Kelsey** for reading and feedback.

Bennetta Adamson for her very thoughtful case study on ethics and dealing with interviewees.

Elly Bradburn and **Mike Sanders** at the Edit Store for their guidance and input on post production.

The chapter on CGI could not have been written without the huge collaborative contribution of **Mike Davis**, for which I am extremely grateful.

Paul Gardner, Archive Producer, for sharing his passion and vast knowledge in his interview on archive and copyright.

Very grateful thanks to **PC**.

Jenny Mauthe and **Pete Hirst** for their help with the chapter on deliverables, and Jenny also for her input into the Health & Safety chapter.

Ulla Streib, Head of Operations at Darlow Smithson Productions for allowing me to reproduce the best cost book ever invented.

Emma Parsons, for her help on H&S and also for work above and beyond the call of duty in checking the cost monitor.

Simon Anderson from Audio Network for his scrupulously fair and hugely informative chapter on music copyright.

Mike Coles for his fully comprehensive camera format list.

Phil Bax for the equally comprehensive sound format list.

Richard Moore at Media Insurance for all his kind help on the insurance chapter, and for saving my professional bacon on more than one occasion!

Ceri Smith, for assistance with holiday pay calculation.

Barry Kim at PACT for her advice and wise counsel over many years.

Janet Watson for her flair, imagination and positive feedback.

Neal O'Keefe, Programme Manager at Channel 4 for help on deliverables.

Mark Vermaat at Silvermouse for information and help about their organisation.

Bapty & Company for kind help on weaponry.

Leon Goswell at London Underground Film Office and **Sue Hayes** at Film London.

Greg Lanning, mentor, who taught me so much about people and their funny little ways.

And finally, but very importantly, **Caroline Fleming** who runs the PMA so efficiently and with such a wicked sense of humour.

Introduction

A man in a hot air balloon realised he was lost. He reduced altitude and spotted a woman below. He descended a bit more and shouted, 'Excuse me, but can you help? I promised a friend I would meet him an hour ago, but I don't know where I am.'

The woman replied, 'You are in a hot air balloon hovering approximately 30 feet above the ground. You are between 40 and 41 degrees north latitude and between 59 and 60 degrees west longitude.'

'You must be a production manager,' said the balloonist.

'I am,' replied the woman. 'How did you know?'

'Well,' answered the balloonist, 'everything you told me is technically correct, but I have no idea what to make of your information, and the fact is I am still lost. Frankly, you've not been much help so far.'

The woman below responded, 'You must be a producer.'

'I am,' replied the balloonist, 'but how did you know?'

'Well,' said the woman, 'you don't know where you are or where you are going. You have risen to where you are due to a large quantity of hot air. You made a promise which you have no idea how to keep, and you expect me to solve the problem. The fact is you are in exactly the same position you were in before we met, but now, somehow, it's my fault.'

I don't know where the above anecdote, joke, call it what you will, originated from, but most production managers have heard it and love it. If it seems a trifle cynical, well, it probably is, but I make no apology for it – so there!

I'd just like to say a couple of things about the book that follows. Firstly, I have been hugely privileged to work in the television industry for twenty-odd years and the opinions and working practices outlined in this book are my own, very personal response to situations I have found myself in. Much of what I have learned has come about in response to disasters, calamities and bad experiences – one learns more from negative situations, I find, than from when things go right. I have tried to outline what I consider to be good business practices, which sometimes take longer than the short cuts that we take when we're in a tight corner. As my old mum used to say, don't do as I do, do as I say!

But the main point I'd like to make is that, despite all the hard work, stress, unsociable hours, insufferable egos, cock-ups, disasters, tight budgets, un-doable schedules and problems that will undoubtedly dog your efforts during your working career as a production manager, the satisfaction of doing a job well and producing a great programme or series on time and on budget will be unmatched. It will also – especially if you help the process along – be bloody good fun. And what more can a mere job offer you?

Linda Stradling

1 The role of the production manager in documentary and factual projects

Lots of what production managers do is common sense – though often, sense is not so common – and attention to detail. In fact, attention to detail to the point of being anal. The key word is organisation. The following chapter refers mainly to documentary and factual projects; for guidance on working in drama, please see Julie Clark's excellent chapter which follows.

What is production management? Well, how about facilitating a project so that it gets made smoothly, efficiently, properly, on budget and within the schedule. We need to ensure that everything from budgeting and setting up the team through to delivery is as problem-free as possible.

There will undoubtedly be cock-ups – but as long as you can think on your feet, you can cope. The following are some key qualities required by the job.

Anticipation
Looking ahead as you move through the project to anticipate what the various team members are going to need, putting the necessary measures in place, and anticipating possible problems before they occur. This becomes easier the more experienced you become.

Facilitating
Ensuring that all team members have easy access to what they need – be it stationery or contact details, courier booking numbers or purchase orders, call sheets and tech specs for the edit.

Communication
Talking to people constantly and passing on information to everyone who needs it (for example, the editor *and* the director will need a set of interview transcripts in the edit). Make sure that you sit right in the middle of your team so that you can overhear what is

going on too – eavesdropping is a useful tool for when people forget to mention the huge spend they are about to commit to or the recce (a location visit – see also pp. 92–3) they are planning. Consider yourself the conduit for information and hold regular meetings (Monday mornings are a good time, but keep it brief) with your production team so that you know what everyone is doing in the coming week, and can see where additional help might be needed and guidance given.

Lubrication!

Oiling the wheels of social intercourse so that colleagues, even if they don't particularly like each other, can work together efficiently. Team-building events of any kind; lunches, picnics, afternoon tea – whatever is appropriate. Alcohol helps. But leave it until after work.

Diplomacy

Being able to coax, encourage, wheedle or bollock where necessary, to get things done properly and on time. And a word here about playing to people's strengths and recognising their weaknesses – if you know that a director is great at directing but hopeless in the edit, try and make the most of their skills by giving them two shows to direct back-to-back and getting someone else to run their edits. Explain as you do that their directing skills are so amazing that you want to make the most of them and not waste precious time merely editing. This may also make it possible to give that good assistant producer (AP) a golden opportunity to edit a show along with an experienced editor.

Flexibility

Things will change as you move through your project and they will go wrong despite your best efforts. But you need to take changes in your stride (smiling as you unpick a schedule that's taken you days to put together!), handle stress and errors without panicking and minimise the fall-out. Save the blame-game for later and concentrate on getting things back on track.

Professionalism

Never be afraid to ask questions and check things. Consult all the experts you can find and try always to maintain a professional attitude when meltdown is going on around you. Courtesy at all times – ask instead of tell.

A sense of humour

Possibly your most useful tool. It's only telly! Step back, take a deep breath and keep a sense of perspective. Losing your temper is not going to fix it – though sometimes a strategically placed tantrum can remind colleagues that your patience is finite. But if you can laugh (eventually!) about it and then carry on you will save yourself and others a huge amount of energy and stress.

Confidence

The confidence to ask questions when you don't know the answers, and to say 'I don't know, but I'll find out'. There are so many elements to the job that you can never hope to be an expert in all areas, but if you know the right person to ask then you can always learn. You can find experts you need by scanning relevant websites, checking out a production guide or, better still, asking someone who has the relevant experience – often another production manager whom you can track down by scrolling through the Production Managers Association membership list.

The production manager's most useful tools

Call me old-fashioned, but I still think a piece of paper is a useful item to have, just in case the computer crashes and burns and everything is electronically wiped out. You need to leave some sort of trail so that if you are absent for any reason someone else can find out what they need to know. If paper is not your style then just make sure you keep everything clearly labelled and filed on your computer's hard drive. (Back it up regularly and keep a memory stick at home for safety.)

Keeping things noted down helps the memory when it gets overloaded and spontaneously combusts. For example, I always work with a hard-backed A4-size note-book (my bible) which is open on my desk at all times and goes into every meeting and home with me when I think I may need it. Make notes when you are on the telephone or discussing issues, particularly in meetings – names, telephone numbers, email addresses, details of negotiations made; I usually write on the right-hand side and keep 'To Do' lists on the left, ticking items as they get done (I did say it was anal). The deal letters and contracts can be done when things are quieter in the office, using notes that you made when chatting on the telephone with the director of photography, for example. Prioritise your tasks accordingly and slap a big name and address label on your bible so that if it gets left somewhere it will find its way back to you. I can't over-emphasise the importance of putting labels on things: one of the first things you should do is to print sticky labels so that all your raw stock is labelled with the company name, address and telephone numbers before they are handed out to crews. Losing rushes can lead to all sorts of problems!

Production files

Keep all your bits of paper (or electronic equivalents in files on the computer) in properly labelled lever-arch production files, logically filed with those nice coloured-card file dividers for ease of reference. I find it useful to have (a) a finance file for all the expenses, float reconciliations and company credit card statements and reconciliations, (b) a file for insurance paperwork, including any claims, (c) a CGI (Computer Generated Imagery) file with delivery details of the various graphic items, storyboards, etc., (d) an archive file, with logs of the archive in each programme, their sources, costs and, ultimately, licences, and (e) contracts and deal letters which should be kept locked away. The time spent getting these organised will be repaid when you can put your hands on vital details quickly and easily. And I keep the budget, schedule and contact list in one of those flimsy plastic files on my desk because I am constantly referring to them and don't want to keep having to drag a heavy file off the shelf. I am assuming here that you are running a large and lengthy series of programmes, but even if it's only a one-off job the same principles apply.

Keep copies of everything and bugger the paper-free office. I always copy invoices and keep them filed alphabetically; this saves you the trouble of wading through your accountant's files to find something, and can be useful if they lose an invoice – something that does happen, particularly in a large company. And problems with people or companies should be committed to paper along with relevant dates in case of trouble later on – keep these notes confidentially, maybe at the back of your bible. When you finish your project all these files become useful archive material for the company.

Electronic organisers

These are popular and can be hugely useful – but take heed! You must find the time to regularly back everything up, and this applies to all the telephone numbers on your mobile too. I have seen grown men weep because they have lost a professional lifetime's contact details through said electronic item being lost, stolen or just malevolently malfunctioning. And as I move from freelance job to freelance job I always keep a contact list for each project so I can reference that terrific editor or director of photography (DOP) who did such a good job, or recommend them to someone else.

Logs

I love a good log! Keep them for bikes and cabs booked (check them against the invoices when they arrive), purchase orders, rushes tapes, material coming into the office from contributors or companies, contracts issued, signed and returned – anything, in short, that you might lose track of in a long project. Your co-ordinator can set them up and update them, and they will save you precious time because you can access information at a glance. When a team returns from a shoot, take the rushes and log them – tape number, date shot and briefly what is on each tape, what format and frame rate they are shot at and any other details you need. This will help you figure out what the next tape number is on the next shoot, which avoids duplicated tape numbers, and the log can be copied to the editor when he or she starts work. You may also need to send them to your graphics house so they know which rushes contain their 'backplates' for their CGI work. You should also add to this the location of the rushes as they move from the office to the edit and then on to the post facility.

Refer to website 💻.

Refer to website 💻.

USEFUL TIPS

Logging is especially important when contributors are lending you personal items for your shoot, to avoid the embarrassment of not knowing who lent what or, worse, losing something precious and irreplaceable. It might be a good idea to visit the edit suites in the last days of your project to pick up all the detritus that lurks there before the facilities house dumps it all in the rubbish!

You need some method of keeping the contact details of everyone you want to be able to recall: a rolodex, filing box, filofax, address book – whatever can be alphabetically filed and added to easily and carried from job to job. This will cross-reference your contact lists.

Roles within the production team

We will now look at the roles and responsibilities of your production team.

Production co-ordinator

Your right-hand person. Choose them carefully – not only should they be brilliant at their job, but you should also be able to get on with them, trust them and rely on them to be cheerful at all times. It's part of the production manager's and the co-ordinator's remit to be chipper – the last thing you want is someone sitting opposite you with a face like a bag of spanners. They will be worth their weight in gold and you will buy them flowers, chocolates and thank them when they have done a particularly good job because they will be near the bottom of the food chain, not very well paid and do much of your work for you. They will set up lots of the systems, logs, call sheets, shoots and anything else you throw at them. They may also do transcriptions and post production scripts if they have time. In fact they can do everything that you do except manage the budget – that's your job.

Production assistant

May be slightly junior to the above, but does a similar job. If you have a big project you may need at least one of each.

Production secretary

Similar to the above but probably less experienced and cheaper. Useful for real grunt work when the going gets tough!

Runner

Often someone very low on the pay scale who is hired for the duration of a shoot or by the production company to fetch and carry and save on courier/bike bills. They are often keen to get some work experience on shoots or edits, so as well as giving them menial stuff to do, try also to reward them by giving them some exposure to real work – i.e. helping the DOP with something specific, or sitting in an edit and observing.

Accountant

Your best friend! You will work very closely with this person, who may be part of the company you are working for or may be from an external organisation that comes in regularly to manage the company accounts and do the VAT returns. You should sign off your own invoices and pass them, before together arriving at some sort of cost report that you both agree on. You will also produce some sort of variations text which will explain where and what your budget variations are; the attendant paperwork that goes with the cost report will be your joint responsibility.

Executive producer

Someone who may work within the independent production company who will be overseeing your project and ensuring that the programme or series is what the Broadcaster wants and is on schedule and on budget. Also a 'big gun' to call on if you have a problem with a member of the team or with the Broadcaster.

Series producer (SP)

If you are making a number of programmes, the SP will be on board (and possibly directing one of them too) to ensure that the 'look' of the series is consistent. Since there will probably be a number of different directors, the SP will be formulating a template for each programme, editing scripts and watching rough cuts and fine cuts before they are viewed by the Broadcaster. They should also work closely with you on budget and content. I find it useful to have them sitting near you so you can discuss issues as they come up, and make sure you are always invited to the 'creative' production meetings (or send your trusty co-ordinator) to listen to what the individual director wants in his or her episode and make sure that this 'wish list' is affordable and possible within the time frame you have.

Producer/director (P/D)

In documentary TV these two roles can be done by one person, responsible for the creative content of the programme with an eye to the spending as well. If you find yourself working with just a director, they will be focused on the visual overview of the project and may not be very interested in the money, except in spending it. You will always strive to give them what they want but it will need to be within the budget, so try to avoid saying 'no' – negotiation is always the best route. So, for example, they can have a couple of extra days' filming if they are prepared to give up some of the 'toys' budget. You can move money around within the budget to a certain extent and as long as you don't change the original remit of what the Broadcaster will be expecting. If, for instance, you have promised 8 minutes of archive then you can't suddenly spend most of the archive money on something else and leave it with only 3 minutes – the Broadcaster will get understandably annoyed that the programme being delivered is not what was originally agreed. You need to be a bit cleverer than that, and as you get to know your team you might try and squirrel away some money to be pulled out of the hat when it's needed.

A director or P/D may ask for a copy of the budget. This is a sticky one. If you know them, and know that they will 'get it' when reading it, then it may help – but some directors or P/Ds are just confused by budgets so you may want to produce an edited version. It isn't any of their business what other staff are getting paid, for example, and they really only need the bits of the budget that they have some control over. So you might fillet out these schedules and talk them through it. Most directors, in my experience, are happier with just a general indication of what money is available where.

Assistant producer (AP) or researcher

A word of warning here. If you take on a researcher for a job, they may want a change of role when it comes to credit time. They might argue for an assistant producer credit, which you should be wary of bestowing unless they have made a significant contribution to the project in terms of using their research material creatively with the director. If you credit someone as a sort of treat for being good then you may well do them a disservice when they apply for their next job, since they may be under-qualified for an AP job and find themselves out of their depth. A good AP will be doing the work of amassing factual information and 'packaging' it for the director, speaking to possible contributors and assessing whether they will make good 'talking heads'. Indeed, they should build up a good relationship with contributors, be they witnesses, interviewees or academics expert on their subject – and they should find out whether these people will want a fee for their contribution to the project. If the process of negotiating a fee looks as if it might be sticky, then offer to take over this task, which will free them up to be just a nice person who is interested in their story. You can be 'bad cop' and do the money and paperwork things.

Researchers and APs should always produce a minimum of paperwork – and I would require a full list of all their contributors' contact details and a note of any personal items they have passed over like photographs or home movies. When they are interviewed, the AP should get their signature on a release form plus an accurate spelling of their name and the preferred wording for their 'strap' on screen (sometimes called a lower frame super or caption – the writing that gives the name and role of the person being interviewed). If the AP is being helpful, they could also put a brief description of the contributor on the back of their release so that you and the co-ordinator can work out who they are when the paperwork is being processed and the AP has left the team (for example, 'green sweater, beard and glasses' for an interviewee whom you have never met). A good AP should prepare the contributor for what to expect, warn them not to wear a tee-shirt with a slogan on it or stripes, greet them and look after them before and after filming, and finally send them a nice thank-you letter when the shoot has finished. One last point: if for some reason the contributor has been omitted from the programme then someone – preferably the AP, who has a relationship with them – should let them know. If the AP has left, then you or the director should do this. Failure to do so means that when the programme goes out and the contributor is missing from it (having invited all their friends and family round to watch it as it goes out) they will be puzzled and upset, and that isn't a good way to treat people who may have given their time and energy for very little. Courtesy at all times is crucial.

Unit manager

I haven't come across these very often, but in bigger organisations you may find yourself with a unit manager above you who will want regular reports from you on how your project is running. They may be a good sounding-board for any anxieties or moans you may have, or this may, in a smaller company, be the role of the head of production.

Head of production

He or she will be overseeing the production aspects of the projects within the company, and should be a good point of contact for you – someone to moan to and help address problems within the team or to do with money. They should be your ally, so try and keep them on your side. They may want to sit down every month and look at your cost report, and you should mention any over-spends you may see coming. Don't keep these sorts of problems from the head of production; they must be able to trust your cost control.

Hierarchy

Broadcast television is very hierarchical and there is sometimes a tendency for the 'creative side' to lack respect for the production staff. For some reason they think that shoots get set up as if by magic, and often have little idea of how much work goes into producing a realistic schedule and an informative call sheet. One day I will have a tee-shirt made that says, 'If you can read this, you can read your call sheet.' But fat chance – they don't, preferring instead to ask endlessly irritating questions of your team. You have my permission to shriek, 'Read your call sheet!' at least once on your project. One way of encouraging them might be to tell them (and the crew) that there will be a prize for the first one to find the deliberate error – gets 'em every time.

Roles of crew – filming personnel

Briefly, when we talk about a DOP it means a director of photography (or cameraman or -woman), and this is the person or people you hire to shoot your project. They may or may not own their own camera equipment, and you should check their CV to make sure that they have relevant experience in using the camera you want and the genre that you are working in.

Sometimes, especially in the days when film was used, you work with a camera assistant, but if you are filming with a lot of kit or with rudimentary lighting or camera accessories that aren't too specialised then you may need them to carry out these extra duties.

Sound recordists usually have their own sound kit and attach themselves to the DOP quite literally, by plugging into the camera and recording sound – either with a boom (one of those long poles with a fluffy thing on the end which is for baffling things like wind noise) or with radio mics which are attached to the interviewee's person. You can also ask them to record interviews for transcription, in which case try and get them talking to the transcriber so they use a compatible sound format.

Sparks are electricians, and you may need them on a shoot that has a big lighting set-up.

Grips are the chaps who arrive on location with vans bursting with bits of kit which may include wind machines, smoke machines, and various dollies of differing size and complexity with attendant tracking.

Editors are the people you hire to off-line your project, and are chosen for their expertise in the edit format you are using and their ability to take a bunch of random material and cut something exciting and beautiful from it!

A production manager's overview

You will be working closely with the producer or P/D to make sure they are aware of their budget. You must be able to justify your budgetary decisions (keep notes; there is a lot to remember and as things progress you may not recall why you decided on a particular course of action). Once your budget has been agreed at the start of the project, you may have to draw up a cash flow – which the Broadcaster will authorise (see website 🖥) – and you will also need a week-by-week schedule (see website 🖥). You and your co-ordinator will set up all the paperwork and logging systems that you need, and make sure that the team know where they are and how to use the ones you want them to complete.

Holiday pay

You will at least oversee, but probably assist in hiring staff and crew and also negotiate their rates of pay, working conditions and contracts. Make sure that you are fully conversant with the paid holiday credits working regulations; you will need to pay both freelance and payroll staff a total of 28 paid holiday days per year on a pro rata basis (as of 1 April 2009). For help on this, call up PACT and ask them to talk you through it – though you can only use PACT if the company is a member, so if they aren't, you should encourage them to join. You will also need to be clear about who can and can't work freelance (this is controlled by which roles the Inland Revenue will allow to be freelance and thus pay their own tax and NI contributions). Briefly, no person who is fulfilling an assistant role can be freelance, unless they have a letter of dispensation from the Inland Revenue – ask to see it if they say they have. And anyone hired on a freelance basis will only be allowed to work for a 9-month period before being shifted on to the payroll, unless, again, they get a letter from the IR permitting this to happen. It is their responsibility to get this, not yours, and again you need to see this written permission. Any staff members who are on the payroll will need to have 12.8% of their total fee calculated and put into schedule 18 of your budget. They will then be taxed at source (PAYE) and a National Insurance contribution deducted (unless they are over 60, in which case they cease to pay NI – and you need to see evidence of this, too).

To find out which grades can legitimately be freelance, either call 0191-225-0040 or go to www.hmrc.gov.uk and then type in 'Film and TV Guidance Notes 2003' (the latest version). Do consult the IR if you are unclear about any of these stipulations, and don't forget to allow money in schedule 18 to cover both the employer's NI contribution (check the current rate, because it does change from time to time) and the holiday credits you are obliged to pay. (Use the Holiday Chart Calculator on the PACT website for a simple calculation guide for holiday pay.)

VAT

If a crew or team member is registered for VAT, make sure that they show this item on their invoice separately along with their VAT number. If you get any of this wrong, the company for which you are working will be exposed – so check. And if any crew member argues with you over any of this, refer them to the head of production.

Cost control

Set up your cost book or cost monitor. This will be some method of keeping a running account of your costs and committed spend, and there is an example of an excellent one in the Visuals section 💻. Check with the accounts department how they run their company and projects accounts; see if they will need access to your cost book, and discuss how this will work with them.

Systems

Set up your contact list, purchase order system, tape log, contract log, an archive log if you are using archive, and templates for call sheets and purchase orders. Make sure that each member of your production team knows what they are responsible for, and set weekly meetings with them to establish who is doing what during each week. Ensure that all the research people know what you expect from them by way of paperwork. Some sort of social meeting early on might be a good idea – perhaps a working lunch where you supply the sandwiches and drinks, so you can meet everyone and establish codes of practice.

Pencilling staff and facilities

Start asking directors which DOPs and editors they want, and begin the process of contacting these people and asking their rates. Get in touch with equipment hire places and get quotes, and start exploring where you are going for your off-lines and post production. Find out whether the directors want their rushes transferred to a viewing format that they can view at home (providing you have the cost of this in your budget), whether they want transcriptions and if translations are required. Then start the process of looking for people to do this.

Financial practices

When you start to issue floats, make sure that the recipients sign for them and put them in your budget as a float to be reconciled – remember to remove these gross figures when they are; otherwise, you will be double accounting (and scaring yourself witless when you do your monthly cost report). You could do the same with company credit card amounts too, so you never find yourself forgetting a large amount of money that has been committed, even if it hasn't quite been reconciled yet. And make sure that all team members *always* give you a piece of paper to cover every spend they make, especially if there is a VAT element on them. You might prefer to collect all credit card receipts and float receipts and reconcile them yourself, or to get your co-ordinator to do it: sometimes this is quicker and easier than trying to unpick a reconciliation done by someone who's no good at them. It's up to you.

Supervision

Oversee your co-ordinators as they set up each recce and shoot. They won't be dealing with the total budget but you might give them relevant parts of it to help them as they book hotels, flights and other items. If you become aware that you have a weak co-ordinator on board you may want to nip the problem in the bud sooner rather than later.

It's easier to get rid of someone who is not up to scratch before the series really gets into its stride, otherwise you may just have to suck it up for the entire series.

Post production

Once you start to move into the post production stage, ensure that information makes its way out to all the edit suites. Editors should have a file containing possible transcripts along with all the tech specs issued by the Broadcaster, guides to duration of programme and the placing of each break. Visit the edits from time to time to check that the editor is happy with how things are going and to spot bits of archive or music that may have crept into the episode from a 'dodgy' source. Sometimes you will meet a barrier of resistance to these visits because the editor and director will be very busy and stressed, and may see your visits as intrusive. It's a difficult one to handle and will draw on all your people skills – don't outstay your welcome, but don't be forced out either since you may spot potential problems on these visits. I have been into edits and seen scary material culled from books and music used by a director who has been browsing through HMV at lunchtime. I'll deal with music in more detail in Chapter 17, but in the meantime you might consider providing mood music from a clearable source that can be replaced later.

Remind editors that various deliverables are due on certain dates in advance, and check to see if they can extend their contracts in case of an edit overrun. Sometimes they have booked their next job in the week following the end of yours, and this can cause you a problem if you are running late. Make sure that the facilities house doing your voice-over record, dub, on-line and grades have pencilled dates early on, and keep in touch with them if and when dates slip.

If you are making a series, it might be a good plan to arrange a viewing of the first finished programme for the whole team – at, say, a convenient lunchtime. This helps clarify what the shows are supposed to look like, and may inject some energy into a tired team. Provide some food and drinks while viewing it and encourage discussion afterwards. Remember to thank all concerned for their efforts at the end; this can make for a useful bonding exercise.

Handover notes

Towards the end of your project the team may well begin to shrink in numbers, so make sure you get everyone to do handover notes as they leave. These should detail what bits of business are unfinished and give clear instructions about whom to contact and what to do. Read the notes before the person goes, and clarify if you need to. And make sure that company property is handed back (keys, production mobiles, outstanding paperwork, etc.). It's time to plan the wrap party too (which you will have already set some money aside for!). This can be lavish or modest but is a good way of thanking people for their efforts over the course of months – it should always be paid for by the project or the company, involve alcohol and some food to soak up the booze, and be in a nice venue that is easy to get to. You might also arrange cabs for people so they get home safely, and give some sort of gift to each of your production team as thanks for all their hard work and devotion to duty.

Only then can you collapse into a heap and sip on a gin and tonic. And then, of course, you have to start looking for your next job.

2 Working in drama

Julie Clark, a very experienced line producer in high-end TV drama and a number of British feature films, has written the following chapter on drama – which outlines how working in the drama genre of film and TV changes the role of the production manager into the more common title of line producer.

There's nothing quite like the offer of a new job, especially if you're freelance! The excitement of a new script, different cast, the opportunity to work with a fresh crew and the knowledge that you're going to be instrumental in making a new drama (be that for TV or the cinema) keeps us returning to production again and again. But before we can launch into production, there is a lot of pre-prep work to be done.

Months before the green light is given, the Broadcaster or commissioner will insist on signing off a budget that is realistic according to the script they have accepted. This is when a line producer can get involved at the very early stages of a production. The script may be in a rough draft form and may change substantially before filming starts, but it is a good basis on which to budget and schedule the show. (More about budgeting and scheduling later.) The line producer will ultimately be responsible for managing the production from pre-prep through to the completion of filming. This involves people management and budget control, while still keeping the editorial side of the script in mind.

Once the production company gets the green light (i.e. when all the finance is in place), it is usually full steam ahead, as often there is minimal lead-up time before filming needs to start. This may be because of a lead actor's availability, a transmission deadline, perhaps a key location that is free only for a certain period of time, or just because it's best to strike while the iron is hot! The chances are that there is just a producer, script editor and line producer (yourself) on board. Sometimes the director and other heads of departments have been chosen before the line producer; other times, not. On many occasions it might not have been you who did the original budget, so assuming you've read the script, the next important task is to scrutinise the budget and reallocate it according to the latest script(s). This may also mean producing an initial draft shooting schedule. Once you feel confident with the budget, it's time to start employing the crew in conjunction with the producer and director. An average TV drama would employ approximately 50–70 crew, and larger series or cinema films substantially more than that, so there is a lot of work to be done.

Imagine the production as a huge cartwheel. The line producer is the centre of that wheel, with each spoke leading to a different department. Each department needs overseeing in terms of budget, and each head of department (HOD) needs a point of reference to return to regarding department spend (script versus budget), any crew issues they may have and general production logistics. The line producer is often the primary liaison between these HODs and the producer, who in turn feeds relevant information to the director. This doesn't mean that the director or producer never speak to the HODs, but it is important that the information is filtered so that the director does not have to deal with general logistics and minor budgetary issues. It's a matter of knowing when to involve a director with a decision, and there is no hard and fast rule on that since it depends very much on what sort of director you are working with.

Let's look at the different departments and crew involved in making a drama.

Production department

The roles in the production department regularly overlap depending on the experience of the production team and the requirements of the production. There may well be a line producer as well as a production manager on a large TV series or big-budget film, as there is so much to be done. The delineation between these roles varies. It may be that the line producer makes most of the decisions and negotiates the main deals with regard to HOD, crew, equipment and facilities, with the production manager following through those decisions and contracting the other crew. One line producer may choose to oversee every part of the budget, while another line producer may give their production manager more responsibility, leaving them in control of certain sections of the budget. On a one-off drama or lower-budget film or TV, it is usual for the line producer to fulfil the role of the production manager as well. There is no right or wrong way of spreading the workload, so it is impossible to give full job descriptions here. What is important, however, is communication, so you all know what is expected of each other and nothing slips through the net.

The production co-ordinator is based in the production office and is the main support to the line producer (assuming there is no production manager), initiating cast and crew contracts, overseeing clearances, booking additional daily crew and extra equipment, managing the production team and generally fielding all calls which come into the production office. This role covers such a huge spectrum of different responsibilities that a whole chapter could be devoted to the production co-ordinator alone. But in short, whatever back-up the line producer needs, the co-ordinator is there to do it.

The assistant co-ordinator works to the production co-ordinator, but also keeps cast, crew and supplier contacts lists updated, arranges equipment transport, organises car hire, travel and accommodation, writes purchase orders, buys in stationery and performs general office admin. Depending on the size of the production, there could be a production secretary or travel co-ordinator as well.

The production runner also works to the production co-ordinator, collecting paperwork from set for the production office (such as continuity notes, camera and sound sheets), and will often deliver last-minute requests to set such as costume, prop or equipment requirements. Of course, other runner duties include making tea and coffee, post office runs and copious amounts of photocopying!

Accounts department

The production accountant is key to the line producer being in control of the production budget, and will manage the budget based on information supplied by the line producer on a daily basis. They will also take budget information from cast and crew contracts, and purchase orders (POs). If these aren't written regularly for every item hired or purchased, and kept up-to-date, then it is easy to lose track of the budget. It is imperative that every department write their own POs, which should be signed off by the line producer before being sent to the supplier so that every purchase or hire is approved. All cast and crew contracts should also be pre-approved by the line producer. The accountant and line producer will have regular budget meetings to discuss the overall production spend at any given time, and the line producer will inform the accountant of any anticipated deviations from the budget due to script or schedule changes. The producer will be updated on the overall financial position at a weekly cost report meeting.

The accountant (with the help of an assistant accountant or several assistants, depending on the size of the production) will also prepare the cash flow, manage the flow of funds, ensure that cast, crew, locations and suppliers are paid, and deal with floats and petty cash. They become the crew's best friends, as they hold the purse strings!

Casting

The casting director and casting assistant may well have been talking to actors' agents long before the line producer came on board, as many productions are commissioned or based on a leading actor/actress being attached to the project. However, casting will still be required, and will continue until the first day of principal photography (the main filming period). The casting director will negotiate deals with the agent on the production's behalf, based on a cast budget, but with the approval of the line producer, who will have a clearer idea of dates required and if safety cover days are required.

(Equity is the name of the actors' union and you will find a brief description of an Equity contract towards the end of this chapter.)

Assistant directors

The first assistant director (1st AD) works alongside the director during both the pre-production period and the shoot. During prep, it is the 1st AD's task to create an achievable shooting schedule based on the final shooting script and taking into consideration any specific requirements of the director. This could be anything from a request to shoot a stunt sequence in chronological order (sometimes not possible due to location or cast availability), to allowing additional rehearsal and shooting time for a particularly emotional scene. Once the script has been scheduled into an agreed number of days, it is discussed with all HODs in order to fine-tune it, taking into consideration other departments' requirements. During the actual shoot, the 1st AD is on set at all times, liaising between crew and director, thinking one step ahead to ensure that everything is prepared in advance for the next scene, and keeping track of time with the intention of completing every set-up for every scene within the shooting day. (A set-up is a camera position – for example: high or low angle, pan or track, etc. – so there will be several set-ups for the same scene, and the actors will have to repeat the same lines over and over again.) If the shooting were running behind schedule, the 1st AD would discuss with the director possibilities for simplifying, or even cutting, certain set-ups. It often helps for the line producer to step in at this point.

The second assistant director (2nd AD) is not required on set and usually works from a mobile office at the location base, dealing with the co-ordination of day-to-day requirements of the set. During prep the 2nd AD is mainly concerned with the cast and background artists, organising rehearsal schedules in conjunction with the director, as well as costume fittings and special tuition if required (such as driving, horse riding, dialogue coaching or playing a musical instrument). The 2nd AD also breaks down the script alongside the schedule to identify days for background artists, stunt or body doubles, action vehicles, etc. – the list is long. During the shoot, the 2nd AD is responsible for creating the call sheet, giving every member of cast their daily call-time, booking background artists (generally through reputable agencies), managing transport of cast to and from set, informing caterers of times and numbers, and also passing on numerous other pieces of vital information. The 2nd AD is the main link between the set and the production office.

The third assistant director (3rd AD) has less prep – maybe enough to familiarise themselves with the script and to attend cast rehearsals. Their main role is to be on set during filming, working to the 1st AD, setting the background action and generally keeping the set quiet. The 3rd AD is responsible for handing out and keeping tabs on all the walkie-talkies and head-sets.

As with all the assistant directors, the floor runner is linked by walkie-talkie to the 1st AD. There could be one or more floor runners depending on the number of cast and background artists. They are generally set-based, and inform cast and crew when the camera is turning, while on location help with control of the public, often deliver lunch to cast in their trailers, make numerous hot drinks and do general grunt work! This role is a coveted starting point for youngsters wanting to get into the TV and film industry.

A stand-in should be similar in height and colouring to the lead artist. They are useful to allow the artist more time away from set while lighting and camera positions are being set up. Many stand-ins are happy to fulfil runner duties too, to make their day pass more quickly!

Script department

The script supervisor is responsible for timing the script before filming begins, and also for timing the script during the filming. Timings are especially important for TV drama, as a Broadcaster will insist on a programme being a very specific length. Although a lot can be done in the edit, keeping scenes to time during the shoot means less wastage and ensures sufficient footage to work with in the edit. The script supervisor is also responsible for continuity on set. Continuity is crucial, and a whole scene could go to waste if there is a continuity error that has slipped though and not been discovered until the edit, such as a hairstyle mis-match or a missing prop.

The script editor is often on the staff of the production company. They are the main point of contact between the writers and producer, and keep track of storylines and threads. They can also implement small changes such as story days and times (i.e. when a day in the script ends and becomes the next day, or two or three days later – particularly important for costume and make-up) and also name-changes due to clearance issues.

Location department

The location manager will be one of the first crew members you employ, and occasionally they may even be on board before the line producer. This is because the key locations often determine where your production office/base may be, particularly if you are shooting in London where it could take a couple of hours to get from one side of the city to the other. The location manager will find suitable locations (sometimes with the help of a location scout), photograph them and present options for the director to choose from. The skill in being a good location manager is not just having a creative eye, but also being able to assess the practicability of shooting at a particular location. The role also requires the conviction to charm potential location owners into letting a crew of 60 or so on to their property.

The location manager will have their own location budget, which will have been agreed with the line producer and which will include location fees, dressing and striking costs, unit base fees, technical vehicle parking costs, security, police charges, council charges and many other incidental costs. The location manager should give you regular cost updates on the location budget, and it is important that you discuss cost implications almost daily, as it is very difficult to rein in a location budget if it is not tightly controlled from the start. There will be times when you will need to have editorial conversations with the producer and director and suggest more cost-effective ways of shooting a particular scene. Perhaps turning a night scene into a day scene could save several thousand pounds in security, night lighting, and gratuity payments for local residents, but that would need to be weighed up against the accessibility of a location during busy daytime hours and interference from the general public. The cost of shooting in central London can amount to anything up to £10,000 per day for location fees, technical vehicle parking, crew parking and security, so it's always preferable to shoot outside central London unless the storyline makes it unavoidable.

The unit manager will have sufficient prep time to recce all locations prior to shooting, to write up 'movement orders' (directions to and from locations) for the crew, arrange parking for technical vehicles, and organise the unit base where the facility vehicles will be parked (i.e. catering and dining facilities, costume and make-up trucks, artists' trailers, mobile production office, honey wagons and generator, etc.). Once filming, the unit manager should be the first to arrive and last to leave, to see facilities vehicles in and out, and park up technical vehicles at the location and crew vehicles at the unit base.

There is often one or more location assistant(s) to help the location department, particularly when there may be a 'split' location within the day, which entails moving the whole crew from one location to another.

Camera crew

The director of photography (DOP) is the person in charge of the overall look of the production. They will be key in choosing which format to shoot on (if this is not already stipulated by the Broadcaster) and which camera to use. There is a vast choice of cameras these days, which includes anything from the traditional 35mm and 16mm film cameras, to High Definition cameras and tapeless formats. Of course, there is always a cost implication in this decision, so the input of the producer and line producer is essential. Very often, a line producer will be asked to prepare various cost comparisons of the different options, which would include the cost of stock (film or tape) and the post production routes available. The DOP will sometimes operate the camera as well, but if budget allows, a camera operator will be employed. The other members of the camera department will be the focus puller (or 1st assistant camera, 1st AC), clapper loader (or 2nd assistant camera, 2nd AC), camera trainee and sometimes on larger productions a video assistant, the person whose main task is to record what is being filmed on to tape for quick reference playback. If shooting on a tapeless format, a DIT (data information technician) will be required. This role involves regularly backing up and downloading the shot footage throughout the day, so if anything goes wrong with the camera, the rushes are always safe.

The clapper-board is the familiar black and white board (with the name of the film, the director, the DOP, shot number, take number and date) which is clapped at the beginning of every shot in order for the editor to sync the picture with the sound and to easily identify each shot. It is operated by the clapper loader or 2nd AC, and generally used whatever format is being shot. ('Clapper' refers to the clapper-board, and 'loader' refers to loading the film on to the film magazine.)

Grip department

The key grip is the person who controls the movement of the camera dolly, by physically pushing the dolly along the track; they will also oversee any rigging of the camera on to a camera crane or jib arm. The dolly is a wheeled platform on which the camera and camera operator are mounted. The dolly usually sits on a track that can move around the action, and is extremely heavy: it is the grip, along with the assistant grip, who has to manoeuvre the dolly into position for each camera set-up at every location and lay the track that the dolly runs on in the appropriate place for the action.

Lighting department

The gaffer is the most senior electrician in this department. He will work alongside the DOP to help create the required lighting look. The best boy (no idea why they are called that!) is the liaison between the gaffer and the other electricians, and will be the main point of contact between the lighting department and line producer. There can be anything from two to twenty-two additional electricians (or sparks) required on a location plus a lighting generator operator. For Health & Safety reasons, electricians need to have the requisite qualifications, and, as such, have formed their own section within the technicians' union BECTU in order to standardise pay and working practices.

Sound department

The sound recordist oversees all recording of sound on the shoot, be it dialogue, music or 'atmos' (background or atmosphere sound). He/she is assisted by a boom operator who holds the boom pole and microphone, and who attaches radio mics to artists when appropriate. There is often a sound trainee who labels up discs and generally helps the department with changing batteries, etc. Most productions record on to hard-drive and keep a back-up for safety purposes. DATS are old technology!

Art department

The size of an art department varies enormously depending on the size of the production and whether it is a period or contemporary show. The production designer creates the look and design of the drama, and will invariably have an art director to follow through the designs. There could also be an assistant art director, graphic designer and art department assistant. The stand-by art director is employed to stand by on set while filming to adjust any last-minute design issues, and to check continuity for props. The art department budget is probably the most fluid; there will always be set pieces that are script-led, but equally there will be expensive or more cost-effective ways of creating a particular look. The line producer must discuss with the production designer the allocation of the art department budget in the early stages of prep, because, as with the location budget, once a commitment has been made to a set, it is very difficult and often not cost-effective to pull back.

Props department

The production buyer is responsible for hiring or buying all props required for the production, and sometimes a set decorator will fulfil this role too. On larger productions there will also be an assistant buyer. The props master checks in all received props, whether purchased or hired, and organises the transport of props to the right location at the right time. On larger productions there will be a separate store master for this. There are generally two dressing prop hands who pre-dress locations before the crew arrive and 'strike out' (take out the props which were dressed in) once filming is completed at that location. Two stand-by prop hands stand by on set for the duration of filming.

Construction and set operations

Depending on the size of the production, there could be any number of construction crew. A construction manager might be employed to oversee all set construction, often through a dedicated construction company.

A stand-by carpenter and stand-by painter are often employed to stay with the shooting crew throughout filming. The stand-by carpenter will help lay camera track and ensure that it's laid evenly. The stand-by rigger's duties fall between various departments: lighting might need a rigger for rigging lighting towers or lamps on to cranes and cherry pickers, and the art department might also need a rigger for set construction.

Costume department

The costume designer creates a look for each individual actor as well as creating an overall look for the production. Again, there will be budgetary constraints which will need to be discussed and agreed with the line producer during the prep period. The number of background artists will have a huge impact on the costume budget, particularly if it is a period show, and every individual extra will need to be specially fitted for a costume. The rest of the costume department could consist of a costume supervisor, set dresser(s), dressmaker and wardrobe assistant(s).

Make-up department

The make-up designer will have a team consisting of a make-up supervisor, a varying number of make-up artists, and possibly specialised hairdressers. If the production is heavy on special effects, there would be prosthetic artists too.

With all of the above departments, daily crew ('dailies') are often employed as and when needed.

Editing department

Generally an editor will have either one or two edit assistants. The current, most accepted equipment to edit on is the non-linear Avid, although with tapeless work-flows fast becoming more prevalent, this may well change in the foreseeable future.

On larger productions a post production supervisor will be employed to take over the management of the post production process. This role often overlaps with that of the line producer, but once production is completed and all equipment, props and costumes are wrapped and returned, the line producer hands the production over to the post production supervisor.

Transport department

Unit drivers are regularly employed to bring artists to and from location. Delays in filming would be inevitable if actors were expected to get themselves to location in the early hours of the morning for their make-up and costume calls. Having regular drivers who can also run errands for the production, such as picking up and dropping off equipment, can save time and money. Many well-known artists request their own driver.

Truck drivers are often employed specifically to drive technical vehicles such as the camera truck, grip truck, prop truck and lighting trucks, etc.

Health & Safety

Although there are no hard and fast rules regarding having a unit medic on set at all times, it is a legal requirement to have at least one qualified first aider. A dedicated unit medic is usually present at location filming where there are greater risks of accidents happening.

A Health & Safety adviser is sometimes offered via the production company. If not, it is advisable for a qualified Health & Safety consultant to attend all technical recces prior to filming to advise on any potential hazards. A risk assessment for every location is required, and although these can be prepared by the line producer or 1st AD, a professional opinion is a distinct advantage.

Miscellaneous crew

Every production is different, and has its own special requirements. Here are some of the other crew you may need to engage on an ad hoc basis, to name but a few:

Armourer (someone who supervises weaponry on set and off)

Stunt co-ordinator, stunt performer, stunt double

Crowd co-ordinator (for controlling large groups of actors/extras)

Child chaperone and/or **tutor** (to ensure that children's hours and duties are monitored and their education continued while filming)

Publicity photographer

Animal wrangler (a trainer who supervises any animals on set and off)

Dialogue/dialect coach (one of the most expensive hourly rates)

Driving instructor (check that the artist can drive before filming!)

Choreographer

Music tutor

Steadicam operator (operates a special camera that is physically attached to the cameraman, so long, fluid and complex follow shots can be achieved – less cumbersome than a dolly)

Special effects designer, special effects technician

Paramedic

Now you know who does what on a drama, let's look at scheduling and budgeting.

Scheduling

'Movie Magic' Budgeting and Scheduling is the most common and accepted way of presenting budgets and schedules for both TV and film. It is made by a company called Entertainment Partnership, and some older versions of Movie Magic are known as 'EP'.

Before starting to write a detailed budget, the overall production will need to be scheduled, the script will need breaking down, and a basic shooting schedule created.

Overall production schedule

This will take the form of a week-by-week breakdown, which includes the number of prep weeks before filming commences (including start dates for crew members with prep), number of shoot weeks (5-day weeks, 6-day weeks or 11-day fortnights), and post-production weeks (including assemble editing, fine-cutting, grading, track-laying, sound mixing and delivery dates). This week-by-week schedule makes the budgeting process easier, as it clarifies how many weeks a particular crew member needs to be contracted for.

Breaking down a script and creating a shooting schedule

EP provides a package called EP Scheduling, which enables every element of a script to be broken down and input into a document that can produce lists in a variety of formats. The information required to produce a first draft shooting schedule on which to base the budget could include the following:

a) Scene number
b) Set (as described in the script)
c) Day or night scene
d) Location (if known, or could be studio/location/abroad)
e) Cast
f) Supporting artists
g) Stunts or animals (if featured heavily)
h) Page count

'Page count' warrants a little further explanation, as it is generally accepted, for ease and consistency, that every script page is broken down into 8 x ⅛ of a page. This enables you to schedule more accurately, and the size of the production budget often determines the size of the daily page count to be shot. A very basic rule of thumb is that 1 page (written in the standard 'Final Draft' script format) roughly equates to 1 screen-time minute. A high-budget feature could expect to shoot 3 screen-time minutes (or approx 3 pages) per day, whereas fast-turnaround TV can shoot anything up to 8 or even 10 pages per day. An average TV drama might expect to shoot around 5 pages per day. A very short scene might be just ⅛ of a page in length, whereas a long scene could be around 5⅞ pages. So you could be shooting many scenes within a day, or just one. Of course, there are many other elements to take into consideration when scheduling: ⅛ of a page could also take you a whole day to shoot if it involves a complex stunt or many supporting artists. Consider the difference in shooting time for the following two ⅛-page scenes:

> 'The army emerges over the brow of the hill through the pouring rain.'

> 'He arrived at his front door, key in hand.'

Then there is the order of the day to consider:

Imagine, for example, that there are two locations that have to be filmed in the same day. One location involves a camera crane which takes a couple of hours to set up in a street; the other needs a couple of hours pre-lighting the interior of a manor house. Which would be the best location to start the day? Issues to consider would be:

i)   Weather – would the crane-shot be lost if it were to rain, in which case having it ready for the start of the day would give the option of a.m. or p.m.?
ii) Is the manor house location charging by the hour?
iii) Are there background artists involved in either scene, and how long might they take to get ready?

So an understanding of the script and the complexities of filming is crucial for scheduling.

Once all the basic elements have been input into Movie Magic Scheduling, it is then possible to pull scenes together to make full shooting days. Obviously, shooting in story order is not always practical, and the first step in scheduling might be to put all scenes involving the same set or location together. Then you may need to consider whether the scenes are to be shot day or night. Other considerations are likely to be artist availability, location availability, whether it is possible to double up on background artists within a day, children's legal hours – the restrictions can be endless. The first draft schedule you do is primarily for reference (to work out the number of days filming, artist deals, crowd budget, stunt days, etc.), and there may be a variety of configurations. Eventually, when the 1st AD comes on board, the schedule will be fine-tuned according to the latest script and in consultation with other HODs. At this point you will be able to access reports on anything from artists' working days (referred to as 'Day-out-of-Days') to daily props requirements.

Budgeting

With an overall production schedule and shooting schedule to refer to, you are now in a position to start budgeting. The chances are you will have been given some guidance as to the expected budget figure, although it is better to budget for every single thing you can think of to start with, even if it puts you over budget, as it is always easier to cut back than to add.

Budgets are broken down into above-the-line and below-the-line costs. Above-the-line refers to: development costs, story and script costs, producer and director fees and principal talent fees. Below-the-line is everything else including production, post production and other costs. Unlike most documentary budgets, there are many different budget templates for drama or film with a variety of category numbers, although the order in which a budget is laid out is often similar.

Above-the-line

DEVELOPMENT

There is likely to have been a separate development budget agreed before confirmation of the commission, but the total for that budget will be shown here in one line. It will include such costs as the initial budget and schedule (which you may have done), research expenses and other possible related production company costs.

Writers' fees will have been pre-agreed, and they should incorporate a specified number of script rewrites together with number of episodes where applicable. There could also be an option payment here, or format fee. Writers are entitled to a contribution to their pension if they are members of the Writers Guild of Great Britain, and this is set at a percentage of their fee. There should also be an allowance for writers' expenses, particularly if writers have to travel to script meetings, etc.

This budget category might also include title or copyright report costs that may have been carried out by the production company.

PRODUCER/DIRECTORS

There could be a number of executive producers who have been involved in development and purchasing of rights relating to the production, all of whom should be included here. There could possibly be one or more producers. The line producer is sometimes included here, and sometimes under production.

The director's fees could be based on a buy-out for the production, or shown as a weekly fee. Most directors have agents who negotiate their fee on their behalf.

As with a documentary budget, expect some internal company costs to cover staff salaries and overheads.

PRINCIPAL ARTISTS

Principal cast are shown here, and they can be contracted in a variety of ways:

i)   Buy-out fee for the production – this form of contract is usually reserved for the leading roles only.
ii) Weekly engagement fee, plus set rate for additional production day payments.
iii) Episodic fee – used for TV series.
iv) 75% rule – also used for TV series and longer-running productions where cast are required on and off over a period of at least 12 weeks.

There is a different agreement for films and TV, and many other purchase percentages which are too complex to go into in detail here. (Seek help from someone who has done this before, or call up PACT for advice and guidance.)

Other cast-related costs which should be included in this budget schedule are:

- *Read-through fees*
- *Rehearsal fees*
- *Costume-fitting fees*
- *Overtime* (it's worth remembering that all cast and stunt contracts are based on an 8-hour filming day, as opposed to the usual 10 or 11 hours for crew, so it is likely that overtime costs will be incurred. The overtime rates vary according to the time of day or night and number of hours; however, a full explanation of overtime rates can be found in the PACT/Equity Agreements)
- *Holiday pay* (obligatory)
- *Additional dialogue recording (ADR)* (this may be required if an artist's dialogue recorded on location is not clear, or if some new dialogue is required to clarify something. This can also be called 'post-synching')

Below-the-line

Other cast

Non-principal cast are shown below-the-line, but also include the above additional costs. Equity contracts are the same regardless of whether they are above- or below-the-line. Equity publishes some very useful contacts books – *Spotlight* for artists, and the *Stunt Register* for stunt co-ordinators and stunt performers; these publications are invaluable when it comes to finding agents, previous credits and general contact details of Equity members. The books are expensive to buy, but most production companies subscribe to online access.

STUNT CO-ORDINATORS AND STUNT PERFORMERS

These are also classed as cast, and contracted on an Equity agreement. Stunt performers usually double for an artist and will often be entitled to an 'adjustment fee' based on the risk factor of the stunt they are performing, and the number of times they are required to perform it. For example, a jump from the top of a block of flats on fire would attract a substantially higher adjustment fee than a choreographed fight. The stunt co-ordinator can give you an estimate on the stunt recce, but the final fee will be decided on the day. It is important for the line producer to be present on set during a hazardous stunt to agree the adjustment fee, the number of times the stunt is to be performed, and also to oversee safety. Recce days for a stunt co-ordinator cost the same as a shoot day, even though the stunt person may be required only for one hour. So stunts can be extremely expensive, and are therefore often one of the first things to be cut when trying to reduce a budget.

CROWD AND SUPPORTING ARTISTS

Supporting artists should be engaged through a respected agency (of which there are many). Their rates are specified in the relevant agreements – PACT Cinema and Film, PACT TV, BBC or ITV. In many cases there are likely to be additional payments which need to be budgeted. For example, special skills such as driving and dancing can attract additional payments, as do performing minimal dialogue, working overtime and night payments. For period dramas, the crowd will need a costume-fitting day in advance of filming. Trying to fit crowd remotely (over the phone or by email) doesn't work, as people regularly seem to think they are a few inches slimmer than they really are! The costume team can end up having to hire additional costumes in varying sizes to allow for the unexpected kilos, which costs time and money.

CHAPERONES AND TUTORS

Remember that all children, even if employed as background artists, are legally required to have a chaperone for monitoring hours, and if necessary for tutoring to ensure that their teaching hours meet the required quota.

TECHNICAL ADVISERS

These can cover a multitude of technical advice depending on script requirements, and their fees are open to negotiation.

Health & Safety

This category includes people and equipment. As mentioned earlier, it is a legal requirement for every production to have a first aider on set. Sometimes, one of the production team is first-aid qualified, but it is still recommended to employ a unit medic – firstly, because much of the dangerous rigging is done pre- and post-shooting hours, and secondly, should an accident happen, filming can continue while first aid is being administered. If all is going well this role can become extremely boring, so it is not unheard of for a unit medic to put on a pair of rigger's gloves and help out on set! In extreme situations, such as stunt work, special effects, pyrotechnics, filming near water and so on, more specialised medical cover will be required: a paramedic with ambulance, fire fighters with fire engines and water bowser, or safety divers with the relevant safety equipment. As risk assessments won't have been carried out before the budgeting stage, it is up to the line producer to make an educated assessment of what might be required and the cost to the production.

If locations are likely to be unusually hazardous, then it is also advisable to have a Health & Safety consultant attend the recces, and to advise on risk assessments. The cost of this can be negotiated as an all-in fee or on a daily basis. Their knowledge and expertise is invaluable and can highlight problematic areas well in advance.

Health & Safety equipment also needs to be budgeted and again depends on script requirements. Examples can range from stunt mats and harnesses to protective clothing and general medical kit supplies.

Earlier on we looked at the roles and responsibilities of the production crew, but now let's look at the requirements for each of the other departments.

Art and props department

The art department crew varies enormously depending on script requirements. Similarly the art department budget can range from minimal to extensive. When budgeting for the art department, it is often wise to get advice from a production designer, particularly if there are studio construction builds involved. The areas which need consideration are as follows.

Props hire and purchase

For specific looks and dates, props hire companies are probably the best bet. Most props are hired out on a weekly basis, which gives some flexibility if the shooting schedule has to change (due to adverse weather, for example). They charge a percentage of the value of the props, but beware of loss and damage notifications. It is important that crew respect the props they are working around and not lay equipment on prop tables, nor put coffee cups on prop furniture. These unforeseen costs can cripple a budget.

Purchased props are good for the less expensive contemporary look. The production buyer will probably need longer prep to outsource the items; however, at the end of the production it may be possible to sell the props and make some money to put back into the budget. Don't rely on this though!

Other areas to think about are:

Action vehicles – period or contemporary, these need to come with a driver, and must be added to the production insurance.

Action props – such as mini wet downs, smoke/haze effects, action drinks.

Special effects – such as rain, wind, fire, smoke, snow, explosions.

Road coverage – for period drama to cover those yellow lines, etc.

Graphics – such as signage, dressing pictures, newspapers and magazines.

Consumables – paint, timber, art department materials.

Stand-by equipment – (things not seen on screen, but very much needed) such as black drapes, artists' chairs, fire extinguishers, easi-ups and tarpaulins.

Strike costs – reinstatement (repainting, making good), skip hire, etc.

Transport – this is often under-estimated, as props need to be transported from hire house to set on a daily basis. The average props department transport budget will consist of the following (all of which need a driver): a props runaround vehicle, dressing props truck for pre-dressing and striking sets, stand-by props truck for on set and daily props pick-ups as and when needed.

It is very important to keep back a contingency for the art department budget, as unforeseen circumstances and schedule changes may mean extended hires or recalls on props, none of which the production designer will accept as part of their allocated budget.

Studio hire

Some productions will be studio-based, some location-based, and some a combination of the two. Generally speaking, if a set is required for more than two weeks, it is probably more cost-effective to build it on a stage. Studio shooting gives far more flexibility, as sets can be built with floating walls and ceilings to enable the camera to get more depth. It is a more controllable environment, often sound-proofed and with no interference from the public. Things to bear in mind when budgeting for a studio shoot are: the cost of studio power, overtime and weekend additional costs, costume and make-up rooms, equipment, props and costume storage, and whether the studio insists on employing a studio manager on the production's behalf and thus passing on the cost. Cleaning at the end of a shoot day is the task of the stage hand.

Construction and rigging costs

Set construction will be overseen by the production designer and is often sub-contracted to a specialist construction company. Similarly, if a particularly complex scaffold rig is required, such as a large blackout tent or studio rigging, both equipment and labour can be hired on an as-needed basis.

With budgets becoming increasingly tight, greenscreen shoots are becoming more popular. This is also called 'colour separation overlay', where two images are mixed together to create the illusion that actors or presenters are on location instead of in the studio. So for far-flung locations, it is a relatively inexpensive and simple way of achieving what may otherwise be impossible. The downside is, of course, that there will be restrictions in the camera movement, as the backdrop is only 2D.

Location costs

As with the art department budget, the location budget amounts to a significant percentage of the overall budget. It is therefore extremely important that you can trust your location manager, who will be responsible for managing the location budget as well as being able to find suitable locations which please the director.

When costing out the overall location budget, the following areas need to be considered:

Location fees – i.e. the actual cost of the location, including dressing and strike-out days.

Unit base costs – where the facilities vehicles will be parked up, and where the crew will park their private cars. Remember to include days off, as facilities vehicles still need to park up somewhere between shoot days.

Green rooms on location – artist resting areas when not on set.

Location heating or air-conditioning – if required, depending on time of year.

Cost of local power and water facilities.

Night-time safety lighting – if shooting in unlit areas.

Rubbish clearance.

Structural surveys – if filming in old or derelict buildings.

General gratuities (small payments to local residents can smooth the way if you need to block a driveway, for instance).

Location stills – costs of consumables such as mounting board, print cartridges and library search fees.

Security – the location manager is also responsible for hiring security. Generally, insurers require a security presence thoughout the shooting day and overnight if filming in unsafe areas. These costs can escalate quite quickly, especially when additional costs are added such as overtime, evening meals, etc. Make sure the location manager has agreed all incidental costs before contracting the security firm.

Police presence – this will be required if filming takes place on a public highway and particularly if the road needs to be closed for a period of time. Again, these costs can escalate, as police often come in pairs and for a minimum of 5 hours!

Production equipment

Camera equipment

Because there are so many different cameras out there for the choosing, it is beyond the scope of this book to give comprehensive advice. They range from 35mm film cameras for big-budget cinema films, through to High Defininition and tapeless cameras for lower-budget films and television, and Standard Definition for much cheaper productions.

In most instances a second camera – or at the very least, a second camera body – should be part of the camera kit. This is mainly for back-up should the main camera break down, but it's also useful to use a second camera when coverage is crucial. An example of this would be while shooting a stunt or special-effects sequence that requires a lot of reset time for another take. If you were shooting a scene on a lake and you had two actors jumping in to rescue somebody, imagine how long it would take to get them back to shore and dry them off completely, ready to do the shot again. In order to save on employing additional camera crew for a small number of 2nd camera set-ups, and if your DOP is in agreement, it is possible to pay an upgrade to your camera crew. This gives them the valuable experience they need in order to move up a grade. One additional camera assistant would need to be employed in this instance.

Your DOP will give you a list of camera equipment with their wish list for lenses and filters, etc. and you may well find yourself negotiating with the DOP as well as the camera hire company in terms of the camera package deal, and what you can and can't afford.

Grips often have their own equipment, but very rarely own their own dolly and track. This is because dollies are extremely expensive and such large items to store. The additional grip equipment required may include varying height tripods, different attachments to the camera (fluid heads and sliders), ladder pod, mini monitor, plus an array of levelling equipment to ensure that the camera track is level – especially on uneven surfaces.

Other requests in the camera and grip department might be: camera cranes for high, moving shots; low-loaders or A-frames for shooting action in a moving vehicle; steadicam for long, fluid camera movements. These additional requirements can cost more than £1,000 each, so necessity of the shot versus budget considerations should be kept in mind.

The camera and grip equipment will be stored and transported in a camera truck with dedicated driver while on location, but can be off-loaded if shooting in a studio.

Lighting equipment

Unlike camera equipment hire companies, there are very few lighting companies to choose from. Their rates vary enormously, not just between companies but also depending on the type of production you are. Commercials have relatively higher budgets and the lighting companies can charge top whack, whereas TV drama budgets are often tight, so the lighting company may adjust their rates accordingly. It's best to get the lighting list from your gaffer, then send it out for quotes.

The deal should include a lighting generator (genny) and a large truck to transport all the equipment. Every electrician who drives a truck or genny needs to have an HGV licence. And fuel for these trucks soon mounts up: the genny will take red diesel and probably costs around £10 per hour to run, and there will also be road fuel on top.

Additional lighting requests which might come your way are: lighting balloons (large inflatable lights which shed a soft overall light – great for ballrooms, court rooms, etc.); and consumables such as lighting gel, black wrap, polystyrene boards, extra bulbs, crocodile clips – the list is long, and you will not have an accurate costing for it until the end of the shoot, so make sure you keep a separate section in the budget for lighting consumables.

Cherry pickers, genie booms and scissor lifts are all machines designed to reach heights. Lamps are often positioned on these machines, which requires the help of a rigger and licences to drive.

Other miscellaneous lighting requirements may include blackout drapes and scaffolding, often used to build a 'tent' around a doorway or windows if you are shooting night scenes during the day. It's often cheaper to do that than to turn your shooting day into a night shoot.

Sound equipment

It would be very rare to employ a sound recordist who doesn't have their own equipment. Most sound these days is recorded on to hard-drive and backed up, then synched to the picture by the editor in the cutting room. Additional sound equipment which may be requested could include playback equipment for music playback, additional radio mics and lots of batteries.

Walkie-talkies are hired by production and enable the assistant directors on set to communicate with each other and with those at the unit base.

Costume and make-up

Costume

The costume designer is responsible for the costume budget. Costumes can be hired or purchased. As with props, hiring is the best option for a period drama; specialist tailors can make to measure, but with late casting and tight lead-up times individual makes can be tricky. For contemporary drama, experienced costume designers shop around, and often get good discounts with suppliers they use regularly. One of the bonuses for the crew at the end of a shoot is the costume and props sale: many items are sold off at 50%, with the proceeds going back into the budget. It's a winner all round!

Other things to remember when setting the costume budget are: fitting room hire, haberdashery, cleaning and repairs.

Make-up

The make-up budget will be managed by the make-up designer. If it is a fairly straight-forward shoot, then the budget should be minimal. However, for period drama, a lot of money can be spent on wigs (and wig fittings), facial hair, hair cuts and colour, etc. Prosthetics are also expensive and need to be created and applied by a reputable prosthetic technician.

Most make-up artists bring their own kit with them, which is usually charged to the production on a weekly basis as 'Box Hire'.

2nd Unit

On larger films and TV dramas, employing a 2nd Unit crew is an economical way of shooting additional footage. It may be useful for mute (no dialogue) background footage or for picking up sections of a scene which don't involve the principal artists. A 2nd Unit could range from a minimal three-man crew to a whole shooting crew with a 2nd Unit director.

Travel and transport

Within this budget category are the following subheadings:

Facility vehicles – which include costume and make-up trucks, artists' trailers (single, double or triple, depending on star status!), dining bus, production/AD office, honey wagon (portaloo) and generator. These vehicles travel to every location and form the 'unit base' for the production. They need to be in position well before the cast and crew arrive in the morning, and leave once everyone has wrapped, so the drivers' days are long. They may also end up having to travel to a new location on a day off, so this needs to be accounted for when budgeting.

Technical trucks – including the hire of camera truck with driver, grip truck, lighting trucks (hopefully included within lighting package deal), sound vehicle, props and art department trucks, stand-by construction and rigging trucks.

Costume pick-ups – an allowance for collecting and delivering costumes to and from hire houses.

Rushes transport – at the end of every shooting day, the rushes (be they on film, tape or hard-drive) need to be transported to a film lab or edit suite. These rushes are the day's work and are invaluable, so it is imperative that they are transported reliably and safely.

Allowances should also be made for:

Parking and Congestion charges (if shooting in central London).

Fuel – for technical vehicles, production vehicles and crew (if the locations are outside a 30-mile radius of the production office).

Artist transport – including unit drivers and artist taxis, and flights if required.

Bikes and taxis – for general production use.

Hotel and living

Catering – on a drama, cast and crew are provided with breakfast, lunch and tea. The meals are prepared by unit caterers, who travel to every location and park up their mobile kitchen at unit base. Within the 'price per head' deal you negotiate, you should expect breakfast, lunch, sandwiches and cakes at tea time and running tea, coffee, biscuits and fruit. Water is often charged as an additional cost, as is cooking gas, overtime, and additional snacks, such as a hot late break if shooting late or at night.

Off-set meal allowances – these are paid to crew who are unable to eat with the on-set caterers (for example, the props dressing team or location department, who usually have to be one step ahead of the shooting crew).

Per diems – a daily allowance paid to cast and crew if required to stay away from home.

Hotel accommodation.

Post production

Budgeting for post production needs experience, as there are so many different post production routes these days. The safest way to get an accurate budget is to acquire a number of quotes from different post production companies. Some 'post houses' specialise in picture only, and others in both picture and sound. A post production supervisor often takes over from the line producer at this stage, in which case you know the programme will be overseen in safe hands.

If you have shot on film, then the daily rushes will have been processed (negative development) overnight at a reputable film laboratory, transferred to a format which is compatible with the off-line edit equipment, and sound-sync'd. You are likely to end up with an amount of 'short ends', which is film stock that hasn't been shot but has been loaded on to a magazine. Many film schools will be delighted to receive your short ends, and you certainly can't sell them on to anyone else!

If your drama has been shot on a tapeless format, then the rushes will need to be downloaded daily on to a back-up hard-drive and then imported into the off-line edit equipment. This process is time-consuming and can take anything from 4–8 times actual running time (depending on resolution).

If you have shot on High Definition (HD) or Standard Definition (SD) tapes, then the process is a lot simpler. The rushes will need to be digitised into the off-line edit equipment on a regular basis, which takes more or less the actual running time.

Tapeless formats are becoming more popular, and they have the ability to create a more filmic look with a higher resolution.

The post-production route is very similar to that of any programme, and involves the following stages:

- *Off-line edit* – the rough cut (remember to budget for the cutting room if you are dry-hiring equipment).
- *Conform* – when the final picture assembly is taken from the off-line.
- *Despot* – where any dirt, scratches or unwanted marks are removed from the picture.
- *CGI (Computer Generated Imagery)* – particularly needed for special effects, and on period dramas where certain modern tell-tale signs such as satellite dishes and yellow lines need removing.
- *Grade* – usually attended by the DOP, the colourist (or grader) will give the programme an overall look by colour grading every frame.
- *On-line* – the final edit of the programme, which will include adding titles and credits.
- *Track-lay* – this will probably be happening at the same time as some of the above, and involves various sound tracks being pulled together including dialogue, atmos and possibly music.
- *ADR* – additional dialogue recording may be necessary if the sound recordist was not able to record clear sound on the day. This may be because of extraneous noise (aircraft, traffic, etc.), or if additional dialogue is needed for the script. In these instances, the artists will be called into a studio for a 'post-synching' session.
- *Foley* – sound effects such as footsteps on gravel, keys in locks and birds tweeting can all be added at this stage.
- *Pre-mix and final mix* – when all of the above come together.

Once all post production is complete, the programme will be mastered on to whichever format has been requested by the commissioner or financier. If there are a number of financiers (as is often the case with a feature film), a number of masters will need to be created. Remember to include these costs in your budget, along with publicity copies and any other requests. Feature films will need show prints and release prints too.

Archive

As with documentaries, all third-party material needs to be cleared for use within the programme. This includes TV clips and stills.

Other clearances, called negative checks, are also required for things such as: names of characters, names of places, names of businesses, addresses, telephone numbers, and art work (e.g. paintings, book covers and the like). This can be a long-drawn-out process, and often the script will need to be amended to accommodate a name or place change. Specialised 'neg checkers' are often employed to do this for the production.

Music

Music clearance can be a minefield. If your production is contracting a composer who will create specially composed music throughout the programme, then your life will be a lot simpler! If the composer chooses to use an orchestra or a variety of musicians, then they need to be cleared too.

However, if the script demands commercial tracks, then every track will have to be cleared. The rules are the same as for documentaries.

Other production costs

This category covers a multitude of miscellaneous costs including, but not limited to:

The PACT fee.

Rehearsal and read-through rooms.

Props and costume storage.

Production office equipment – which includes personal computers, stationery, photocopiers, safe hire, phone charges (mobile, land-lines and fax), postage, etc.

Legal fees.

Bank charges – plus accounting software, audit costs.

Insurance – including cast medicals, errors and omissions and an allowance for loss and damage which may be too minor for an insurance claim.

Publicity – including stills photographer (plus related expenses) and publicist.

Screenings and viewing theatres.

Delivery items – including production script and associated delivery paperwork.

Fringes – National Insurance accrued on relevant individuals.

There will always be numerous other miscellaneous expenses – too many to mention; but forethought, research and common sense are the key to successful budgeting. At the end of the day, no line producer can accurately predict the cost of bringing a script to the screen. However, the skill is in managing the production to fit within the final agreed budget while keeping the on-screen value at its maximum. This inevitably involves making decisions and implementing changes throughout production in conjunction with the producer and director. It's a huge jigsaw puzzle waiting to be played out!

A STEP-BY-STEP GUIDE TO THE LINE PRODUCER'S ROLE

Pre-production

- ☐ Finalise overall budget with financier(s).
- ☐ Create shooting schedule in conjunction with 1st AD.
- ☐ Choose and negotiate deals with crew.
- ☐ Allocate budgets to location manager, production designer, costume designer and make-up designer.
- ☐ Oversee casting in conjunction with casting director and producer and director.
- ☐ Negotiate major equipment deals.
- ☐ Choose caterers and facilities company.
- ☐ Negotiate any special effects and/or stunts.
- ☐ Attend location recces.
- ☐ HOD production meeting.
- ☐ Health & Safety meeting.
- ☐ Finalise equipment lists.
- ☐ Oversee location risk assessments.
- ☐ Get feedback from camera, costume and make-up tests.
- ☐ Attend script read-through.
- ☐ Check the first day's call sheet – and you're ready to roll!

The Shoot

- ☐ Visit the set daily so the crew can have access to you and air any problems. Be available and willing to listen to any grievances.
- ☐ Check the daily call sheet.
- ☐ General Health & Safety checks on location or in the studio.
- ☐ Keep in touch with the editor to ensure that all rushes are clear and that you are not missing any shots.
- ☐ Daily progress reports will be completed by your co-ordinator or production manager, but checked and signed off by the line producer. A daily progress report is an essential document which details the day's work in scenes, minutes, stock ratio, cast called, special equipment hired, catering figures, crowd figures, faulty equipment, accidents and near misses, and much, much more. In fact, everything that happens within the

shooting day should be documented in the daily progress report. This report is sent to the production executives, commissioners, financiers and insurance company, and will be used as evidence if any issues arise after completion of filming.

☐ Weekly cost report meetings are arranged with the accountant and producer.

☐ If shooting multi-episodic programmes, casting, scheduling and editing could all be happening at the same time. Juggling your time is an important skill for a line producer, along with problem-solving and people management.

Post Production

☐ On most productions, the line producer would not be required to stay on for post production, unless you are taking on the role of post production supervisor (which, of course, is possible). One or two weeks of wrap will cover the clear-up process of checking in all equipment, finalising loss and damage bills, completing a final production cost report with the accountant, and saying farewell to all the crew who have worked so hard to help bring the script to the screen!

3 An introduction to budgeting a documentary

This chapter concentrates on documentary budgets, though it does include passing reference to drama schedules (for more detail, see Chapter 2 on drama).

The budget templates for most UK and US channels are similar, and are divided into around 37 possible schedules. The first four of these don't contain figures but do impart information about schedule dates and production fees, as well as the clearances specified for the project. The costing schedules start from schedule 5 (see website 💻).

Budget templates

The Broadcaster will usually supply you with the format if you need it; alternatively you can use an Excel worksheet and custom-build it for smaller budgets. Before you start out, get an idea of the figure the Broadcaster has in mind. There is no sense in writing a budget that they don't have the money for.

Budgeting is the key to production management, because along with scheduling it forms the heart of the job. Having a realistic schedule and a budget that more or less matches it will mean that you set off on your project with a reasonable chance of getting it made on time and for the right money.

Budget schedules

The first schedules in a Broadcast budget will refer to items like the production fee. The production fee is the profit line that the independent production company makes on each project and will probably be a percentage (agreed by all sides) of the 'direct costs and overheads'. Be aware that the Broadcaster will keep in reserve a part of this fee to be paid only when *all* the deliverables have been received, so if you fail to do this you will not be popular.

Schedule 5 – Development

Sometimes the Broadcaster will give you an amount of money – anywhere between £2k and £40k – to develop a project. Draw up a mini-budget and cash flow for it. If and when the main budget is done you must remember to include the development costs.

Development funding does not qualify for a production fee, but if the project is subsequently commissioned you can include the (paid) development advance in your full budget and retrospectively claim the production fee. The Broadcaster will probably want a mini-cost report on how you spent the development funding, and you may have agreed that you will deliver a taped interview or a much more detailed treatment, which should also be submitted within a specified time. Remember that having some development money does not necessarily lead to a commission, though you shouldn't have to return the funds if the project doesn't go ahead.

Schedule 6 – Producer/director

If you are not sure of the current rates for these personnel, try asking around – enquire of other production managers or your head of production, for example. Or call up the Production Managers Association (PMA – contact details are given under 'Help Agencies' at the end of this book) and ask advice from production managers who are familiar with the genre you are crewing up for. The contract for producers, directors, series producers and other production staff may outline hours to be worked, but in reality they will probably work the hours that are required to get the job done with no overtime costs. And if you suspect that they will want to work from home, even though you have provided a desk, telephone and computer, you might want to make it clear that any home costs will not be covered by you unless it's a pre-agreed phone bill (in which case you will need an itemised copy of the bill and the refund can't cover any portion of the line rental, only calls made).

You may also have in this schedule an amount for, say, the executive producer who is employed by the company you are working for. This will be an internal payment and will probably be taken with or without sight of an internal invoice. Either way – wave it goodbye. These sorts of internal costs are the company's way of paying the salary of their payroll staff, so you may also find a portion of money reclaimed for runners, receptionists and the like, and possibly internal services too. There is no point in arguing, even if you don't actually see much of the said personnel or services.

Schedule 7 – Artists/actors and extras/stuntmen or women

DRAMA ONLY

See Chapter 2 on drama, where the rates, fees and contracts for these personnel are explained more fully.

Allow for a casting director in your budget so that they can suggest likely actors for your casting session, and then do deals with the relevant agents. This saves you much aggravation, time and energy and will be worth the fee, although you will have to produce the contract for the actors (call PACT for advice).

Supporting artists and extras can be hired through agencies using the Film Artists Association (FAA) Agreement or Equity Walk On rules, or sometimes you may be able to approach one of the many re-enactment groups that abound. Alternatively, friends may help out for a beer voucher! Do make sure that you don't offer less than the minimum wage (£5.73 per hour at the time of writing). However, take care not to alienate Equity, as they are vigilant about the practice of hiring non-professionals to take part in drama sequences since it threatens the livelihood of their members – again, take advice from PACT.

Employing children is full of constraints and you need to be aware of all the regulations governing it. PACT will help with initial enquiries.

Schedule 8 – Interviewees and contributors/narrator

You will probably have to pay interviewees for their contributions. Offer them only what you can afford unless, of course, they have you over a barrel.

If they travel to your location they must always have their travel expenses paid and be fed, watered and overnighted if necessary. Academics will usually want an hourly or daily fee, plus expenses. And if you are hiring several for your programme, be aware that they will probably talk to each other and compare fees, so standardise them as much as possible. (Favoured nations doesn't just apply to music!) As a general rule Broadcasters don't like paying fees to contributors and still think they will do it for love (indeed, a few of them will). But increasingly, contributors want money – so get the researcher to broach the subject when making initial contact. You may want to take over the negotiation at some point. Once you have agreed a fee, email or write confirming the amount and how it will be paid. Offering cash on the day may make negotiating a bit easier.

Voice-over artists' fees can vary, so call up a couple of agencies and ask how much they charge. Any of the standard V/O agencies will happily send you endless options, and you can listen to samples of voices on their website. Standard narrators are generally quite negotiable. However, if the Broadcaster wants a 'name', this will be more expensive. Try to pin down a couple of options and ring their agents for a quote.

> **USEFUL TIP**
> Voice-over artists or narrators should have a standard narrator contract unless they are narrating in character, in which case they will need an Equity contract.

Schedule 9 – Production staff

Production co-ordinators, production secretaries and accountants, plus researchers, assistant producers, location managers and casting directors (and possibly fixers) are included here. Check the current rate of pay for each of them – a documentary production manager will be less than a drama PM – and the PMA will help here. You could just call up an experienced production manager and check the current rates for all these roles, and they may also help with possible candidates; personal recommendations are always a good idea.

Your production staff rates will vary depending on seniority and experience. Never, ever disclose rates within the team; such information should be confidential. Always keep invoices face down on your desk to avoid prying eyes, and enter them yourself into the cost book/manager and file contracts under lock and key.

Accountants may come from an agency with a set rate (if you are working for a small production company) or they may be in-house. You will need to put around one day of their services per week in the budget. Check with the accountant themselves, or with your head of production. The company will tell you exactly what sums you should put in your budget for all their 'internal' charges (as previously indicated, these may be for payroll staff or services within the company). This is sometimes known as the 'margin' for the production company.

Location managers reside in the Schedule 9 if you're doing a drama.

Schedule 10 – 1st assistant directors/2nds and 3rds

See Chapter 2 on Drama for help with these roles.

Schedule 11 – Camera crew

A good director of photography (or cameraman or camerawoman) will be worth their weight in gold. A word of advice here: if you negotiate hard for a lower rate than they have asked for, you may find that they will not go the extra mile on the shoot or that their invoice will curiously contain extras that take the daily rate back up to the original quote. Be clear about the length of working day you are asking for (8, 10 or 12 hours).

You might try to get a buy-out deal to save yourself overtime, but they may not go for this – possibly having been badly screwed in the past. Their working day will include travel and an hour for lunch, so you may only end up with a very short day if you book them for 8 hours. And it's not possible to get a cameraman to do a half day. Who else is going to hire them for the other half?

If you have a sizeable block of filming you can discuss a mutually good deal, remembering to factor in some rest days so they are not on their knees by the end of the shoot. For travel, recce and rest days I would ask for a lower rate – say, half of their working day figure or a little bit more than half. And if you are flying them home from your shoot on an overnight flight you will need to pay them for the day when they arrive home, since they will be too knackered to work that day. In such a case I'd try and get some work out of them for the morning of the day they fly (GVs on the way to the airport?); otherwise you have two full days which have been paid with nothing 'on the screen' to show for it.

Some cameramen will own their own kit and want, understandably, to use it and include it in their daily deal. If the format is right for you, this will save you having to hire separately.

Make sure the crew get fed and watered properly; film crews, like armies, march on their stomachs. Film days can be long and arduous and subject to all weathers, so a hot lunch is preferable with time to eat properly – and keep the hot or cold drinks going during the day with snacks to keep up sugar levels. And if you are filming a long day you should offer dinner as well – it really isn't fair to expect people to work well if they are hungry or thirsty, and a grumpy crew will not work to their full potential and are not a joy to be around.

If you are filming in the UK you might find that your DOP will own their own vehicle and will hire it to you for the day for a daily fee, which may include a number of free miles. If you can negotiate a fuel receipt rather than mileage for the rest of the journey you will probably save some money. Owning their own production vehicle will mean that they will probably have the correct insurance in place, so their vehicle is insured for work purposes – always worth double-checking with them.

Protocol dictates that you ask the producer/director which cameraman or camerawoman they would like to work with. If they are not available (and good camera crews get booked up early) then call in some CVs and showreels for the director to look at, and get recommendations from other production managers.

GUERRILLA FILMING

One-man crews for certain jobs. You must agree with your cameraman beforehand that they are happy to record sound, and be prepared for them to decline this sort of job. Ask around to find people who are used to working like this.

SECRET OR COVERT FILMING

If you are asking a cameraman to film secretly, then there may be an element of threat attached. In such a case you might also need to think about having a security person around, heavily disguised perhaps. And, of course, the details of such filming must always be discussed beforehand with your Broadcaster, since you must have their permission (in writing) for this. There are some invaluable guidelines to be found in the *Independent Producer Handbook* issued by Channel 4 and 5, which you should consult for this and all sorts of other advice and instructions.

UNDERWATER FILMING

This will require specialised underwater protection for the camera (costed under production equipment). You should probably find a specialised underwater cameraman and you will need to allow extra money for person and equipment, so check costs with an experienced operator.

FILMING FROM HELICOPTERS OR AIRCRAFT

Check with a specialist company, because filming in a helicopter (for example) will require a special mount for safety. (And don't forget to tell your insurers.) Helicopter shoots are expensive because you will pay for time by the hour and you will need to factor in the flying time between their base and your location and back again. It's a good idea when sourcing these kinds of facilities to find possible suppliers on the Internet or in a production guide, and then call around and get them to talk you through the process and give you a quote. Ask for a copy of their Health & Safety procedures so you can incorporate it into your own risk assessment when you come to do it.

CAMERA ASSISTANTS

More normally used if shooting on film; also in some circumstances when tape is being used (for example, if there is going to be a lot of moving around or lighting set-ups to do). The cameraman will prefer to work with an assistant they know, so respect that. Camera assistant daily rates can be surprisingly expensive.

GRIPS AND GRIP EQUIPMENT

There are good companies who will supply a vehicle with lots of equipment on it as well as the personnel. Usually you pay for the kit as it gets taken out of the van, but remember to check this. You will probably also pay for the mileage of the vehicle. It might be difficult to anticipate what this will cost you in advance so make a generous estimate and put it in your anticipated costs. (See also Chapter 2 on Drama.)

Schedule 12 – Sound crew

Based on a daily fee (again, specify the hours you need) plus their sound kit. As with the cameraman/woman they should also offer a recce/travel day rate. Check with your DOP which sound recordist they prefer; indeed, the two may come as a package that includes their own sound equipment. Don't forget to tell them if you need them to record interviews for transcription purposes, and ask them to liaise with the transcriber to get a recorded sound format that is acceptable to both parties.

Schedule 13 – Lighting crew (gaffers and sparks)

If you have any big set-ups you may require chaps to light them. Companies like Film & TV Services are excellent because they will supply men and a van with gear which you will pay for only as and when you take it off. It's difficult to predict exactly how much this will all cost, but talk to them and over-cost it slightly. *(Film & TV Services on 0208 961 0090; mail@ftvs.co.uk)*

Schedule 14 – Art department crew

You may require a production designer, art director or props master, possibly props buyer and a couple of assistant props – depending on the size of the project. Ask the production designer about staffing and s/he will probably suggest names and hire them on your behalf. Be clear about what budget is available and make sure they stick to it (or inform you in good time if they look like over-spending). See Chapter 2 on Drama for more details.

Schedule 15 – Wardrobe and make-up

You will need a costume supervisor and possibly an assistant; also possibly a dresser(s) depending on how many actors or supporting artists and extras you call on a specific day. Also required will be a hair and make-up supervisor and assistants – once you have details on numbers they will help you decide how many staff are required. Don't forget that if you have a large number of cast to get ready for a start time that demands all of your cast, you will need more assistants to get them ready in time – otherwise you'll have the whole crew standing around waiting for three people to sort out 90 cast members.

Schedule 16 – Editors

Suitably experienced editors will be almost as highly paid as your directors. In the past, editors traditionally worked long hours and often weekends as part of their remit, but times have changed and they will probably want a five-day week contractually confirmed. Make sure that if your director is intending to work really late or on a weekend they let you know in advance so you can check with the editor how much this is going to cost you.

USEFUL TIP

The aim of negotiating rates and extras beforehand is to make everything as predictable as possible, so you know what your final costs are going to be with a minimum of nasty surprises.

Schedule 18 – Wage-related overheads

The difference between staff who are self-employed or freelance (they used to be known as schedule D) and those on the payroll (they will be employed on a PAYE basis) will affect this schedule. The Inland Revenue has the final say on who can be taxed on a freelance or self-employed status; only certain roles qualify. No one who is an assistant (e.g. assistant cameraman, production assistant, assistant producer) can be self-employed; they must be on your payroll unless they can get a letter from the Inland Revenue exempting them, and you will need to see this and keep a copy. I know it may seem fussy to hire an assistant cameraman for four days on the payroll, but that is how it has to be unless they come as part of the package deal that your cameraman is offering. Check with the IR if you are not sure how to apply this rule.

Put simply, anyone who is hired on a self-employed basis will be responsible for their own tax and NI contributions, and will invoice you for their total quoted fee. Anyone who is hired on a PAYE basis will be added to your payroll and the company then becomes responsible for deducting their income tax and the employer's National Insurance contribution. The employer's percentage is 12.8 at the time of writing, but it does change, so make sure to check it. You will need to calculate 12.8% of the total fee for each individual PAYE person hired and put it in this schedule. If you get it wrong you will put both the company and your budget at risk – so don't.

If you can't be sure at the budgeting stage which staff will be on the payroll, then err on the side of caution and allow 12.8%. Then you'll have some small change to play with if they turn out to be self-employed.

You should also allow holiday credits here – current EU rules are 28 holiday days per year for all employees. Holiday credits should be applied to every member of your team and crew, whether they are freelance or PAYE, and you should encourage them to take the holiday within their contract wherever possible. If this proves impossible then you will add on their holiday credit as money when they leave. You can also stipulate when they take their holiday – for example, over the Christmas break. If it's a short and frantic schedule then it might be difficult to give people time off, but the holiday credit plan was introduced precisely because we all need a break, so you should encourage people to take them. Editors and directors, for example, might find it helpful to take a few days off when the rough cut has been submitted to the Broadcaster and they are waiting for comments back. And try and take your own holidays too – a few days off can clear your head and renew your energy (and frankly, you deserve it!). To help you calculate holiday pay on all five days per week contracts, see the PACT website where there is a nifty little calculation mechanism. Or you can do it yourself by dividing 28 (days per year) by 52 (the number of weeks in a year) and multiplying the result (.5384615) by the total number of weeks in the contract. You can round up the figure if it's a pesky decimal point of a day. Thus if someone has been contracted for 6 months (26 weeks), 28 divided by 52 and multiplied by 26 will equal 14 days' paid holiday.

Schedule 19 – Production design

See Chapter 2 for guidance.

Schedule 20 – Wardrobe and make-up materials

You will need to discuss the costume and make-up requirements with the staff you have hired once they have a clear idea of what the script requires. This is difficult at the budget stage, so bear in mind that in general, wardrobe will cost much more than make-up and talk to both sets of specialists for help in estimating these costs.

Schedule 21 – Production equipment

Camera and sound-kit costs are included here. The cameraman may have his/her own kit and s/he or the hire company may do a deal of four for seven days, for example. Also, you shouldn't be charged kit costs for travel or recce days, where the camera doesn't 'turn over'.

If you hire kit from a hire company, your cameraman will almost certainly have a preferred company and be able to get a decent discount. Get a list of the equipment they want and ask them to talk technical to (a) your producer/director and (b) the handler at the hire company. Then talk money – remember it's the cameraman's wish list so you may not be able to afford all the things they think they want! If they want a dolly and some tracking, for example, you will need to allow for hefty delivery and collection charges on these extras and also check insurance. If you use a large dolly you will need a grip – cost in schedule 11.

The cost of crews' mobile phone bills go here if you have agreed to pay them. You will need a copy of every phone bill with the relevant calls highlighted, and agree that you will pay this before anyone starts their contract as it's now not necessarily a cost covered by the budget. You should pay only for the cost of calls, not line rental. It might be better to supply a production mobile and insist that they use that. If you are shooting in America you can get the crew to buy an American mobile when they arrive and they can put some credit on it (remind them to tell you the number!). You should discourage crew members from using hotel phones to call their nearest and dearest unless they buy a local phone card. Most hotels mark up their phone calls by a huge percentage and that's just wasted money, so it's worth researching these sorts of items for your crew before they depart.

Schedule 22 – Crew/camera kit

When the crew and all their equipment come as a package you can put the total cost in here. If you are shooting abroad and want to hire equipment there, then check sources very carefully. If you hire PAL cameras in the United States, for example, you may find them easily on the east or west coast but less easily in smalltown America, which may result in costly courier bills. And remember that a PAL kit in America may not be cleaned and maintained as well as a PAL kit in this country, so insist on a camera test at the start of the shoot.

Schedule 23 – Studio package/outside broadcast

Cost here for an agreed price for any studios that you have negotiated. This will generally apply more to drama projects, so see Chapter 2 for further information. However, studios may be needed for drama inserts into a drama/doc project so you would normally approach a studio, discuss your project with them and agree on what is required in the way of space, lighting rigs, staffing, use of telephones and broadband services and other facilities, any in-house catering costs, and clear-up and rubbish disposal services. You may find yourself budgeting an outside broadcast project, in which case your best plan is to approach a company who specialises in such projects to talk through your project with them. I would also advise you to speak to another production manager who has experience of these types of shoots, as they do require that you understand the process very clearly so you don't under-budget them.

Schedule 24 – Other production facilities

This schedule is for items like location fees, office and equipment (if required) gratuities and security and other odds and ends. Location fees may be very high, particularly if you are hoping to film in anywhere like an English Heritage site, any National Trust property or public building.

If you are budgeting a drama or drama/doc then you may need to set up a temporary production office on a site other than your base – so allow money for hire of equipment and machinery and possibly a generator to power it all. It is wise to allow something for gratuities in the UK – you may need to pay someone to stop using a pneumatic drill when you're trying to interview a contributor on the roadside! This figure might be substantially higher in a country which functions on tips, so consult your fixer. You might also need to allow something for overnight security if you will be leaving any kit on site overnight.

Schedule 25 – Stock

Shop around stock suppliers for quotes and check if you can get a discount through your Broadcaster. Check with the sound recordist to see if they need any sound stock.

The film stock used in documentary television is usually 16mm – check with a film-stock supplier for current prices and don't forget that you will need to factor in processing and telecine costs too. Film stock can usually be purchased on a sale-or-return basis. See Chapter 2 on Drama if you are budgeting on Super 8, 16 or 35mm film stock; also see schedule 26, below).

Tape stock should also be kept cool and can be ordered in bulk to save money. For High Definition (HD) stock, remember that post production may be more expensive if you are using this format, especially if you are also delivering on it. We now have P2 cards which you record on to and then download on to your computer, so you may need to take a quick training course on these. The best course of action for costing any shooting material is to ring up a supplier and ask them, not only about prices but also about any possible attendant costs.

You will also need stock for editing (dump stock) and possibly for press and publicity copies. Don't forget to allow for delivery stock and check the contract for the format the Broadcaster requires. Do you need to buy tape stock for the transcription of interviews?

USEFUL TIP
Can you recycle old stock for dumps and transfers during the edit? Budget new, use old.

Schedule 26 – Film post production

If by some miracle you are shooting some or all of your project on film, contact a good laboratory and get them to talk you through the process and cost it for you – they're very good at this. Check with your director about how s/he wants the material treated and whether s/he wants it telecined to tape for the edit with or without VHS viewing copies.

Schedule 27 – Tape post production

This schedule will form a substantial proportion of your budget – maybe a third. In here will go all the transfer costs/digitising/off-line edits/on-line editing/dubs/voice-over recording/colour grades, etc. Ring round some facilities houses and compare prices. Does your director prefer one in particular? The rates should be negotiable, especially if there's not much work around. See Chapter 18 on Post Production for more information.

The technical aspects can be problematic here so try for a crash course from your director or editor and check out the potential facilities house with one of them. Make friends with the client contact because you'll be talking to them a lot when you're trying to change the dates you've made! Set time limits for the expensive on-lines/grades and dubs to control costs – otherwise the director will sit there forever tweaking!

The off-line edit suite is usually 'dry-hired' and you hire your editor separately. Check when booking what hours the suite is available for, as the company may not be happy, for example, for you to have access over a weekend. The more expensive post production time – like on-lines and sound mixing – are usually hired by the hour and include an expert operator. In fact, some directors will specifically want a particular operator to do the grade, so get these people pencilled as early as possible.

Some facilities houses will offer a per-programme deal if you are making a lengthy series, and this might well be worth considering. You pay a set price for the whole of the post production process following picture lock, and provided you don't go too wildly over your predicted hours it can make economic sense.

See Chapter 18 on Post Production for more details.

Schedule 28 – Archive and stills

The Broadcaster, when they commission your programme, will probably give you an indication of how much archive they want, although the subject matter will, of course, dictate this to a certain extent. Much footage is negotiable – as a rule of thumb allow £1,000 per minute, more for a more extensive clearance than 2 x UK. Add in some costing for possible transfer costs and DVD viewing copies. Some archive, like NASA footage, is free (though you'll pay for transfer and courier costs). Feature film clips will be hugely expensive and you will need to clear any music on them separately. Determine what clearance you will require for the Broadcaster: Worldwide, for example, will be very expensive and Worldwide in Perpetuity will bankrupt you!

> **USEFUL TIP**
> Does it need to be cleared, or clearable – there is a difference!

See Chapter 15 on Archive for more explanations on archive and stills.

Schedule 29 – Graphics and rostrum

Graphics can be hugely expensive so if you know there is a demand for CGI (Computer Generated Imagery) in your programme/series, be prepared. Shop around for quotes and try the bigger graphics houses as well as the smaller operations; this will give you a better idea of the range available. Try to approach a graphics artist/company who is 'hungry' and keen to negotiate a deal or all-in package. It's difficult to give a rule-of-thumb cost for CGI since there are so many different styles available, but you and your director will need to spend some time with the graphics house that you eventually choose, and make sure that the wish list for graphics fits the budget you have given it.

See Chapter 16 on CGI for more information.

Rostrum camera is a fixed or bench camera which will capture, on tape, still images that you want in your programme (photographs, newspaper headlines or text, for example). The tape can then be used as a source tape in your edit. Talk to a rostrum house and calculate approximately how many items they can capture in an hour. Then you can estimate the cost of, say, a dozen items per episode. Usually you can book rostrum in 15-minute portions; check if you can take your own stock to save their mark-up on the stock they supply.

If your project has been shot on film you will need to find a rostrum house which will use film for your rostrum.

Schedule 30 – Music

There are three basic choices here – composed, library or commercial. Composed will make life much easier for you because all you have to do is find the composer and do a deal. Cost will depend partly on the length of your programme(s) and the fame of your composer but, as ever, it's negotiable. I would think that £3,000 for a one-hour programme would be a good starting point.

Library music is also straightforward. Call up the MCPS/PRS for Music to get their set rate-card for the clearances you need. You can get endless free discs from companies like Bruton & Chappel, or visit their websites for examples.

The third option, commercial music, is where madness lies. If you can possibly dissuade your director from going down this road, then do. Commercial music will need two lots of clearance – publishing and recordings rights (i.e. you pay a fee to whoever wrote it and again to who performed it). In particular, American commercial music will be a nightmare to clear. If you have to use commercial music you need to budget for some professional help in clearing and paying for it, so I would call up a few examples of such companies and take their advice about what amounts to put in your budget. But before you do any of that, read Chapter 17 on Music for the easy way out!

Schedule 31 – Travel and transport

You will need a clear idea of where you are going to film the various elements of your programme. Call up a good media travel agent (like Screen & Music Travel – or get your production secretary to do it!) and get quotes for flights, hotels, excess baggage, visas, etc. A good travel agent who understands that there will be last-minute changes and cancellations is invaluable and someone like Screen & Music Travel's sister company Samfreight also handles carnets (see also below).

Don't forget possible inoculation and visa costs for your crew. There are organisations that will help you gain visas, or check with the relevant embassy. Read the chapter on foreign filming for more information.

A carnet, put simply, is a passport for your camera and sound kit and you will need one if you are taking camera/sound kit to any country outside the European Community. They are issued by the Chamber of Commerce and I would strongly advise that you get a carnet company to do yours for you; it's very time-consuming to do it yourself. And if you are shipping your kit outside the UK you will probably need to pay for the excess baggage on it, so allow for this item on flights to *and* from your destinations.

It may be a good idea to split this section into the recces/prep period, the filming period and a little bit for the post period to more clearly calculate these costs.

You will need to allow some cash to cover recces to the locations, though a way of saving money is to run the recce into the shoot and thus reduce flights and overnights. Bear in mind, though, that the director may feel this doesn't give him/her enough time to plan the shoot. Allow some money for hire cars, trains and taxis for UK-based recces and find out who will be going on them. There may be recces to check out suitable locations as well as visits to possible contributors, and you can't calculate the exact cost of these – but you will need to put in a lump sum that is based on shrewd estimates.

The bulk of this schedule's money will probably be spent during your shoot period(s). Allow money to cover flights for all the people who are going on the shoot, their journeys to and from the various airports (surprisingly expensive – can you save money by doubling up people who live near each other?), and their excess baggage if you are flying out the kit too. Carnet costs will need to be calculated and some costing for any visas you need and inoculation costs. You will need to budget for the team and crew vehicles while abroad and a driver if you are in a 'difficult' area (see Chapter 12 on Foreign Filming) plus money allowed for fuel, tolls and parking. (Hazard an informed guess about fuel use – for example, for each vehicle – then multiply it by the days the crew are away and add a bit.) Don't calculate these amounts too tightly; err on the side of generous.

Do you need to pre-book airport parking or is it cheaper to use a driven vehicle that can drop off crew and kit?

Allow for excess baggage if your crews are taking their own equipment. You can get quotes from the travel agent or airline, but some cameramen are brilliant at bargaining at check-in so you may save money here.

If you are making a drama or drama/doc you may need production vehicles – make-up and costume trucks, catering vehicle and possible dining buses, a honey wagon (toilet truck), Winnebagos for your cast – see Chapter 2 for more details.

Finally, allow some money in the post period to cover late-night cabs for directors and editors. Add a line across the schedule period for taxis generally, plus a weekly amount to cover bikes for ferrying tapes, graphics and any other bits and pieces. If you are working for an American Broadcaster then add in a hefty amount for couriers (i.e. Fedex) to get masters and possibly rushes back to them, and a lesser amount for delivering within the UK.

Schedule 32 – Hotel and living

Try to get a clear idea of who will be going where, and know that every time they step out of the office you will be paying for their food, overnights, coffee and snacks –

everything, in fact, that they need to keep them going. If your crew are travelling abroad get estimates for hotels (remember to allow for breakfasts because this is not always an included item in an overnight cost) and don't forget laundry, newspapers and telephone calls, especially if your crew are going to be away for a while. Remember that hotels mark up telephone calls enormously, so it may be worth getting some sort of telephone discount card. It would be worth advising crew (in writing, on the call sheet) that you will not pay for their mini-bar costs or porn films in their hotel room!

Allow per diems for every filming and recce day – PACT have suggested rates for per diems (a set amount handed out to cover food, drinks and snacks for the day) but they're very low so don't undercut them. I would base per diems fairly on local cost-of-living rates. Remember you are feeding and watering your crew but not paying for them to get drunk. Another option is to pay for everything while the crew is on the road, which will involve giving a float to someone responsible if you are not there yourself. But the amount of the float should be based on your per diem amount plus a bit for extras.

An example of calculating this amount would be to assume that if you are filming in the UK and you are paying for breakfast within your hotel bill, then allow, say, £10 for lunch and £20/25 for dinner (to include a beer or glass of wine). Add on another fiver for hot drinks, water and snacks throughout the day – a total amount of let's say £40 per person, per day. The total will be £40 multiplied by the days on the shoot (include travel days) multiplied by the number of people on the shoot.

Allow a little bit for hospitality (a useful cushion of money to cover unexpected costs) and also late meals if the production team are likely to be working very late in the office or in the edit. Don't forget to allow an amount for feeding and possibly overnighting presenters, contributors and interviewees who will be on the shoot, and be aware that they may bring a companion with them in certain situations and you can't not pay for them too.

If you're doing drama you will require catering (I think most catering companies will have a minimum plate number). Call up some catering companies and get an idea of meals per day per head cost. Good catering is worth it in terms of a happy crew. (See also Chapter 2 on Drama.)

If you work long filming days on a shoot (beware, there are contractual limits and Health & Safety limitations) you will need to feed the crew an evening meal, so budget for that. Otherwise your catering will need to include at least lunch costs, breaks and possibly breakfasts.

If you are shooting at night on a documentary type of shoot, ask yourself where you will feed your team. Is it open late and will it cost you more? Don't risk leaving these kinds of things to chance; a hungry crew will not be a happy, or efficient, one.

These two schedules (31 and 32) are usually around a similar total and form a large part of the total budget. You will need to tread a fine line between keeping costs down, because it's money we don't see on the screen, and not under-budgeting, because every time a team member leaves the office you're paying for where they go and what they eat and drink on trains and in airports, as well as when they get there.

Schedule 33 – Other production costs

Transcriptions are budgeted here – the expensive process of transcribing interviews for your director to read and select sound bites from.

If your project requires translating, check out some agencies who offer this service and you may have to pay for both translation and transcription. Don't forget to add in the services of a translator in the edit to check that you have edited sound bites properly so that they make sense in the original language. Different languages may also require subtitling and this should be costed here. (Sometimes the Broadcaster will want a foreign language segment dubbed instead of subtitled, in which case that cost will go in schedule 28 – sound post production with a possible extra narrator to do the foreign bits costed into schedule 8. Though you might save money on this by dragging volunteers from the team to the dubbing studio!)

Research materials are also costed here: books, magazines and newspapers, sometimes CDs or videos – any special requirements in your programme (like transcriptions from a medical hearing or accident reports)?

Check with your Broadcaster about whether they require production stills and if this should form part of the budget. If so, budget for a person plus their stock and processing costs.

Transmission postcards seem to have been superseded by electronic postcards, but if they are required they should be costed here.

You should budget for your post production script here, which will be part of your deliverables – get a quote to have them done commercially but, when it comes to it, can your production secretary do it? (Some American Broadcasters now demand that their post production scripts are done by a particular company, so get a quote from them.)

Schedule 34 – Insurance/finance and legal

Check with your Broadcaster to see if they pay for insurance or if they allow a budget amount for it. If it's a co-production, double-check who is paying for insurance and then get a rough quote from an insurance broker.

Allow a fee for setting up the bank account – usually projects will require a separate trust account. Allow for currency commissions if filming abroad.

You may want a lawyer to check the contract or there could be contentious issues in your programme. The Broadcaster may have people in-house to deal with this or you might have to hire a compliance lawyer to check your programme (and you'll need to send them a DVD and the script for this purpose).

You may also require E&O (errors and omissions) insurance, especially for a US-funded project.

See Chapter 10 on Insurance for more guidance on E&O.

Schedule 35 – Overheads

Check with whoever runs the production company to confirm what they want included here. There should be an amount to cover rent, rates, electricity, postage, photocopying, telephone costs, and computer and Internet use, etc. for the full production period.

People sometimes ask me if you can put a contingency amount in a budget, and the answer is usually no. A contingency is more often an amount of money which is included in your budget for a specific item or event. If for example you are hoping to secure an interview with, say, a significant interviewee but you don't know, when you are doing your budget, whether this will be possible, you can calculate what it would cost and draw the money down only if you get the interview. In other words, it's specific to a particular item and you can't draw on it just because you're over-spent or would like the money!

Calculate your grand total.

Check and double-check everything and then write up some text to explain how you arrived at various costings (i.e. a front page covering format for shooting, schedule, staffing, etc.). This will help you to justify how you arrived at your figures.

You may, of course, be given a target cost by the Broadcaster which you have to match your budget to – check whether they will require regular cost reports or whether you need only do internal cost reporting.

 Check the budget with your executive, series producer or director – whoever is creatively running the project – and discuss any changes, reductions or increases.

Make notes of where you think you can save money or move sums around to counter any possible over-spends, and keep this in your production file for future reference.

When the budget is authorised, do a cash flow (see Chapter 5); and when *that* is authorised, set up your cost book in good time for controlling your costs from the very first spend.

Good luck!

4   Scheduling

Each project that you work on needs to be divided into three basic periods:

- Pre-production – development and research
- Production – which is mainly the filming period, and
- Post production and delivery – editing and finishing your project and sending it to the Broadcaster.

If you have been given a TX (transmission) date then you will need to work backwards from that to determine your ideal pre-production start date. Alternatively the Broadcaster might demand delivery by a specific date, in which case your first job is to grab a calendar and see whether you stand a chance of fitting everything in by then.

You will then need to discuss with your producer/director some key questions:

- Exactly how long is your programme(s)?
- How many filming days are required for your project?
- Is there any archive or CGI in your programme, and if so, how much?
- How long do you need to edit (off-line and post production)?
- How many different versions are required (i.e. is it a co-production)?
- Which format(s) are you shooting/delivering on?
- How much pre-production time can you afford, and can it overlap with production?
- Can you start your edit before you finish filming?
- Will your producer/director want the editor to attend the on-line and mix?
- And the major question: How does this all fit in with the funding available?

I have included a draft schedule on the website 🖳 for you to use as a template. It's an Excel document and ideally uses colours to make it very easy to read. Your first draft will be just that – a draft. And I would suggest that you call it Draft/1 and date it. After that you may well find yourself redrafting the schedule all the way through the project (sometimes every day as things shift and change), so don't forget to update these details so that every team member is always working from the correct draft.

Let's work through my suggested template.

The left side of the document gives you a visual representation of the number of days, weeks or months that your schedule runs. The first column indicates the week number (you might also, if your schedule is lengthy, add this column again on the right-hand side to make it easier to read). The second column indicates the Week Beginning date, using Monday as the W/B day.

Along the top of your schedule you can list the programme(s) in your series (using episode 1, ep. 2, etc. rather than their working titles, which might change, or programme order, which might shift around). This column should be wide enough to describe briefly what is happening in the week. Later on in the schedule, for example when you start the post production, you may want to issue a daily schedule as a supplement to this, to describe the finer details of what is happening on each day. If you are only making one programme, or if you have a fast turnaround, you may start off with a day-by-day schedule. You can colour code the production parts of the episodes to separate them from the post period, and the delivery week can be highlighted in another colour followed by the TX dates as and when you know them – there's nothing like a TX date to motivate the team!

If you are making a series you will probably need to 'stagger' the start dates of each episode. This means that your production team will have some lead-in time for each shoot, rather than having shoots running concurrently, and you may also be able to use a particular director or editor to do more than one episode, which will help set the style and keep up consistency. Their dates will be easier to juggle when shown in colour on a handy chart. If your series is a long one, I would suggest that you try to add an extra 'stagger' in the middle – to give your team a bit of a breather and maybe fit in some holiday time, but your delivery dates may preclude this. By setting out your schedule in the way I have suggested you can see at a glance who might be able to do two episodes and where people may be able to take breaks. Believe me, if it is a long project some breathing space at intervals, even if it is only a week here and there, will help your team keep their momentum up.

If your schedule runs across public holidays, mark them clearly in yet another colour. Christmas especially will mean a period of down-time; although you or your team might want to work, the office may be closed – as may other facilities.

On the right-hand side of the schedule you will see a chart of columns which indicate the lengths of contract of each member of the team. You can put their initials or their role at the top of the chart and colour them differently. This can show at a glance when people start and finish their contract and how you might save money by snipping contracts by a week here and there while still covering the tasks to be done.

Circulate this schedule to all team members, and when reissuing it, let them know that the updated schedule replaces all previous drafts.

You can overlap your three major periods of production if necessary. For example, you may do some essential filming during the prep period because of a contributor's availability or because a researcher on a recce can capture with a small camera some timely incident that you may need. Pick-up days of filming can be saved for use when the edit is under way in case the director finds that s/he has 'black holes' (i.e. no pictures to cover the point being made in narration or pieces to camera). And your edit may have to start before main filming is completed if time is tight: the rushes can be couriered back to the editor, who can start digitising and assembling ahead of time.

If your episodes are approximately one hour each, then a rule of thumb for prep time might be six weeks – unless there has been some significant research and development done already, in which case you might be able to shave it a bit. Very approximately (and depending on how much archive and CGI is planned for each episode) you will probably require at least 10 days' filming per episode (so you could add two weeks as the filming period, which will give you a bit of time for travel). An off-line edit will need to be at least 5/6 weeks long, more if you can afford it. With the post production requirements which bring your project up to broadcast quality (on-line, grade, voice-over record and sound mixing) added on to this, say an extra week allowed which your editor may or may not stay on to supervise. Remember that if you are working for an American broadcaster there will be the inevitable delay while they view the rough cut and fine cut, so you may need to build extra time into your edit for this process. (If you decide to close the edit for, say, a week for this to happen then you need to agree storage with the post production house and whether the editor is happy to be unpaid, or take some paid holiday for these periods.) So an approximate time required to make each episode would be, say, 15 weeks. The directors may want a paper edit (perhaps a week or so for them to 'draw sync' and produce a rough script to edit from) so you may need to add this in or suggest that it happens while the editor is digitising.

During each production period your workload should look something like this:

Pre-Production	
Finalising the budget/getting the cash flow approved/ obtaining a Broadcast contract, agreeing and returning it or asking for a trust letter if the contract negotiations are getting lengthy/opening up the trust account at the bank (if required) and getting first monies paid to you.	Some or all of this may be done for you by the head of production and/or accounts department.
Setting up your cost book and establishing who is going to be in-putting purchase orders and invoices and other costs into it.	Work this out with your co-ordinator, but the ultimate responsibility of cost control lies with you.
Establishing contact with the insurance broker and discussing your project in detail. Identifying key personnel, getting them medically checked out and registered as essential cast. Discussing any dangerous activities or hostile locations.	Known as the cast list – who exactly should be on this?
Setting up your systems and establishing how the project will run. Systems will include: a contact list, purchase orders, call sheet template, cost book, rushes log, etc.	Helped by your production secretary, production assistant or co-ordinator; discussion about who is responsible for what.
Hiring research staff, directors and anyone else you need at this stage, and establishing what they will be responsible for.	A written job description might be a good idea for research/ production staff – or at least talk them through what you require of them.

Loan Receipt
Liverpool John Moores University
Library Services

Borrower Name: Thomason,Billie-Gina

Borrower ID: ******

Production management for TV and film :
31111013327091
Due Date: 30/09/2016 23:59

Total Items: 1
12/09/2016 14:16

Please keep your receipt in case of
dispute.

Writing contracts for self-employed and payroll staff. Calculating paid holiday allowances for each team member. Putting these commitments into the cost book.	Probably in conjunction with the head of production for the payroll staff.
Getting to know your team and ensuring they all work well together/establishing lines of communication/setting up production meetings.	Meetings for production team only and/or whole team.
Making initial contact with contributors and negotiating any fees/adding their details to the contact list.	Will you need to make travel/accommodation arrangements for your contributors?
Booking kit and buying stock. Getting wish lists of kit from your directors and cameramen and setting up good deals with hire companies.	What different formats will you need for shooting/editing/delivery?
Checking flights, excess baggage deals, visa and inoculations requirements, and establishing the carnet company.	Much of this done by your production staff but directed by you.
Supervising roles and demarcation of duties. Issuing 'milestone' requirements and paperwork required from each team member.	All team members should be clear about what they are responsible for.
Organising and attending any recces and tech recces (don't forget to do a risk assessment for them).	Or sending people in your stead, fully briefed, so they can report back to you.
Setting up shoots/hotels and transport/drafting call sheets/maps and directions/attending to carnet and excess baggage requirements/setting up per diems or floats/obtaining currencies.	Your production team will largely be doing all this but you must check them and ensure they are within your budget parameters.

Writing risk assessments in consultation with the directors and distributing to insurance company, executive, series producer, crew and anyone else who should have them. Keep a copy on file.	Checking on shoot activities and supplying first aid kit and any extras like cold weather gear, anti-malarial medication or high-factor suntan lotion!
Thinking about which editor(s) you will need and pencilling them and exploring options for post production facilities.	Pencil dates at post house.

Production Period

To go or not to go? If you stay in the office can you make occasional visits if practical? Where would your time best be spent? Keeping in contact sensitively! Is the insurance broker happy with all the information you have given them? Do you need any Accord certificates for shooting in the US?	Do the team require local mobile phones? Satellite phones? Hired-in laptops?
Is a shot list required?	Who will do it?
Do they need more stock/money?	How will you get it there?
Being on the end of a telephone or email to organise and rescue.	This may mean at home during unsociable hours.
Supervising the return of the rushes, logging them and getting them stored safely. Do any interviews need transcribing or translating?	Are viewing copies required by the director?
Collecting and disseminating relevant shoot paperwork. Ensuring that no vital release form or location agreement is missing when each shoot returns; chasing immediately if they are.	Log releases and location agreements and file.

Find and contract editor and make sure they have up-to-date contact list/treatments/script/paper edit and copies of call sheets, shot lists, rushes log, I/V transcriptions.	Does the editor have everything they need, i.e. stationery and files, pens and pencils?
Ask Broadcaster for possible narrator choices and get clips for them to hear.	Check narrator's agents for their availability during your post production period.
Supervising the reconciliation of floats as soon as team returns from shoot. Collecting company credit card receipts for when the statement comes in.	You may want to do these jobs yourself, or get your co-ordinator to do the donkey work!
Maintaining cost control POs, invoices, cost book and liaison with accounts department, etc.	
Ensuring systems are being maintained properly.	Curbing the tendency for this to get a bit sloppy when it's manically busy!
Sending out thank-you letters and/or gifts. Starting a log of people who will require a copy of the finished programme (some archive sources may contractually require this).	Or making sure they get done by the relevant director or researcher.
Organising up-coming shoots and edits if more than one programme is being made.	This is where logs for contracts issued, signed and returned come in handy.

Post Production and Delivery

Producing a post production schedule and circulating it along with details of all venues where off-lines and post production are taking place.	Address and telephone numbers and directions for how to get there.
Establishing contact with the narrator's agent, pencilling dates for voice-over sessions and agreeing fees. Issue narrator contract(s).	Make sure these dates are checked with the agent if V/O dates are changed during the edits.
Supervising incoming rushes and sound tapes, CGI and archive material.	
Delivering to edit suite along with some blank stock for dump tapes and viewing copies.	Any sound reports?
Using your own stock saves money.	
Making music decisions : Composer? Commercial music? Library? Or a mixture?	
Choosing and negotiating with composer/contacting and supervising delivery of sound tapes to edit in time for relevant dubs.	What format will composer deliver on?
They will need a DVD of the rough cut to work to.	
Checking any music clearances and other 'alien' material, and finding substitutes for any that can't be cleared (or cheaper sources, perhaps).	Check any blanket agreements available?
Booking rostrum time.	Can you supply your own stock here and save money?

Organising any translations or translators required in the edit.	Checking that final foreign language inserts are correct.
Liaising with post production house(s) and facilities, pencilling and shifting dates of on-lines, dubs and V/O recording sessions and liaising with V/O artist and sending them scripts in good time.	Is V/O artist recording to picture? They will need a time-coded script.
Visiting edit to make sure that edit is running to schedule and facility is working properly.	
Arranging with commissioning editor viewing dates and times.	Keeping an eye on what 'alien' material is in there, with time to clear and cost it – or tracking down alternatives.
Supervising archive fees and ordering in material; ensuring you know all source details and costs.	Your archivist or archive researcher may do this, but you will need to supervise it.
Producing and sending licences to be signed and returned to you; these are part of the delivery paperwork.	Final timings can be done only when the programme is finished and you have a BITC viewing copy.
Deciding on what your title sequence will be. Getting credit rollers approved by Broadcaster(s) and arranging for them and the logo tape and end board to be at edit for on-line. Checking the spelling of ALL names in the credit roller and on the straps.	Liaising with the Broadcaster if your programme is part of a strand for the appropriate logo to be sent.
Keeping abreast of costs – this is where the budget can go mad in the most spectacular fashion!	Keep track of your facilities house invoices – check them with the editor/director .
Organising a compliance lawyer and sending them a copy of the programme along with a script in good time.	Or can the Broadcaster help with legal checks?

Checking all delivery paperwork and underlying documents, and chasing any missing releases, location agreements and licences and filing them in appropriately labelled and organised files.	NB If you don't guarantee possession of ALL the required paperwork, the Broadcaster will retain a large chunk of your production fee!
Anticipating the final cost report and any budgetary problems.	Are you over- or under-spent – and which is worse?
Organising master delivery, paperwork and supervising the clear-up.	Ensuring that all staff who leave before the end give you handover notes.
Finishing off the tidying-up process, passing on your files with notes about anything problematic or outstanding.	Doing comprehensive handover notes and maybe a final report to help with a subsequent series (if there is one) and keeping a copy yourself.
Organising the wrap party (having put money aside earlier on to pay for it). Writing thank-you letters to anyone you think deserves one, and buying gifts for your hard-working team.	Try and organise the wrap party for the end of the project, before everyone has departed to their next contract.
Taking a holiday and looking for your next job.	Updating your CV!

5 Cash flow – what it is and how to do it

The term 'cash flow' is often mentioned, and it's the item that I most frequently get asked to explain when I'm training people. I have prepared an example of a cash flow document 💻; you will notice that it follows the standard media budget format, and I will refer to it as I explain how to do it. It should, of course, be done in an Excel format so that it will add up and cross-cast for you.

When you agree a budget with a Broadcaster they won't, sadly, give you the entire budget monies up front, so you will need to do a cash flow which specifies at which point you will need each portion of the budget. The top line of the cash flow in my illustration indicates the schedule you are working to, and the line down the side indicates the schedule number of the budget. Bottom right shows you the entire budget and this should cross-cast both horizontally and vertically.

You can customise this document on Excel. Pull up a new worksheet and title it (a small point, but you would be surprised at the number of documents I see without a title!) and date it. Using the budget template, fill in the budget schedule numbers down the left-hand side. I have assumed that your schedule is a fairly long one and made it ten months – from the beginning of January until the delivery date of 31 October. Include all schedule numbers even if some of them are not being used.

At the top of the chart should be a line for the production fee, which will also be claimed in portions.

At the bottom of the chart you can see a line for the total outflow (which will be the sum of the figures above it in that column) and you should add a line underneath for contingencies (see also Chapter 3 on Budgeting) if you have any. Underneath that goes a line for total budget, and below can come the requisite number of lines for co-funders – one line for each if you want to see it separated out.

Across the top of your chart the first column will be for any development costs. This should be followed by ten columns for your ten payments (dated each month from January to October in my example) followed by a column for the final payment and then a final column for the total. You will need to set up a sum in the cells that total down and across – a quick way to do this is to use the 'auto-sum' symbol from the toolbar, placing it in the cell where you want the sum to be. Once you click your mouse on this symbol it will outline a suggestion of the figures you want totalled, and when you confirm these it will automatically do the addition for you. Now your cash flow chart is set up.

The purpose of a cash flow is to predict when the various areas of the budget will be spent, so you need to work through your schedule and estimate when you will need each bit of your budget. For example if your schedule shows your main filming period taking place in May, then much of the money in schedules 11 (camera crew), 12 (sound crew) and 22 (crew/camera/kit) will be allocated to this payment, along with a hefty part of schedule 31 (travel and transport) and 32 (hotel and living). You will also need to draw down some money from schedule 25 to pay for shooting stock and perhaps some cash from schedule 8 to pay contributors and interviewees, and so on. If your schedule for post production is set across the months of July onwards, then much of schedules 16 (editors) and 27 (post production) will be drawn down here. The aim of this exercise is to put enough money into the project's bank account to cover payment of invoices for the various items and services taking place at each stage of the schedule. Simple, really.

Let's start by looking at the line for the production fee. The Broadcaster will almost certainly withhold a proportion of this fee until delivery and release it only when they have received every master tape and attendant piece of delivery paperwork, or its electronic equivalent. This might be something like a third of the total fee, so start by putting this figure in the final payment column. The remaining production fee (i.e. what is left after you have deducted the final payment) should then be divided into ten equal payments and entered into each of your ten payment columns – check that they cross-cast to the same amount as your total production fee payment.

Next let's look at schedules 6 and 9 – your production and creative staff schedules. Anyone who is on for the full term of the schedule (perhaps yourself and the series producer or director) can be apportioned across the ten columns in more or less equal payments (i.e. their total fee divided by ten). Put those figures in and then look at your contracts for each of your remaining staff. This is where the coloured columns on the right-hand side of your schedule come in handy, as you can see at a glance when each of your staff are on board and put them in the appropriate payment place.

In a similar fashion work your way through each schedule number and enter your figures in your sub-chart – the one with several lines per schedule number – and then in your master chart. It might be a good idea to work at home when doing something like this; somewhere you don't have constant interruptions to distract you.

You will probably need to add lines to your cash flow chart to cope with the various internal lines within each schedule number. For example within schedule 31 (travel and transport) there will be money set aside for pre-production, production and post, especially if your project is a multi-programme one, and within these parameters there may be even more internal lines. You could create a second and more detailed chart to work through these many lines and then enter the sums in your master chart. This is a fairly time-consuming and concentrated task, but once it's done you will have a clear idea of when you will need your money, which will be reassuring for you and for the company that is employing you. You might want to run the chart past your head of production when you have completed it and get her/his agreement.

I would also say that if you can 'front load' the cash flow a bit (i.e. put little bits of cash up front where you think you can) it will ensure that you don't get caught in the awkward situation of being out of funds with invoices still to pay. The Broadcaster, however, will authorise your cash flow and will query anything that looks like front loading, because they want to hang on to their money for as long as possible before handing it over to you. So during this process keep notes explaining how and why you have estimated the funding in case you have to justify your calculations.

Your finished cash flow will probably show that the funding required will be lower in the pre-production months – with money for paying your team of researchers and directors during the research stage of the project along with some funding to cover recce trips and research materials (schedules 6 and 9 followed by 31, 32 and 33).

The shooting or production period will be heavily funded because you will be drawing down cash for camera crew and equipment, travel and living on the shoots along with major stock costs. And the post production period will be high too, because editors and post production costs form a large part of the budget.

Once you have completed the cash flow and your head of production has checked it over, it should be sent off to the Broadcaster for authorisation. You should then be able to draw down your first tranche of funds. You, or the accountant or head of production, will then invoice for your first payment as per your cash flow. Usually this figure is exclusive of production fee, which should be shown as a separate line on your invoice. These two items should be sub-totalled and VAT added at the correct percentage (at the time of writing this is 17.5%) then total all these figures and add your bank details if the Broadcaster is paying through a BACS system straight into your bank account. Send off your invoice and wait for the money, which won't be paid until the contract for your project is signed. (Some UK Broadcasters may pay some money on a trust letter if there are lengthy wrangles about the contract.)

Thereafter you may need to submit a cost report along with your invoice in order to draw down subsequent payments and also, perhaps, copies of your bank statements. The Broadcaster retains a right of access to your trust account, so make sure that you keep all your dealings completely kosher. Only transactions for your particular project can go through your particular trust account; this account mustn't be used to subsidise other projects when their coffers are low.

You should also submit a variations text along with all the figure paperwork to the Broadcaster. This explains any variation of each budget line (usually if the variation is more than about £5,000) and justifies it. For example, if you are running over-budget on salaries for the production team, then you need to explain that the projected over-spend will be mitigated by under-spends elsewhere. As long as the bottom line is pretty much on budget you will be solvent.

A brief word here about VAT. As a production manager you will *always* work exclusive of VAT. Your budget will deal with figures which are exclusive of any VAT element. When you receive invoices for fees and services, you will be entering the net figure into your cost book; when you send off invoices to the Broadcaster for your monthly cash flow you will add a VAT element to your invoice, and when it comes in you will ignore it. The accountant who deals with your project will fillet out the VAT elements of your project and create a VAT return for the Customs and Excise people every three months. If they don't do this regularly and properly then they will be in trouble. A word of advice here: if anyone ever asks you to get involved in VAT in any way, say no. You are a production manager, not an accountant, and VAT is not your responsibility other than to make sure you treat it with respect.

For advice on ongoing cost control, study Chapter 7 on Systems. For a brilliant cost book example, see the website 💻.

6 A guide to essential documentation

There are a small number of useful documents that you should produce to help with running the project, and they should be easily available to everyone on the production team. I like to print them as hard copies but that's just my personal preference. Some of them will be ongoing and need to be maintained regularly – and documents like the contact list should also be archived at the end of your project. So let's start with that.

Contact list

See my example on the website 💻. Use a Word document with three columns of tables inserted: the first is the role of the team member, the second is the name of the person or people in that role, and the third column contains some of their contact details. (Mobile numbers only; using home numbers is against the Data Protection Act. You should also leave out home addresses from this document, as it may get seen by all sorts of people.) You may add more personal information to another list for your own purposes – setting up contracts, for example – but always keep it in a secure place. I usually date this list and make sure it gets regularly updated as people come on board. It can either be circulated to everyone concerned with the project, or kept in an accessible place on the hard drive. It will also help in the compilation of the credit roller and in compiling the list of people who will have been promised a copy of the programme, including any archive sources, as they often include a copy of the programme in their contractual requirements.

Call sheets and movement orders

A call sheet is a comprehensive document which details everything that is going to happen on a shoot, from the moment individual team members leave their homes until their return. A movement order is more usually the paperwork that a location manager will provide on a drama shoot, and consists of maps and directions to locations as well as shoot details. Call sheets are a detailed blueprint of who is going where and doing what on a shoot, and might include recce details too if the recce runs into the shoot (see website 💻 for an example of a documentary call sheet). Call sheets must be circulated to every team and crew member, the head of production, the executive, series producer, your insurance broker, and anyone else you can think of. In these convenient electronic days they can be sent by email but do follow up with a phone call to check that they have arrived with each critical member of the team, and make sure they know where they are meeting and at what time. You should also print up a number of call sheets and send them on the shoot with the assistant producer/researcher for those people who didn't print them out or have lost their copy. File a copy of each in your production folder as a useful archive reference. As the production manager you should check through the documents for possible errors before they are sent out, and it will help to talk them through with the AP and/or director before they leave to make sure they each understand what they are responsible for. The call sheet should have an equipment list attached so the crew don't lose any kit and, if there is hired-in kit, it gets returned to the right place. The call sheet *must* also have a risk assessment attached to it which every member of the team should be encouraged to read – more on this in Chapter 13 (Health & Safety).

You should include emergency contact details on the call sheet, for the nearest police station and hospital to each location, and the out-of-office-hours telephone number for the insurance broker so accidents or camera fault problems, for example, can be promptly reported. You should also specify technical instructions to the cameraman or sound recordist along with the number of the next tape to be shot; this becomes even more important as the shoots progress, to ensure that you don't get doubled-up tape numbering. A recent weather report can be useful along with a reminder about cold weather gear and protective clothing or, conversely, hats and sun protection. Anything, in short, that the team could possibly find useful when away from home.

Include maps and directions to the various locations, but beware of just grabbing these off the Internet: I remember going on a shoot once to Birmingham where the two young and inexperienced production assistants had done just that. Arriving a bit early at the hotel, the series producer and I decided to travel to the first location and write specific notes to be circulated to the rest of the crew to save time the following morning. We sat in the car and looked at the instructions, which said something like 'proceed to the Something-or-Other roundabout, take the third exit and proceed for three-eighths of a mile'. The producer turned to me and asked, 'Is that left or right out of the car park?'

The AA route finders can be helpful and where it is at all possible these directions should be checked by actually driving them. Of course this applies only to UK locations, so if you are sending crews abroad, check out directions on the Internet and also encourage them to buy map books (or, if funds permit, employ drivers along with crew vehicles). This is especially important when the crew are in countries where driving can be confusing or downright frightening. I was once asked which side of the road they drive on in India, and I had to say that I never did work it out! Scary. Of course if the location is volatile or potentially dangerous you will need to hire drivers and, possibly, security people to help your crew stay safe (see Chapter 12 on Foreign Filming).

When the crew is away take a call sheet home with you, or email it electronically to save paper, and keep it handy. And give one to the person who answers the office phone so they know who is absent and when they will return.

Contracts and deal letters

If you are struggling to keep up with contracts which have a tendency to all come at once, as a holding measure email a deal letter. The wording might be something like 'I confirm our intention to hire you as a …' and include the dates of engagement, the fee you have agreed, any kit or vehicle that comes with the individual – and a request for the recipient to confirm that they are in agreement with their terms of hire. When you have more time and a quiet office you can bash out the more formal contracts using PACT templates as a basis for them or the preferred contracts of the company or Broadcaster you are working for. Send two copies signed by the company representative (or yourself) and ask them to sign and return one and keep one for their records. Try and make sure that you have a signed contract in place before people leave the office for a recce or shoot, and don't pay their first invoice until you have it – otherwise you might never receive it and that could pose a problem with your deliverables paperwork. Sometimes people think that by not signing their contract they have some 'wriggle room' in negotiating something else further down the line. But, legally, once they have shown up for work they have tacitly accepted the terms you have offered and that constitutes a legal contract.

Purchase orders

These are simply promises to pay and as such should always be completed and, where appropriate, sent out to the person or company supplying the services described. They serve the dual purpose of giving the supplier all your details to invoice to, and providing instructions for payment (e.g. requesting their bank account details so you can pay by BACS). POs are vital for keeping track of commitments to pay, rather than being surprised by costs which you weren't expecting. The company you are working for might have a preferred format or you can design your own on the computer (see example 💻). If the company has pads of carbonised POs then you will probably have to use these, but I prefer to build my own on a computer because they are quicker to prepare and are always legible.

Via POs you can keep tabs on what spending has been committed to by any member of the team until the invoice or credit card statement arrives, and they should be completed for any spend excluding perhaps bikes and taxis (which should be kept in a Bike Book) and petty cash. When an invoice comes in it should be checked against the PO and signed off by you. Any disparity between the amounts payable can be queried. I usually attach the PO to the invoice before submitting it to the accounts department for payment.

I think it is also good practice to draw up a purchase order log, which should contain: the number of the PO, the date it is issued, the supplier, brief details of the transaction, the cost (different currencies can be noted), the budget schedule number(s) it refers to, and the date the invoice is received. When a purchase order is required you can go into the log first and pick up the next number when you fill in the details of the transaction (unless you are sufficiently computer-wise to work out how this log can automatically produce running numbers, in which case please let me know!). You might fill them in using red print and then change them to black when the invoice arrives. The purpose of this log is to keep a record of what has been issued which you can access at a glance. During a long project you can check and see which purchase orders haven't been invoiced and chase them up.

In order that your cost control is up to date you will need to regularly enter your purchase orders in your cost book. See Chapter 7 on Systems for more details.

Rushes log

You will need to keep a list of all the material you have shot (the rushes) when they are returned to you at the end of each shoot. A Word document with tables in is ideal, or an Excel sheet. Divide the worksheet into at least three columns. In the first goes the date the tape has been shot; the second column is the number you have given the tape; and the third column should have as detailed a description of what is on the tape as possible. Sometimes you can get the AP/researcher to do this on the shoot – perhaps in the evenings if they're too busy during the day. Further columns could be added if you want to record information about where tapes currently are (locked up in the office, in the edit suite, on their way to post production, etc.). The rushes log is then sent to the editor at the beginning of their edit.

Float reconciliation and expenses sheet

A basic expenses sheet can be made to do a number of jobs: it can detail out-of-pocket spending which needs to be claimed back from the company; comprise a float reconciliation, which is a paper explanation of where a float, given by the production, has been spent; or detail a company credit card reconciliation, which itemises where and what payments have been made. *All* these documents must be accompanied by receipts or some sort of paperwork that backs up the spend; in the case of goods bought on the Internet a confirmation print-out will suffice. Receipts prove that the expenditure is pukka and, more importantly, will include a VAT number so that this item can be reclaimed (without the VAT number you can't claim the VAT element back, which means that you have to absorb it into your costs). Try never to issue a second float to a team member until they have reconciled the first; reconciling it yourself, or getting your co-ordinator to do it, might be quicker and more efficient in the end. For team members who are engaged in the creative side of a project, filling in forms and stapling bits of paper together are low priority, but the longer these bits of paper get left kicking around, the harder they are to balance.

Logs in general

You will notice that I advocate the use of logs a lot. But what may seem like extra work setting them up can make organising the various items much easier and accessing them quicker. When you're busy you can see at a glance where you are in the process, but they do have to be regularly updated. I always keep a contract log, for example, because working on a large series might require dozens of contracts and you need to know whether they have been written, issued, returned or forgotten. A log makes this a simpler process than leafing through dozens of bits of paper.

Deliverables

This is the term given to those acres of paper, now more usually replaced by acres of electronic files, that the Broadcaster demands be completed and returned to them at the end of the project. They can be extensive and complex and you won't receive the final tranche of production fee until they are delivered – so I have devoted a whole chapter to them later in this book.

7 Systems and cost control

Cost monitor

I have included a template ⌨ of what I think is the best and most simple-to-use cost monitor that I have ever come across (supplied, very kindly, by Darlow Smithson Productions). You can use it for your own cost control and compare it at regular intervals with the system used by the accountant to make sure you are both on track. The accounts department can also use your cost monitor for their input. I will explain how the system works in both instances.

Setting up your cost book

Once your budget and the cash flow has been approved, you should open a blank template of the cost book on your computer. You will notice that each schedule (indicated by tabs along the bottom of your Excel document) is laid out in a similar fashion and also that many of the cells within each schedule have calculations in them. Someone much cleverer than I spent hours linking all the relevant calculations and totals to the summary page at the beginning of the document, from which you can see at a glance exactly where you are financially at any time during your project. As you fill in the narrative of your spend and committed costs in the relevant budget schedules, the cells operate to show you how much you have spent and what you still have left. In this way, if a director asks whether they can have more filming days, for example, or an expensive 'toy' (a piece of filming kit outside those normally used, like a dolly or a helicopter, for example), you can look at the costs so far, what you still have left to spend and make an informed decision rather than a wild stab in the dark.

Let's imagine we are setting up our cost book at the beginning of our project. The summary page contains lots of complex calculations and links to each individual schedule; it is 'locked' so it can never be written over either deliberately or accidentally. Working in the individual schedules (indicated by the numbered tab at the bottom), begin to fill in the budget amounts for each schedule and sub-schedule in the appropriate cell(s). If you are looking at the schedule, there is a lilac-coloured line across the top of each, at the right-hand end of which it says (funnily enough) 'Budget' – enter your budget figures beneath this as a figure (i.e. no equals signs or anything). You can, if you wish, add some narrative as to how this budget figure is reached by using the 'Description' line lower down. You might do this using italics or a colour other than black or red to indicate that it's a working from the budget. For example: in schedule 12 you might have something like: 'DOP at £400 daily rate x 16 days' filming plus 4 days' travel at £250 per day' here.

Assuming that my sums are correct, this figure will read £7,400, which you will enter in the budget space. Easy so far.

Work your way through the cost-book template filling in these budget figures and any relevant narrative about how the figure is arrived at. It's perhaps a good idea to save this job for doing in a quiet time or at home, but bear in mind that if you are compiling a fairly large cost book it might take an age to email back to yourself at the office, so consider putting it on to a 'stick' and downloading it on to your computer at the other end – making sure that both computers are compatible, of course.

Once you have all your relevant schedules with their budget figures added in, check that the summary page compares with your budget and is correct in each schedule.

Now you can start to use your cost monitor. As you amass purchase orders you should put them into their relevant schedule and I suggest that you do this in red so that they are immediately recognizable as POs. Their cost should be entered into the committed costs line and their number and date in the boxes on the left of the worksheet. If you keep your purchase orders in hard copy you can file them in a lever-arch file in number order, and when invoices start to arrive you can marry them together and check that the costs are correct as per the PO. Any that aren't can be investigated before they are signed off. My system would be to staple the two together and enter the invoice amounts in the relevant PO line and turn the print to black, moving the cost figure from the committed line into the actual costs line. As you move through your project you can easily see which invoices have arrived and which haven't, and at the end, if you still have purchase orders left un-invoiced, you can check with the company to get them issued. You may also find that the odd PO has been included in another invoice cost and you can delete it, thus making savings at the end when you may be glad of some extra funding!

One more line to fill in and this will be a sum. Move your mouse into a line under the costs-to-complete section, and enter the following calculation – an equals symbol (=) then click the mouse on to your budget figure top right, hit the minus sign on your computer and click into the total cell at the base of the column marked actual costs, another minus sign and then click at the base of the column for committed costs and hit return – you should then have a sum that gives you your budget figure, less costs committed and spent … and thus what you have left. Hurrah! You can then keep an eye on this figure as you proceed and see where you may have (a) problem areas of insufficient funding and (b) possible cushions of money that can be moved around to help mitigate any overages. When and if this cost-to-come figure ever becomes a minus figure you must delete it, because the cost book will be compensating for nil funds and that's no help to anyone. An absence of a costs-to-come figure will indicate that you are over-budget in this area.

If the accounts department are also using your cost book, they may well change your figures when the invoices are paid – perhaps by 'bolding' them. And any costs that had a VAT element included (for example, a float reconciliation with individual VAT-able receipts) should have been reduced to their net form, which further reduces your costs!

To achieve further control of your costs I would suggest that you enter any floats that you give out in the cost book. If the float is for a recce or shoot, much of it will probably end up in schedule 32, so you could actually 'colour up' a block in this schedule and list each float in it. When the float is reconciled you can remove it from this block or, better still, add a narrative to say that it has been reconciled. But remove the figures, as they will now be allocated to their proper places and you don't want to double-account.

You can be even more organised and do the same with credit card statements as soon as they come in. Reconciling them may take a few weeks, but you will have them covered, with petty cash floats too, until they are accounted for. This means that whenever you have to do a cost report you will be reporting more accurately your outlay and will not be lulled into thinking you have spent or committed less than you actually have.

So now you are moving through your project, adding purchase orders, invoices, floats and any other kinds of spend or commitments, into the main body of each schedule or sub-schedule. You will see how your columns of cost totals and cost-to-come totals give you a clear idea of how much has been spent and how much is left. At the base of each schedule you will find a blue box of figures, which will show at a glance a total of the sub-sections in the schedule for actual, committed, costs to come, final costs and budget; the last column shows a variance – this tells you where you are under or over your budget and by how much. When you start your project your figures will just be simple additions and a sum showing you the costs-to-come figure. However, as things progress you can decide whether the costs-to-come figures reflect actuality. It may be that you think there is not enough in this line or, conversely, too much; this is when you might start to remove the sum in this line (equals budget, minus committed costs, minus actual costs) and enter a more realistic figure based on what you know. This is the tricky bit – putting your expertise into practice and making informed judgements about how much money you need to complete each budget line. In areas where you think you will need more than that which is calculated in costs to come, enter a higher figure and then try and balance the overs and unders so that your bottom-line total is more or less on budget. The theory is that (within limits) you can adjust each individual schedule's costs upwards or downwards as long as they balance out overall and you can justify the changed totals.

When you submit a cost report you might want to protect your costs to come. Whilst you may judge that you don't need all the costs to come in any particular line, you can leave them there and view them as contingencies. This means that you can call on them if you need to when you are over-spent elsewhere, and you can also mark them outside the locked area on the summary page (i.e. make notes for yourself – and your accountant? – in the column after the final one of the summary page). And while we're on the subject of notes, you can make notes to yourself (or your accountant) anywhere within the text lines of each schedule. So if your accountant visits your cost book, you can ask questions like 'Can I have this under-spend?' if there is money left in, say, schedule 18. The company may want to drag back any money left over in this schedule or may, if you ask nicely, give back part of it against an over-spend somewhere else – in which case your note might read 'Can I have this under-spend *please*?'.

This all may sound very complicated but, trust me, once you have been running this cost book for a while you will get the hang of it and may even start to finesse it in other clever ways. I would only add here that if you allow your production co-ordinator or some other helper to add, for example, purchase orders to it, you should talk them through it first and make sure they do so only in the way that you want it done. In other words, you may put some costs in places where they make more sense to you – if your co-ordinator gets cocky and starts changing things around, explain why it must be done as you have set it up – then lock them out of the cost book and do it yourself unless you can absolutely trust them to use it only in the way you have prescribed.

The efficient running of this cost monitor is the basis of your cost control, so you should become familiar with it as early as possible in the project and visit it often, adding information but also just checking through it to make sure that all the figures are being correctly caught up in the sums within each schedule. Being familiar with each section of it will mean that you are always informed and can negotiate when asked if you can pay for more of something. And learn to trust your gut instinct. I find that I just know when the budget is going out of control, almost without checking it in my cost book – I can feel it in my water!

USEFUL TIP

Be aware that if you add any columns or cells to your cost book you must make sure that it still adds and cross-casts. Check whenever you add or subtract any cells that it is still working properly, otherwise disaster may follow.

8 Dealing with the Broadcaster

When I first began my freelance career in television I had much more contact with the Broadcaster than I do now. It was quite usual to submit an idea to a Broadcaster and receive a request for a fuller treatment. When this was forthcoming, if they liked it, I would be asked to draft a budget. I would get some idea of the sum of money the Broadcaster was thinking of paying for the project (no point in writing a dream budget only to find that their intended cost was half my budget amount) and then my producer and I would go in to see the Broadcaster and argue the draft budget, sometimes almost line by line. Their finance person often knew the exact cost of a roll of tape stock (and would red-pencil that budget schedule accordingly!) but would sometimes point out that I hadn't allowed enough elsewhere – it was a very enjoyable sort of dance where we ended up with a mutually agreed cost for producing our programme or series.

As the TV industry has changed and become more 'product'-oriented, it seems that a huge amount of programming is commissioned, or promised, by the Broadcaster asking an individual independent production company to produce 'half a dozen science-based programmes for an 8pm slot on a Thursday evening, 30 minutes long and we need them by November'. The budget will be the amount they want to pay and you will have to make your treatment fit that. Before I get started on a nostalgic hankering after the good ol' days, let's just accept that when you take on a freelance job with your independent production company to produce their intended 'product', the budget amount will be fixed or the budget already written and you will have no real input. So the first thing you should do is to go through it in detail, having closely studied the treatment for the intended programme(s) – and you will have a good idea of whether the two will be compatible.

My advice, when you have done this, is to write a clearly dated email or memo to everyone in the company who you think should know (the executive, series producer, head of production, for example) giving a detailed analysis of whether you think the project can be made for the money available. Detail where you think funds may be lacking and whether there are areas which might have 'padding' that you can move around. Circulate it and invite comments, and print out a copy and file it under 'cover your back memos' so that you can wave it at people nearer the end of your project when the financial shit starts to hit that dirty old fan. Joking apart, unless you are fully in agreement with the way the budget has been written, say so in detail. You don't have to be critical of whoever wrote it; there may have been good reasons for how it was done. Just ask for a meeting so that any major discrepancies can be discussed at this early stage and adjustments made to the treatment (i.e. you might suggest trimming the filming days at this stage to pay for other under-funded areas). Dealt with early enough it will be much easier to change the budget parameters and make everyone aware that there are possible problem areas. You are all in this together – anyone who says 'the money side of things is your problem' deserves a very rude answer and an explanation that 'we' have to make this work: you can't do it on your own.

When you are invited in by an indie company for a chat about a possible job, it's a good idea to ask about the budget and, if they will give it to you, to take it home and get a clear idea of what the project will be. If you think it's going to be impossible to bring the two things together, it might influence your decision about taking the job. Making a silk purse out of a sow's ear can be a daunting prospect, especially if other people on the team regard you as the Voice of Doom and keep insisting it will work out somehow. Be assured, it won't, and as you learn to trust your gut feeling about what projects will cost you can almost smell the problems before they arise.

Whichever route you take, you may or may not have contact with the Broadcaster – and as I've said, in recent years I have had very little. The head of production at an indie usually does all that now, especially at the early stage, but during the course of making your project you will probably have occasion to call them up and ask questions. I have, in the past, had to go through the contract with the Broadcaster, but that hasn't happened for a while and I think contracts have got fairly complex and are now dealt with by legal departments or heads of production. You will probably get given the relevant bits of it: the deliverables section and the technical specifications (outlining exactly how the programme should be produced). You should check this very carefully to make sure that everything in it has been budgeted. I have found of late that contracts from the Broadcaster can have sneaky little extras slipped into them; extra master copies, for example, which all cost money and if they haven't been budgeted for you will need to point this out. Early perusal is also useful so that you know what format you are shooting on and whether a second camera (a Z1, for example, that the director may be thinking of using for adding texture to their film or maximising footage shot in a day) will form an acceptable format for the Broadcaster.

Co-productions (co-pros)

Up to this point I have been speaking about a single Broadcaster but increasingly, as purses are tightening, projects are being co-funded by a number of Broadcasters – often a mixture of British and American. This may mean that your project will require several versions to be delivered and in turn, of course, have an impact on your budget. Your schedule may also need to be extended as you work to provide all the different sets of delivery documents – see Chapter 19 on Deliverables for more details.

So, if your project boasts more than one funder, you can bet that they will want different versions of each programme – 'seamless' copies perhaps (i.e. no breaks within the structure of the episode) or breaks which may differ in number and placing within the programme (American programmes will usually have more breaks, for example). And sometimes 'soft breaks' will be required – these are suggestions of where a break might occur with appropriate signposting within the narration, and will need to be supplied in log form. It will require more edit time to produce these variations and additional master copies and this, of course, will have an impact on your budget.

And co-funders may pose other problems. For example, an American or Canadian company will almost certainly want a North American voice for the narrator; the UK funder, not. So you need to find out whether that American narrator can be someone living in the UK and recorded here, or whether the Broadcaster has someone 'native' in mind – in which case you may have to arrange a voice-over recording session to take place in America (or possibly 'down the line', which is possible, but sound facilities who offer this service here in the UK will need to be checked to see how much it will cost).

Narrators

While on the subject of narrators, it's helpful to check the amount set aside for this item in your budget early, as Broadcasters will usually allow a sum to cover a 'bog-standard' voice-over artist as opposed to a 'name' or recognisable actor's voice. If they change their mind halfway through the project, the cost of a 'name' will be much higher than that of a standard narrator, so this might be one of the rare occasions on which you can approach the Broadcaster and ask for a mutually agreed over-spend to cover it. Call the actor's agent and find out their ballpark figure for voice-over work. Ensure that they are available for when you want to record, as their acting commitments may take them out of action just when you need them. Allow a period of anything up to 4 hours per 1 hour of programme time, though most narrators won't take this long unless your programme is very narration-heavy. I am always in awe of good voice-over artists who can often get it right first time and who when asked, for example, to 'reduce the speed of your delivery by 30 per cent on that piece' will do just that. Very clever. It's worth getting the script to them beforehand not only so they know what to expect but also because the good ones will rehearse it before they arrive and thus save you money on your recording time.

Back to the Broadcaster. You are likely to need to call up their legal department from time to time, so it will pay to make friends with them early on. There are a couple of documents you will need to get signed off by contributors and locations in your programmes (release forms for individuals, and location agreements for locations) and sometimes the recipient will want to make changes to the wording which must be checked with the Broadcaster.

Be aware that some locations will not sign any sort of location agreement that you give them and/or may want you to sign theirs, and this will have to be run past the Broadcaster's legal department. If you present this paperwork at the end and they don't like it then you'll have to embark on trying to get changes done retrospectively – good luck with that!

You may also need to run the script past them if the material you are dealing with is in any way contentious. Programmes may need to have a compliance lawyer check them at the end (send both a script and a copy of the programme); this is sometimes forgotten by the person doing the budget and is expensive, so it's another area to check early on. They should respond very quickly to your material and will point out areas that might be a cause for concern and make suggestions for changes. Don't stint on this – it's not worth getting sued for libel or being economical with the truth.

You will probably also build some sort of relationship with the programme finance manager within the Broadcast company. It almost goes without saying that you should always deal with these Broadcast personnel with courtesy, despite the fact that they may be making you wait for months for payment of your last invoice. Try not to lose your temper with them; rude is not the same as firm. But payments from Broadcasters often take a long time to pay so getting your cost report and next invoice in on time is a good plan. Even large indies can have enormous cash flow problems, especially when many of their projects are with the same Broadcasters. A lack of money in the coffers may mean that you are late paying your team and that doesn't do much for their morale or your credibility.

Broadcasters often want a monthly cost report which will include a written report about how the project is going. I usually make this part of a 'Variations on Budget' text which explains why individual budget lines may vary within the project but how, overall, the budget is on track (hopefully!). And I always adopt a positive attitude to what is happening – the teams are bringing back wonderful rushes, the edits are running really well. And don't forget to let them know if you have made an insurance claim.

I am often asked when and even if you should inform the Broadcaster about an impending over-spend. There is no clear answer to this. You will need to warn your head of production as soon as you fear this is happening, and I think one should sow the seeds early with the Broadcaster unless you think it is a temporary thing that you can cope with in some way. They may not care anyway if the total budget sum is fixed and will merely expect you to 'absorb it with savings elsewhere'. (How I love that phrase.) But certainly don't leave it until the final cost report – they will then be very cross and rightly so. As for an under-spend, well, this should be dealt with early too. A Broadcaster may reserve the right to take, say, half of an under-spend (funny they aren't so anxious to share its opposite) and I would look for ways to spend the money, perhaps on more post production (or the indie may want to take some of it to set against expenses that aren't covered in the budget). Between you and your HOP you should work out a plan, but try to put at least some of it back into the project and thus on to the screen. If a director finds out that s/he has scrimped and saved money on their prep and filming and you have money to spare at the end, s/he may be understandably annoyed.

It's always helpful to make relationships with the people who are holding your purse strings and assisting you with other bits of your project, so even though meeting face to face may not be possible, take the time to set up a telephone and email connection and keep the information flowing as much as you can about what is happening on your project. I used to ask if they wanted to see call sheets and risk assessments but that sometimes either confuses them or makes them think they have to respond in some way, so perhaps a little knowledge is a dangerous thing. Try to be positive when speaking to them so you aren't always giving them a problem to solve. And being nice to them may prove useful, because television is a small world and you never know when you might come across them again when you are looking for work.

9 VAT and the production manager

At the time of writing, Value Added Tax is 17.5%. Some items are nil-rated for VAT – for example books and flights, though the latter is subject to a fairly large tax which is non-refundable, to cover fuel charges and airport tax, etc., all of which will have to be absorbed into your budget.

When you draw up a budget you should always assess costs exclusive of VAT – net costs, in other words. Whenever you get a quote for goods or services in the TV industry you will usually be quoted a figure, which is, again, exclusive of VAT, be this for a freelance cameraman or camera kit ordered from a hire company. For the purposes of cash control you should always work with the net figure. I have now said this three different ways and I hope I have made the point that, as a production manager, you don't include VAT in your figures – that makes four!

Accountants and VAT

When you work closely with an accountant, they should pick up the VAT element; indeed, when an invoice is sent off to the Broadcaster for more funds a VAT percentage will be added at the end. When that money arrives you will take the net figure (exclusive of the VAT amount) for your funding. The accountant will keep efficient financial records and calculate the VAT amount owing at the end of every quarter, sending off some money and documentation to the Department of Customs and Excise for any VAT owing.

I once went to an interview at a very small independent production company and part of the duties they wanted from a production manager was completion and submission of their VAT return. I turned down the job. I am a production manager, not an accountant, and I think the two are very different. The VAT return is a responsible job for which I don't feel qualified, and if you screw it up you will bring down the wrath of the Customs and Excise department upon your head. If you submit your VAT return late, or get it wrong, the company can be fined huge amounts of money – not a responsibility I want on my shoulders.

Invoices and VAT

When you receive an invoice, say, from your cameraman if they are registered for VAT, they will also add this percentage on to the fee they have agreed with you. You take the net figure for your cost book but when the invoice is paid it should, of course, be paid in full, including the VAT amount. Years ago, when I was confused about this process, I remember a financial guru moving his hands in a wave-like motion and saying, 'Don't worry about VAT – it all just washes through.' Indeed it does.

Having banged on about VAT you need to be aware that, on certain invoices, the VAT element is included in the total cost and not necessarily shown separately – for example, on hotel bills and petrol receipts. You will have to put the full figure into your cost monitor (especially if you pay with a company credit card) and wait for the accountant to 'fillet out' the VAT. You will then need to work out a method of getting revised costings back from your accountant so you can go through your cost book and nip the costs back by the VAT element. All to the good, as you'll have spent less than you thought!

The importance of receipts and bills

VAT is a major reason why you should be vigilant getting back bills, receipts and invoices from your team when they pay for things on recces or shoots. If they don't back up their expenses, float reconciliations or credit card payments with the proper hard copy bills and receipts then you will not be able to deduct the VAT element and will have to include it in your costs – a large amount of wasted spend on your skinny budget! Not bringing back this crucial paperwork when the team has been away is just careless and costs the whole project money, so make sure you make this point with boring regularity when sending people out of the office. If hotel bills, for example, are forgotten or lost then you can call and ask for copies, but this all takes time and effort so bringing them back the first time is the best way to go. I have added into the templates on the website 🖳 an expenses or float reconciliation form that automatically calculates the VAT element in items that can have their VAT claimed back – thus saving your brain for more important issues!

So, if you pay VAT as part of a bill, providing the VAT number is on the bill or receipt you can reclaim it. When individuals or services submit invoices to you containing an element of VAT you must make sure that their VAT number appears on the invoice. If it doesn't, return the invoice and ask for it to be added. The VAT amount should also be shown separately. The same applies when you submit invoices to Broadcasters or funders of any kind: add your VAT registration number and show the VAT amount as a separate item.

Foreign VAT

If you are sending crews to European countries, you can claim back the European equivalent of VAT in those countries. For help on this, refer to the website given below and look for the reference 723, where you will find an application form to be downloaded and instructions for how to do it. This process usually takes some time but may be worth it if you have a substantial amount of expenditure in the European Community.

If you ever have any anxieties about VAT and how it affects your budget, call the Customs and Excise people – they are there to help you.

Website address: www.hmrc.gov.uk/customs/tax-and-duty.htm
Emails: enquiries.estn@hmrc.gsi.gov.uk
Helpline number: 0845 010 9000 – open 8am–8pm Monday–Friday

10 Insurance

Every project that you work on will require production insurance. There are a small number of insurance companies who specialise in production insurance and their details are listed at the end of this chapter. Unless your company has some specialised insurance deal with a set company I would always recommend that you check out your options and go for the one that offers you not only a good price and adequate breadth of cover, but also a contact person you feel you can talk to – because you will be consulting that person on a regular basis throughout your project. Insurance companies are open 9 to 5 Monday to Friday but your broker needs to be available to you 24/7 in case of an emergency.

The intention of this chapter is not to go into detail about the wide range of insurance that is available to you should your project require it (and remember that every project you will work on will have unique requirements), but rather to advise you of the basic cover you will need and then to reiterate my mantra: *If you don't know, ask.* The people who work in production insurance companies have specialised experience, so whenever you have a query call and ask for an explanation. Your particular problem may be new to you but the chances are that your broker has encountered it, or something similar, before.

Cast insurance

You will need to identify and insure the key members of your team so that if they are incapacitated by accident or unforeseen ill-health (or death!) you are covered for any additional costs to your budget. For example, if the director is unable to continue his/her duties, you will have to put your project on hold while they recover or you find a replacement and claim any additional resulting expenses through your insurance policy. If you have a presenter on your project they will need to be covered under the cast section, as will principal actors if you are making a drama. Think about other team members whose incapacity would cause you a delay as you may want to argue that a specialist researcher with particular knowledge, for example, should be covered. (Interestingly, production managers aren't usually on the cast list – clearly we are two a penny and easily substituted.) Any cast members that you nominate will have to complete a Statement of Health form and possibly undergo a medical, and any ongoing medical condition will become, as for ordinary travel insurance, for example, a 'pre-existing condition' which will restrict your insurance cover. Depending on the condition these pre-existing exclusions may be able to be 'bought out' by way of an increase in the excess (the amount you pay in the event of a claim) or an additional premium.

Videotape/faulty stock camera and processing

This will provide cover for any additional re-shoot costs resulting from faulty cameras, faulty stock or faulty processing plus loss of the raw stock. I have had a number of instances where there has been 'drop out' on rushes tapes which hasn't been spotted until the crew has returned to base. If they can't 'cut around' such faults in the edit, and the material is critical to the programme, then the crew may have to return and re-shoot, in which case your insurance claim will include the additional re-shoot costs. With ever-changing technology you must always make sure that kit and crew are fit for purpose. Insurance does not cover operator error or inexperience.

Extra expense

This provides cover for the additional costs incurred following the physical loss of a property, facility or location. It will also cover the cost of any abortive trips including crew payments, air fares, hotel bills, etc. In real terms if your location gets blown away by a hurricane you may be able to claim costs from loss of location – but this section does not cover you against weather, so if it rains on your outdoor shoot on the only day you can get access, tough luck. You can buy specific weather insurance, but this is very expensive. Check with your insurance broker, if you have a key location, set or intrinsic prop, to make sure cover is sufficient.

Technical equipment

This will cover you for the repair or replacement cost of owned or rented camera and sound equipment which is damaged or stolen during the course of your production. The loss of equipment is covered under this section but the loss of time while waiting for replacement gear would come under extra expense (see above). Always make sure you have a contract of hire with the facilities house that states who is responsible for insuring the equipment and on what basis. If you do not have this you may end up with the insurance company paying you the value of the equipment at the time of loss but the facilities house insisting on the full replacement-as-new value.

Props, sets and wardrobe

Cover is provided for the repair or replacement of any owned or rented props, sets or wardrobe, damaged or stolen during the course of the production. This doesn't mean, of course, that people can be daft with security arrangements for such items.

Third party property damage

Provides cover for the production company's legal liability for property in its care, custody and/or control. The cover operates to provide loss of ongoing charges to rental companies whose property is being repaired or replaced. Most contracts insist on a minimum of 13 weeks loss of hire.

Office contents on location

Provides cover for temporary office equipment in your location offices. Location offices are not covered by the company's usual annual corporate insurance, so this insurance will operate in offices away from base.

Money

Covers your team for loss of cash (including foreign currency) or cheques, travellers' cheques and/or credit cards during the course of the production. There is usually a standard amount for cover of a float, so check what this is. If the crew are going to a country where cash is the only reliable form of payment then you may need to increase the float amount substantially.

Employer's liability

Indemnifies the insured against any claim for damages or defence costs if you become legally liable for any accidents which happen on the production and which cause bodily injury or disease to any UK person employed by you in the course of your project. When filming abroad this will not cover local fixers. Discuss this with your broker, who will be able to advise you on what cover you need and either arrange it for you or put you in contact with someone who can.

This section covers the production company for any costs they are legally liable to pay in the event of death, accident or illness while working on the production. This is not a 'to pay' policy; therefore there are no guaranteed payments. If you are particularly concerned about a dangerous or hazardous shoot it may be advisable to buy personal accident cover. Again, seek advice from your broker.

Public liability

Indemnifies you against claim for damages and defence costs if any accidents occur which cause bodily injury or disease or loss of or damage to property to third parties on your project. Specifically this covers you if, for example, a passer-by trips over one of your camera cables in the street. Again, this is not a 'to pay' policy; you have to be deemed negligent for the accident.

Film union

Provides baggage cover including emergency medical expenses, personal baggage and cash when travelling outside the UK. However, be aware that there is a limit for personal effects, so if one of your team members wants to take along their personal possessions which are not for direct use on the production – an iPod, for example – then you should inform your insurance broker: there may be an additional premium if you need cover in excess of this limit. You should also make sure that people behave in a responsible manner regarding their personal possessions. It might be worth putting some sort of reminder on the call sheet about not leaving possessions in full view inside vehicles, because it's so common to have items stolen in car parks while their owners are busy filming.

Motor insurance

This provides cover for any vehicles used *in front of* the camera. If you hire cars or vans for your crew to use then they should be fully insured at the point of hire. Do remind them of this on the call sheet – they must tick all the insurance boxes when they collect their hire vehicle.

And if, during recces and prep, your researcher wants to go off to visit a location or contributor in their own car, ask if they are insured for work purposes and make sure you see a copy of their insurance document to confirm this. If they aren't then you should make sure they travel in a hire vehicle. If they have standard domestic insurance this will mean that if they are transporting the contributor around during the course of work, and they have an accident, the contributor, and any damage to their vehicle, won't be insured.

Errors and omissions insurance

Known briefly as E&O, this insurance provides cover for legal costs and damages incurred following charges such as libel, defamation and infringement of rights or privacy. This type of insurance has become more used over the last decade or so, particularly if you are working with the American TV industry (perhaps because the US tends to be more litigious) and is a complex business. Part of the requirement for the E&O to be signed off at the end of your project will be that all the appropriate licences for all the copyright material in your project have been received; your broker will help clarify this with you. Overall, though, my advice would be that if you are asked to put it in place, make sure that you discuss any options offered to you with your in-house lawyer if you have one – or take external legal advice if you don't.

Security

You will be expected to keep things under lock and key whenever possible, and you can discuss with your insurance broker how you are going to do this and add these security arrangements to your call sheet. When you book hotel accommodation, for example, you might want to rent an extra, ground-floor room where valuables can be decanted and locked up overnight, or book a bigger room for the cameraman so he can store the camera and sound kit overnight without tripping over it on his way to the toilet.

The above are the standard insurance covers that you will need to be aware of, but if you are filming in the US, in a 'dangerous' area, on a boat or a plane or helicopter, or somewhere where your crew might be abducted or your rushes confiscated then you should discuss extending your insurance with your broker.

When you begin your project one of your very first calls should be to a production insurance broker and you will have a fairly long and detailed conversation about what you are doing and how and where you are doing it. You should be honest about all your activities and when things change during your production period call or email your insurance contact to let them know. At the outset they will want to see a copy of the budget for your project and maybe a treatment as well. They will need to know lots of details: what format you are shooting on, where you will be filming, the period of principal filming, who your cast members are going to be, etc. Make sure that they receive a copy of every risk assessment that you produce, but if you are contemplating anything that is outside the normal risks covered by your insurance tell them about it in good time. They can be incredibly helpful. I once sent a crew to an isolated part of Peru and let the insurance man know this. He called me up and told me to get hold of a map of Peru so I could tell him exactly where the crew were going to be. I confess I was a bit put out (I was busy with other things; why did he need to know?) but I did find a map and when I pointed out the location to him he in turn pointed out that the location was very near the border with Colombia, which meant possible bandit country. He recommended that I should take out additional hostage insurance, which I did. Good thing one of us paid attention during geography lessons.

If your crew are anticipating filming on anything that floats, dives, glides or flies then call up the insurance broker. Companies who own boats, helicopters and planes will have special insurance and you may well have to get sight of their insurance documents to show your broker. There are all sorts of complex rules about boat lengths and such which I won't go into here; the point I am making is that you keep talking to your team to find out what they plan to do, and if anything raises the hairs on the back of your professional neck – pick up the phone and seek advice. The earlier you find out such things the better, and don't be tempted to be anything other than scrupulously honest with your broker. Don't fudge!

Making an insurance claim

If your crew contact you to inform you that a crew member has been bitten by a snake, or eight of them have gone down with food poisoning, or the cameraman has had his wide-angle lens swiped, then you should call immediately to let your insurance broker know. There should be an emergency out-of-office-hours number if the incident occurs in the wee small hours. This number should also have been put on the call sheet so the crew can call direct if need be, but they often prefer to let you know instead.

As soon as you can, write down all the details that you have and email/fax/post them to the broker. Ask your crew member for any additional detail, as soon as possible, and pass this info on too (if it's an accident, for example, where did it happen, what date and time, what was the injury, what medical treatment followed and what was or is the impact on the shoot). People tend to forget details the longer you leave it, or when they go on to their next job, so speed is of the essence. And the broker simply needs the details to process your claim effectively – not to tell you off!

If the incident is about, say, the camera going down then the same applies; inform the insurance broker immediately and in writing as soon as you can. Whether the camera belongs to the cameraman or has been hired from a rental company, you will need to contact a supplier as close as possible to your location to try and get a replacement camera to the crew. Get as much information as possible about the fault: can it be fixed on site or is the problem more extensive? I once had a camera go bang in Dubai on a Sunday and we could find a replacement only in the UK, so I had the co-ordinator primed for a surprise trip to deliver it that very day. He had his bag packed before we managed to locate one in the area, but speed is of the essence — so if that's what it requires then you may need to send someone. His travel and living expenses would have formed part of the subsequent insurance claim.

You must also let the Broadcaster know if you make an insurance claim. The broker will require detailed forms to be completed, a report to be written and receipts to be produced, along with other possible bits and pieces. A claim can take quite a time to process so be patient and make sure you keep and copy every receipt that pertains to the claim. Try and get it all completed and sent to the broker as quickly as you can to keep delay to a minimum, and if the claim hasn't been reconciled by the time you leave the project, explain where you are in the process as part of your handover notes.

US insurance

One of the things you will receive in your 'starter pack' from the insurance broker will be a 'To Whom It May Concern' letter, which advises any possible location that you are covered for Public Liability Insurance. Depending on the production, the limit can vary from £1-10 million and you can send copies of the letter to any person or location requesting it (supply spare copies in the pack that goes with your AP/researcher on the shoot). However, if the location is in the United States this form will need to be replaced by what is known as an Accord certificate, which has to be drawn up for each specific location and which contains their particular details. In other words it will be location-specific. Most production insurance brokers will have a US office and will ask you for the name and address of the location and then get the American office to issue an Accord for you — which will, of course, involve a bit of time due to the time difference between the UK and the US. The location will then want sight of this document.

At the risk of being boring, let me say again that you should talk things through with your insurance broker on a regular basis and check, check and double-check if there is anything you are anxious about. It should go without saying that if you ever find yourself sending a crew to a war zone or hostile area, or asking presenters to do hazardous things for the programme, then you will need to put extra insurance in place. So call up the broker and don't feel bad about bothering them as often as you need to. It might be a good idea to invite them to the wrap party as a thank-you gesture!

Media insurance companies – a small selection

Media Insurance Brokers Limited (Tel) 0207 287 5054 www.mediainsurance.com

Aon (Tel) 0845 070 0387 (E) entertainment.media@ars.co.uk

Torribles (Tel) 0117 300 6161 www.theovalgroup.com

11 Negotiating contracts, hiring and firing

Negotiating with crew

I define crew as being the people that you hire to operate cameras and sound equipment, plus grips, electricians and anyone else who does a 'physical' job. (The production team are those people who work more directly for or with you doing the research and paperwork side of things. Editors fall somewhere in between.)

How to negotiate

You'll find yourself doing a fair bit of negotiating during your career, so it's worth thinking about how best to manage it. This might depend in part upon the type of personality you have – if you are brash and aggressive then your negotiating skills will be formidable and you will drive a hard bargain with everyone who crosses your path. There's nothing wrong with that, but it isn't the only way to go. It may seem a bit soft but I usually try and think where the crew member I am dealing with is coming from. Some people always ask for a higher fee than they think they will get and can then be negotiated down, but quite a lot of folk offer their usual rate and are a bit miffed if you then try to bargain.

When I began my career I usually offered a little bit less than I knew I had in my budget as a starting point: get in first and go low, as it were; you can always go up but not down. Now I tend to ask what rate the person is looking for and then try and gauge whether they are being honest or not. Let's assume that you are dealing with a cameraman to start with; the bargaining process will usually take place on the telephone. I think that part of my job is establishing some kind of a relationship with prospective crew members (or anyone for that matter) – it can be useful for later on when you might need a favour from them, so it's worth spending a little time being generally friendly and interested. Don't overdo it but try a few comments about their brilliant CV or a programme that they shot that you liked. A cameraman's life is quite tough, I think – they often work very long hours, travel a lot, cart heavy gear about in all weathers, and almost all have bad backs as a consequence. For this and other reasons, screwing them down to the lowest rate may not be the best way to go because their subsequent resentment may make working with them more difficult than it need be. I think that if they quote a fair rate for the job, one that meshes with what you have in the budget (and you will also have a good idea of current rates of pay), then you might accept what they suggest at the outset. In the past I have negotiated hard on rates and got a few quid off, only to find when an invoice comes in that it lists a few extras for justified items like filters or basic lights, and, hey, the total amount is what they first suggested. Funny that.

You also need the goodwill of a cameraman and sound recordist on a shoot. There may be days that go belly up and they need to work longer to get the shots you need; if they feel happy with their rate of pay they may just do it for nothing and with good grace, rather than adding a lot of overtime to their invoice.

When hiring a cameraman or sound recordist you should make it clear what hours you are looking for: 8, 10 or 12. You should also check out their overtime rate for when you exceed the hours – it shouldn't be more than time and a half per hour, and anyone who wants extra money for weekend work is living in the past and you should find someone else! If a cameraman quotes a much higher rate than you can afford, or that you feel is inflated, then you need to go back to your director and ask if they will choose an alternative cameraman. Sometimes they are fixated on working with someone who makes them feel secure (or who covers their arse when they forget to get the useful shots for the edit), so this can make negotiating difficult. But you should take a firm line with a director who wants a particular cameraman whatever they cost, maybe by suggesting that s/he can have them if they will do without something else – a shoot-day fewer, for example – to cover the extra cost. You might, in the end, have to say a firm no, in which case you should offer up some alternatives with CVs and showreels and recommendations from other directors.

There may be a case for imposing a camera crew on to the individual directors working on a series. This might be when you make an early decision, probably with the series producer, executive or someone senior within the production company, to use the same camera crew for every programme in the series you are shooting. (Obviously this works only if the shoots don't overlap.) This decision may be made for reasons of continuity of style, or maybe because, on a super-tight budget, you can do an incredibly good deal for what will be a large number of days or weeks of work. Directors may not like this much but they should argue the point with the company, rather than with you.

So, having got your cameraman for a mutually acceptable daily rate, if you are filming in the UK you may want to use their kit vehicle so you should get a quote for this. Usually a vehicle includes, say, 50 free miles per day plus mileage thereafter – can you agree a fuel receipt or two instead of mileage? The very lowest mileage rate will be around 35–40 pence per mile, and the crew will run up a small fortune if travelling long distances (mileage also makes it difficult to estimate travel costs). And while you will normally hire the cameraman the director wants, the sound recordist is likely to be someone the cameramen suggests – which might mean that they will travel together in the same kit vehicle; a good plan all round to save you another vehicle hire, fuel costs and parking. Indeed, they might offer you an all-in package: the two of them, their combined kit and a vehicle – easy. (Make sure that this vehicle is insured for work purposes. You can ask to see their insurance policy – if they carry passengers in a work capacity without this insurance then they, and your company, will not be properly insured in the event of an accident.)

If you are hiring for a trip abroad, remember that you should negotiate a lesser rate for travel, rest and recce days; maybe half of their usual rate or a little bit more than half. If you are sending them to a location where they will return overnight on a flight, you will pay them for the day they land as they won't be in a fit state to work when they get back. When filming abroad the chances are that they will be working consecutive days, so you will need to plan their schedule so that they have sufficient rest days within it, as well as paying them per diems or a living allowance for breakfast, lunch and dinner on those days.

If a cameraman has their own kit they will obviously want you to hire that as part of their package, but you can do this only if it's the right kit for the job; if it isn't you will have to hire from a kit company. They should have a chat with the director and get some idea of what the shooting style is going to be and then furnish you with a wish list of kit. You will pay only what you can afford for this, so you may have to get them to reduce their kit list until it's within your price range. Finally, they may come in for a meeting or two with the director and you, in which case they may charge you for this, or not – just ask them beforehand.

Once you have all this verbal negotiation done you should write an email confirming what you have agreed. I call this a deal letter, and it normally starts with the phrase 'This is to confirm our intention to hire you as …' which covers you if something goes wrong and you have to cancel them – they are on a 'pencil' until final confirmation anyway. You should list all the fees you have agreed and state the hours you have agreed to, finishing the note with a phrase that goes something like 'Please confirm your agreement with the terms of this letter by return'. You could leave out this stage and go straight to contract, but if you are behind on issuing the contract then you have the fallback position of a deal letter. Early in my career I found myself in a situation with a cameraman, whose contract I hadn't got round to issuing, and suffered the indignity of being told, on set: 'Darling, you must be kidding. I wouldn't have agreed that rate for a day's work.' Slap on the wrist for me for failing to get contracts out before starting work. Much of what I recommend here has come about from bad experiences in the past – sometimes a bit of time spent early on can save you time and trouble further down the line.

Contracting crew

Once you are certain that your shoot is going ahead, you can confirm the dates and issue your contracts. I would suggest doing this and getting them back signed before the crew leaves for the shoot. In any case never pay an invoice until you have their signed contract returned, otherwise you may never see it and you may well need it for your deliverables.

The template for the contract will either come from the Broadcaster or from the production company and the chances are that they will both be based largely on a PACT contract. PACT (Producers Alliance for Cinema and Television; see the Appendix on helpful agencies) have a large collection of contracts for everyone from narrators and composers to Loan Out personnel (those self-employed people who will invoice you using their company name for their services). You will need to be a member of PACT to get your mitts on the contracts listed on their website, so it's helpful if the company you are working for is a member because this also means you will have access to the various help and guidance services they offer. If you can't use this then you might call another production manager and ask them nicely for templates that you might borrow (and please don't tell anyone I told you this).

Production staff

When hiring production team – production co-ordinators, production assistants, secretaries, researchers and APs – the negotiation process is slightly different. You will probably interview them first and try, always, to do this with another person such as head of production or series producer. In this way you can discuss feedback afterwards and form an opinion based on more than one impression.

As a production manager you will probably receive dozens of CVs from hopefuls which you should try and read and file away if they look useful. Indeed, if you are waiting for a project to start up and have the time, you could get in a few potential candidates to see how they shape up. Make notes on their CVs to remind you of what they looked like (useful as a reminder when you've seen loads of people), what you thought of them and when they were available, then file them away. Always check out whether a possible candidate has done the kind of job you are hiring for – some experience that qualifies them. And always ask what sort of rate they are looking for just in case they are way out of your financial league. Having said all this I find that the TV industry tends to run on personal recommendation – someone will suggest the name of a good researcher they have worked with in the past, so get them in and see what you think.

Always, and I'll repeat that, *always* get at least two references on anyone before you offer them a job. They may well mention referees in their CV who you can bet will give them a good one, so see if you can also identify a contact that you or someone on your team knows and can ring for confirmation. If you don't get two absolutely glowing references then think carefully about hiring them; good references are not foolproof, but they can give you a good idea of how a person functions.

Interviewing

A word here about what I can only refer to as 'niceness'! It helps if you can work with people you like and who fit in well with a team, as well as being good at their job. You will probably be dealing with at least one 'difficult' or high-maintenance creative person, so it helps if the production staff are sympathetic and supportive, and if possible largely your choice. I would never hire a co-ordinator to work closely with me who wasn't cheerful and 'can-do'. A sense of humour is required, as is a flexible attitude and good problem-solving skills along with an enthusiastic approach and a willingness to work late when necessary. Production staff don't get paid overtime so if they do work consistently long hours then make sure they get the odd TOIL (Time Off in Lieu day) when it's convenient, as well as, of course, providing food to keep them going. However, do bear in mind that when people work very late there comes a point when their efficiency decreases dramatically, so monitor their hours, and your own!

A brief word about self-employed or freelance staff (they used to be known as Schedule D) versus PAYE (Pay As You Earn) or payroll staff. If you hire anyone who has an 'assistant' prefix then they have to be on the payroll, unless they have a letter from the Inland Revenue allowing them to be paid on a fee basis. The Inland Revenue decrees who, in the TV industry, is allowed to be freelance and issues a list of these people, so check this when hiring staff. Anyone who is self-employed should invoice you for their total fee and nothing else (no NI stamp, for example). Their invoice should either include their freelance tax code reference number or state their role clearly, so you know they are entitled to be paid on such a basis. This means that you only pay their fee with no additions, except VAT if they are VAT registered, in which case they must put their VAT number on their invoice and show the VAT amount separately. You will still issue them with paid holiday credits on the term of their contract – this should also be shown separately on their invoices. At present 28 days is the number of paid days annually that everyone is entitled to and there is a very useful little calculating chart on the PACT website which will work this out for you. Or you can divide 28 (days) by 52 (weeks) and then multiply the number of weeks of the contract to get the holiday credit amount. If it's a daft decimal number, just round it up.

If the employee is engaged on a PAYE basis then you will need to put all their payments through the payroll process. This means you (or, more likely, the company accountant) will deduct income tax and 12.8% – the employer's portion of the NI payment (at the time of writing; check it hasn't changed) of their weekly fee – from their payment, showing this clearly on the payment slip. If the employee is 60 years old or over then they no longer pay an NI stamp, but the employer should still continue to make this 12.8% payment. The NI stamp percentage and the holiday credits (payable on all staff, whether PAYE or freelance) should be budgeted for in schedule 18. For extra guidance on this, check with the Inland Revenue. In short, anyone engaged on a freelance basis will cost the company only their fee (plus a paid holiday entitlement). Anyone on payroll will cost an extra 12.8% of their total salary on the budget in addition to their holiday credit.

The inclusion of holiday pay in everyone's contract is a relatively recent one that has come about because of EU regulations, and the spirit of it is that everyone should have regular breaks during their work schedule. You can designate when people take these breaks – for example over the Christmas/New Year period, when the office might be closed – and you should encourage staff to take their holiday if at all possible. If they can't then their holiday payment should be added to their final payment. It may not be practical to take holiday, especially during a short contract, but do remember that the world won't fall apart because someone has gone off for a break; in fact they may well return to work rejuvenated and refreshed rather than burnt out and exhausted. Editors and directors, for instance, may find that they can take a day or so off when they are waiting for comments back from the rough cut, since editing during this hiatus is a bit pointless anyway. Try to encourage holiday taking, in yourself as well as others.

Editors

I deal with hiring an editor in Chapter 18 on Post Production, so I'll just make a few comments here.

Call the intended editor and chat to them about the project, giving them a concise idea of what it's about, where it's filming and how long you think you will need them for. You should also tell them whom they will be working with, since a director might favour an editor but this might not be a reciprocal feeling. Ask them what rate they want and whether this covers any late nights or weekends. It used to be that editors would work the hours necessary to finish a programme, but after years of being exploited they have got wise and now will generally want overtime at least for weekend work. If their rate is high tell them what you have and see if you can agree on a compromise.

The general rule with rates is if someone really wants the work they will agree to accept what you offer – but lately I have found that good editors are really booked up so you may have to keep looking. When people are 'hungry' and the work situation is tight it's a buyer's market, so you can just offer what you have and see who bites.

Before we leave the subject of negotiating rates, a word about your own situation. I have been to countless interviews or less formal chats about up-coming projects and spent an hour or so getting enthusiastic about a project, only to be quoted a derisory rate for the job at the end. At some point you should have worked out your personal expenses, covering everything from mortgage to daily spending money, and will have a good idea of what is the very least you will work for. Accepting less than that is just not clever, unless you are desperate to get your first job or to work after a period of unemployment. Once you have a fair amount of experience then you shouldn't accept significantly less than what you're worth – doing so will probably make you resentful and unwilling to put in any extra effort. This may give you a good insight into how it feels when you do something similar to your cameraman or co-ordinator – goodwill is all.

If the company really want you but genuinely can't afford the rate you are asking and you are keen to do the job, can you work for 4 days a week and spend one day 'working at home'? Or work fewer weeks than is budgeted, or agree, perhaps, to take some unpaid time off in the middle of your contract – a stand-down time, if this suits you? It's all negotiable.

Hiring and firing

Despite the best intentions of everyone concerned in hiring staff, sometimes it just doesn't work out. I do think, especially for longer contracts, that you should try and talk informally and quietly to your production staff about their performance if you have issues about it as early as you can. (Equally, tell them often if they are doing a great job: everyone likes praise.) People often just don't realise things about themselves that are obvious to other people, and though it can be hard to outline someone's faults, it can also be amazingly useful to all concerned if it is done sensitively and with a positive spin. You should, for example, always start any criticism with a positive comment – for example, 'I think you do an amazing job with the cost book and it's great to know I can trust you with it, but I just need to speak to you about your way of dealing with other members of staff.' If things don't improve then you should try again, always keeping notes of the dates and content of these conversations. If this fails too then consider if you can move the person concerned sideways, or into another role where their strengths outweigh their weaknesses? Otherwise you will have to start the process of replacing them, probably sooner rather than later because once you have lost faith in them things are unlikely to get better. Nip it in the bud and move on, and make sure you have alternatives up your sleeve before you proceed.

Be aware that the termination clause in their contract is one that you will have to honour – for example if it's a 4-week period then you may well have to pay them for 4 weeks, even if they have walked out of the door. Always ask for a second person to be in the room when you are firing someone and try, please, to avoid humiliating them as far as possible. It's a humiliating process anyway; don't make it worse. Try to use words that indicate it's just not working out but you wish them all good luck in the future, nothing personal, just unsuitable for this particular project. Be prepared for them to be angry and/or upset and don't let this sway your judgement. Be quiet and firm but fair and regretful and consider whether it is better for them to go more or less straight away to avoid them being negative and bitter with other members of the team. I have been fired in my career, both nicely and nastily – it's an unpleasant experience but you have to try to learn from it and then move on.

I'd always advise you to check first with a legal source to make sure that you have followed the rules for getting rid of a team member, just so you know that you are not opening up the company to subsequent legal action. This might be the ideal opportunity for using the legal service that the PMA offers. An ex-employee may take legal advice and hit you with an action for, say, unfair dismissal, so make sure that you don't expose the company to this sort of action.

If you, or someone you have dismissed, wants to take this further they will need to apply for a Tribunal hearing, and they will have 12 weeks from the date of dismissal in which to do this. If an application for a Tribunal is accepted, ACAS (Arbitration and Conciliation Service, a free government service) will then step in to negotiate neutrally between the two parties. They will work to settle the action before it reaches a Tribunal, so things may well be settled out of court if both parties agree. Do make sure you have your facts right before you fire someone. And be circumspect with the rest of the team by not bad-mouthing the person who has left. A simple explanation that they have gone and will be replaced is the best way to go.

12 'Recces', setting up shoots and foreign filming

I have already mentioned setting up recces and shoots. This chapter will look in more detail about these two important areas of production, possibly the busiest bit of the project for you and your production team. The chapter assumes that you will be sending a four-person crew: cameraman, sound recordist, director and researcher/assistant producer.

The first thing to do

You should get started as soon as possible on nailing your locations. These can take a while to confirm, and if you don't have them in place on time you will be scrambling to make your deadlines. This becomes even more crucial for foreign filming. Finding foreign locations and getting filming permissions from a distance may take lots of negotiating time, so try and pin down the shoot locations with the team as soon as you can and get the process started early. For filming in National Trust or English Heritage properties, for example, you should allow as much leeway as you can for the bureaucratic wheels to grind, and if your budget can't cover a preferred location you may have to spend time finding an alternative and getting the application process started afresh. Pinning down locations at the last minute may force you into paying more than you can afford.

The value of a recce

If the budget can stand it, 'recces' (short for reconnoitre, and sometimes called 'scouts' these days, particularly in the US) are very useful for you and your team. It's a time to visit possible locations, assess any problems they may present and check out the contributors to make sure they won't look like rabbits caught in the headlights once they are on camera. A participant may have the most wonderful story to tell, but if they can't tell it with some passion and without stumbling over every word then they may not make it into the finished programme. Encourage your team to iron out any problems that the various locations may have in signing their respective location agreements, and similarly check that your contributors will sign their release forms without any objections (also that they are happy with any fee being paid).

There may be money and time for a 'tech rec' (technical recce), in which case the director and some of your other heads of department – DOP, sound, lighting or gaffer, art department, rigger, grip and, if you are doing stunts, then the stunt team and a Health & Safety expert too – will need to check the location(s) for things like power sources, camera angles, equipment access, parking, facilities (like toilets nearby), sound levels and any other practicalities that you can think of that are particular to your shoot.

Budgets being what they are, it might not be possible to send everyone you'd like to on a recce. In a perfect world the director and researcher or AP would be the minimum crew, but in a pinch send the director alone. Give whoever goes along a list of questions that you'd like answered. Issue a float to cover the travel and living expenses that you haven't pre-paid and give them some guidance about how much their daily subsistence should be. When they come back they must reconcile the float – or you can do it yourself. There should be a meeting at which they present the fruits of their recce so you can be informed about anything that needs attention, including things like horrid hotels that are miles away from the action or the useful fact that there is an equipment facility nearby that you didn't know about where you can hire extra kit or buy emergency stock. Compile a simple call sheet for the recce and do a risk assessment too. If the director can't be spared from scripting or is busy on something else then it might be a good plan to send the AP with a small camera (a Z1, for example) and get them to grab some footage of places and people, gathering information to bring back for the director and you.

If the budget is too tight to allow a separate recce, it might be possible to tag a short exploratory trip on to the beginning of the shoot (thus saving an extra set of flights/fares and attendant travel expenses). In this way a few days of settling in and looking around can prepare the team for the up-coming shoot. Then there's a bit of time to change hotels if they need to and to meet up with the contributors and check out the locations. You can save even more money here if you send only the director and AP/researcher and arrange for the crew to follow on the day before filming is due to start (but with enough time for them to have a production meeting and maybe a quick look around when they arrive).

If all else fails you will be forced to send the crew and team members into a shoot 'cold' – not the best situation, but sometimes unavoidable. In such a case you should encourage the research team to speak often and in depth to any contributors, to check out potential locations by talking to the people on site, and to explore maps and any of those clever websites that offer virtual tours of places so that the problem of a team arriving in a situation completely blind is reduced.

The shoot

Since a filming day is an expensive item, it makes sense to plan each one very carefully to get the most bang for your buck. Well-planned shoots that squeeze the most out of every day are to be encouraged but, conversely, a crew that is on its knees, exhausted from long hours and no rest days, is not only a Health & Safety disaster waiting to happen but just isn't fair, so plan the days with a degree of consideration for the well-being of all concerned. Try to aim for a day off after six consecutive days of work, and if you know there are going to be long days on some occasions then plan some shorter travel or recce days in between to give the team a break. And know your director: once some of them get the bit between their teeth, meals and rest time go out of the window. They must be made to realise that for a cameraman and sound recordist a two-week shoot is their normal experience, and they won't necessarily have a few days to recover and a week of watching rushes at home before the edit starts, but may well be on a plane heading for the next gig the following day. Talk to the director and the researcher and insist that the hours you have negotiated with the crew are observed and that proper meals breaks are taken. If you think a director is likely to forget these rules in the panic of the day, then speak to them about it again or get your executive or series producer to reinforce the message. If you talk to the crew in advance about hours and rest days they will know that, at least, you have thought about this and tried to consider their well-being. The Health & Safety rules in this country have become much more stringent because of a number of fatal accidents in the industry a decade or so ago, caused largely by fatigue and carelessness. Having such events happen on your watch will be something that could blight your career for ever, not to mention the sense of personal responsibility you will feel until the day you finally pension off your calculator.

I shall first consider the UK shoot and then go on to the particular problems that foreign shoots may pose.

Setting up shoots

To start putting together a shoot schedule you might draw up a simple day-by-day template on your computer and then talk it through with the director and the researcher (or whoever is actually going on the shoot, along with the person who has been dealing with the contributors and locations) to decide who and what is going to be shot in the time allowed. The shoot may run on consecutive days, or be spread across a period with time between set aside for more research or scripting, or your schedule may depend on your interviewees' availability. Your director may also want to save a day or two for pick-ups during the edit, but however it is shaping up, you can start getting it down on paper, or on the electronic equivalent, to work from.

There may follow a more detailed discussion about how long journeys between locations will take and how many interviews, locations or items you can usefully shoot in a day. If you are filming interviews, for example, in a large city, you will need to allow plenty of time for travelling between them, taking into account the problems of traffic congestion and roadworks. Then you should add some time for parking and unpacking the crew vehicle, setting up and lighting (however rudimentary your lighting may be), and then striking the kit, schlepping it back to the car park, repacking it and moving to the next location – not counting coffee breaks, toilet stops, forgetting something and having to go back for it, getting lost, parking problems, a lack of lifts where the kit has to be trailed up three flights of stairs, being kept waiting by the interviewee and said interviewee being very nervous and needing lots of takes before he or she settles down to give the sound bite that you need … In short, I usually find that the 'creative' team will have seriously under-estimated this and are gaily planning four interviews in a 12-hour day. Firstly, your 12-hour day includes travel time at the beginning and the end, and a decent lunch break, so you're down to, say, nine hours by now. If the interviews are geographically close to each other and nothing goes seriously wrong, then it might just work – but err on the side of caution, otherwise you may find that your contributors are kept waiting. This may not only screw up their schedule or put the location out of bounds, but also make them very cross and that's not a good way to begin an interview, even if your crew have had the foresight to call ahead and warn them. And, of course, if a day starts to run behind and everyone has to work longer hours to pack everything in then you are likely to be charged lots of overtime for which you may not have budgeted. If you are filming the next day and you have run very late then, by EEC rules that govern working hours, you must allow your crew an 11-hour break or turnaround (including travel) so if you don't wrap until 11pm you can't begin your following day's shoot any earlier than 10am which might screw that day as well. Am I making my point? Try to be realistic in what can be achieved in a day. Time will never be wasted, because if the crew do finish a bit early a savvy director will get some GVs or establisher shots in the can to help them in the edit and the sound recordist can grab some useful wild-track too.

Call sheet

Once you have set up what looks like a reasonable schedule, the team should check that all the contributors can make their time slot and that all of the locations are available. Then you, or your co-ordinator, can start to set up your call sheet – the bible of what is happening when, where and with whom. Put this on an accessible part of the computer system so that the researcher and director can add contact details and any notes they may want to make on interviewees and locations. They will probably prefer to tell you about it at great length, or write emails – but try to be firm that they do it directly; why do the work twice?

Put everything on the call sheet: travel plans, production team and crew contact numbers, accommodation details (including car park directions), any hire car, taxi or driver details, emergency numbers (embassy, hospital, police – the emergency police telephone code in each country – insurance), how to get rushes back and/or store them, next tape number to be shot, carnet instructions, parking and filming permits, risk assessments, weather, first aid details, schedule, maps and directions, instructions for returning rushes to office on the way home from the airport, taxi reference numbers – in short, everything that the crew may need to know. They probably won't read it and will ask you questions, but at least it is all there and you can be smug and tell them that! (A fellow production manager tells me she once saw someone wearing a tee-shirt saying 'If you can read this, you can read your call sheet'. I want one of those.)

Send the call sheet to everyone who needs it: all crew members, insurance company, production company, etc. and, as a courtesy, crew spouses so they know how to contact their partners if they need to. And give a supply of hard copies to the AP/researcher so they can give them to any of the crew who have forgotten or lost them.

I have included a template for a call sheet ▣, but this is just a suggestion. Use whatever format works for you.

Contracting crew

Earlier in the prep period you will have pencilled the crew that the director has chosen; now you can start to firm up these pencils and make sure everyone is still available. It's not wise to confirm these bookings until as close as possible to the shoot, because once you do that, you are liable for payment if the whole schedule falls apart and you have to cancel. If this cancellation is very late then you will have to negotiate with the crew their cancellation fees, and it wouldn't be unreasonable for them to ask for 100% of their agreed fee if it's the day before your intended start date and they have turned down other work during the run-up. In this eventuality get on the phone as soon as you can and be up-front with them and hope that you can offer another shoot further down the line to mitigate their loss. But it wouldn't be fair to pay nothing for cancelling, even if it isn't your fault. And if you do have to keep putting back a shoot then expect to lose your first-choice crew – don't confirm until things look really definite. It is universally accepted, when pencilling a crew, that if they are offered other work during your dates they will call you and check if your dates are firmed up yet. Try not to take it personally if a cameraman decides to take alternative work if you can't confirm him – it may be that s/he is being offered a dream job. However, s/he should have the courtesy to call and not just jump ship without letting you know. By the same token you must let them know immediately if your dates slip or cancel altogether, and try to do this on the telephone – I think it's more polite and immediate than an email.

Final preparation for the shoot

Be meticulous with the details as you prep your shoot; the smallest thing forgotten or overlooked can tip it into chaos. You will be liaising between the director and the cameraman about what kit they want hired in (if they don't own their own) and making arrangements to have it delivered to you or straight to the cameraman or even location. If it does go to the latter you must make sure that it will be secure, and check the insurance situation on this too. Don't forget you'll also have to get kit back to the hire facility at the end, so make arrangements for that now. All these details should be added to the call sheet. It's a good plan to do a separate list of hired-in kit and which company you hired from, so that bits of kit don't get mixed up and returned to the wrong supplier. Extra charges will be incurred if it is late. And check through this call sheet every few days to see how it's shaping up and to ask questions if there are things that bother you.

Make sure you have more than enough of the correct stock. Your co-ordinator should also be working to set up a folder of necessary bits and pieces like pens, headed paper, envelopes, release forms and location agreements, copies of the insurance certificate, a kit list, maps, props, call sheets and anything else deemed helpful. You will also be organising money for the float (or possibly short-term company credit cards), booking hotels and car hire, and writing and issuing contracts and making sure they are signed and returned. This is when there are a host of things to do and the stress levels can mount, so try to keep everyone cool. Constantly refer to your production check list (see example 🖳) to make sure you don't forget anything. Ensure too that you have told the insurance broker exactly what is happening and get the risk assessment (RA) under way. This should be written by a senior person who will be on the shoot, or by yourself with their input, but the producer will be responsible for Health & Safety on the shoot and they should sign off the RA. Remember to book a stills photographer if your contract demands publicity stills, or get the AP to take them. As you issue floats, get them signed off by the recipient and file the receipt to remind them how much they are reconciling after the shoot. If you and the team find yourselves working late to get everything done in time, remember to order in dinner to keep them going and cabs home if it's really late. A warm thank-you works wonders too.

A word here about Health & Safety. You will have done a detailed risk assessment (this is a legal requirement, so don't stint). I have found it useful to provide the team with a small exercise-type book entitled (in large letters) Accident Book. Hand it to the most responsible person on the shoot and instruct them to enter into it anything that happens that can be called an accident, plus the date, location, what happened, what first aid was given, and whether the injured party accepted or declined any medical treatment that was offered. Even a small cut or graze should be treated with first aid and recorded. I say this because an H&S executive once told me that a minor wound on a shoot he knew of was left untreated and became a fully fledged case of septicaemia before the week was out. Scary.

It is always a good plan to try and encourage your team members to have first aid training, especially when shooting abroad. And you should always provide a proper first aid kit and write on the call sheet who has it, making sure that it contains useful things like antiseptic ointment, tweezers and plasters. Your call sheet should always, of course, include the details of the nearest hospital and police station, and if you are shooting anywhere on or near the sea, the coastguard details. See the Chapter 13 on Health & Safety for more guidance.

Check and double-check *everything*. Go through the call sheet with a beady eye and pin down any details that are waving gently in the breeze. The call sheet should resemble a military operation with nothing left to chance; talk your AP and director through it before they leave and make sure they understand what paperwork you need returned. You can add notes to the call sheet about remembering to bring all vital paperwork back, along with the hotel bill and any other expenditure that you have booked and paid for on the company credit card. You might want to furnish some of those little zipped transparent pencil-case-type things for them to put their receipts in so they don't get lost – separate ones for cash and credit card payments, and separate ones again for foreign receipts. Remember that if shooting in the UK most of the spend will be subject to VAT and without receipts you will be unable to claim it, so feel free to bang on about the importance of bringing all these bits of paper back to you. Then wave them off with a tear in your eye and the instruction to contact you at any time day or night if they need to (but hope that you have planned everything so efficiently that they won't).

Foreign shoots

All of the above applies to foreign shooting but with knobs on. There is an additional range of issues to consider when filming abroad: carnets, excess baggage, inoculations, visas and passports and medication for illnesses particular to some locations.

Where to start

There are a number of things that will take time to sort out, so it's best to get on to those as soon as you can. When you know your countries and locations (or even if they are suggested but not confirmed) check visas and inoculation requirements. Some jabs, like the one for yellow fever, will require time for a course of shots, and visas can take weeks for some countries so get your applications in quickly. And if you are shooting somewhere where a fixer will be needed, start making enquiries about good ones – probably from other production managers who have shot in that area. When you get some names, check that they have previous experience in the genre that you are making. For example, if you are making a cheap documentary and your fixer has done lots of drama, they will send you back a quote that is probably scarily outside your budget and full of items you don't need, so make sure they understand exactly what your project is and what you can afford. Your fixer will be a critical member of your team and many of your arrangements will rely on their expertise and knowledge, so shop around for the best and most suitably experienced one you can find.

Booking flights, trains or ferries – and passports!

Firstly, find out whether the name on your crew's passport is the same as the everyday name they use. If you book a ticket that doesn't correspond to the passport name the ticket will be invalid. Check their nationality, don't just assume they are British, and also check that they have more than six months' validity on their passport; if they haven't you will need to get them a new one. If the location you are sending them to is a problematic one politically then check if they have two passports (lots of crew do keep two), and then ensure they carry a passport that doesn't have 'dodgy' stamps on it for where they are going. (For example, an Israeli stamp on a passport might make getting into Lebanon difficult.) The easiest way to do all this is to ask to borrow their passport(s) early on, photocopy or scan the critical page and keep them safely in the office in case of loss or theft. If you happen to be sending a very large crew on a foreign shoot (a production manager I know regularly ran the Ryder golf tournament, which required getting something like 160 crew and kit to Spain – a task that deserves a chapter in itself!) then you can ask the airline to lay on a special check-in desk for your people. This will speed things up and prevent the passengers queuing behind them wanting to kill them.

> **USEFUL TIP**
> It is now a legal requirement to keep a copy of all your staff employees' passports in your files.

I once had to set up a small and unexpected shoot in Italy. Finding that regular flights were very expensive, I checked out a budget airline and was on the point of booking when I double-checked the excess baggage situation. The airline assured me that they would take all the kit, but maybe not on the same flight as the crew – perhaps the next one? It wouldn't have been a saving to have the crew wait around for who knows how long for their kit, so we went with an expensive but more reliable airline. Also, if you are sending a shoot across the States, or on small domestic flights anywhere, and this involves flying on little toy-town planes, check those carefully too. They may not take excess baggage at all, which will mean your crew having to drive with it or flying the crew and sending the kit by courier – something that makes cameramen and sound men understandably very nervous, but it may be your only option in a pinch.

You will also be responsible for getting the crew to and from airports. These cab rides are always expensive so see if you can save money by doubling up on people who live near each other. When sending a recce you might be able to persuade them to travel by tube or train since they may not have much baggage to carry. If your crew need to drive their vehicle to the airport and want you to pay for long-term car parking, check out how much this will cost and see if you can supply a large vehicle with driver to drop them off and collect them when they return for a similar cost. I have been known to go along to assist at check-in, or to send the co-ordinator, if there is a lot to do and the crew may appreciate some sort of help, especially if you have a presenter or interviewee in tow.

Sending kit abroad

When sending a professional kit abroad it may be a legal requirement to obtain some sort of import/export documentation. The documentation is proof for the authorities in each country you are visiting that the kit is not being sold off abroad, so everything that appears on the kit list at the beginning must be returned at the end. It is, quite simply, a passport for your filming equipment.

Firstly, check if any such documents are required. Member countries of the EU don't require them and there are a few other exceptions (e.g. Switzerland), but never assume! One of the best co-ordinators I ever worked with once sent a crew to Finland, Norway and Denmark and didn't get a carnet for them – well, which country do you think isn't in the EC? It was the only occasion I'd ever seen her cry. But she recovered and got it sorted in no time. That's the mark of a good co-ordinator: cry, panic and then fix it – all in the space of a few minutes. And the answer is Norway.

Next, check if the country is signed up to the carnet scheme. This is a fast and efficient way of satisfying the customs requirements both here and abroad. A carnet is a multi-paged document issued by the Chamber of Commerce which you have to pay for and – don't forget this – you have to return to them at the end of your shoot. It lists the equipment that is travelling in great detail and can be turned around in about a week or less, though don't cut it too fine. A list of the countries signed up to the scheme can be found on the Chamber of Commerce website, or call a carnet company (like Dynamic or Samfreight) and ask them. Any countries that are in the European Community will not require a carnet so you can move your kit freely in these areas. However, you may well need some sort of customs form for this, so check with the relevant embassy what document is required and where you can get one. Be warned: the members change periodically so make sure your information is up to date.

To get your carnet or custom form, first get a list of the camera and sound kit from either your crew or the hire company. Then make sure that this list isn't altered because changes, even changes to serial numbers, will render the carnet invalid. The list will include details like the value of each item and its serial number. You can draw up the carnet yourself but I would heartily advise against this – it is incredibly fiddly and time-consuming; much better to call up a carnet company specialising in compiling them and give them enough time to complete and deliver it. I once cut it very fine and the carnet company representative had to race across Heathrow Airport to present it to the crew who were waiting to check in. I paid extra and my fingernails never quite recovered, so try and allow enough time to do it comfortably. And I usually make the cameraman responsible for getting the carnet stamped in and out of each country, because they have usually done it before and understand the importance of getting it done properly and returning it at the end.

One word of warning: never 'split' a carnet. In other words if you have a carnet for the camera and sound kit together, the cameraman and sound recordist will have to travel together for the carnet to be valid. If one of them decides to stay on for a bit of a holiday, for example, then you're going to have to know that up front and either arrange for a carnet each or ask the cameraman to bring the sound kit home. If you play fast and loose with these documents you will provoke the ire of the Customs and Excise chaps and they have the power to fine you for misdemeanours. If a situation occurs when the crew are away and you need to separate your carnet holders, call Customs and Excise and get advice on how to do it. It's likely that you have to pay extra.

So, your crew are going to the US and taking British kit with them. You will need to allow plenty of time at the airport to meet and get to the customs office for the carnet-checking process. This should be done before check-in/bag drop and may involve removing every single item of kit from every flight box so that customs can check it. The crew then have to repack their flight cases and leg it to check-in – so allow at least three hours before take-off to make sure they don't miss their flights, perhaps even longer in these security-conscious times. It's not a good start to a shoot to miss the outgoing flight. I once heard of a cameraman who changed his taxi pick-up time, believing that he had too much time allotted. On arrival at customs they were irritated that he hadn't left enough time for them to search the bags if they so wished and took the whole kit to pieces. He missed his flight, which caused no end of bother.

If the crew are arriving at the airport extremely early in the morning or very late at night it might be worth checking to make sure that the office will be open. I once sent a crew to Gatwick at 6am. The customs man was off sick, the office was closed, and the crew had to fly into New York with an unstamped carnet, resulting in long and complicated explanations before they were allowed in.

For all other countries each embassy will be able to inform you of their procedures and forms that will need to be complied with. Some of these can be hugely complicated (e.g. Eygpt), extremely time-consuming (e.g. India, Bangladesh), expensive (e.g. Brazil) and even linked to the crew visas (e.g. India, Brazil) so this should be looked into early and before you set your schedule. Oh, and you might need to do it in a foreign language …

If you are filming in Egypt, for example, there is a lot of paperwork and bureaucracy involved and it is not a carnet country, so get started early by calling up their embassy for guidance. In fact, if you are filming in Egypt you should take advice from a production manager who has done it before, give yourself plenty of lead-up time and arrange a good fixer out there to help you through the complex system of gifts, bribes and gratuities that the country runs on. It's a good piece of advice whenever you're filming in a foreign country to talk to someone else who has done it recently and be guided by them – the smallest detail can trip you up and may cost you money to put right.

Your co-ordinator would be well employed making calls and checking websites for unusual requirements in the very early stages of prep, so you have time to sort things out without last-minute panics.

Excess baggage

When you are flying camera and sound kit abroad you will have to pay excess baggage charges. The cost of this (usually for the whole kit or sometimes per flight box) will vary tremendously and should be taken into account when booking your flights – a cheaper flight might give you more expensive excess rates. It used to be that flying your crew in business class, especially on long-haul flights, could be a good investment excess baggage-wise, so if your budget will stretch to that then your crew will love you for ever! And if you send all the crew on the same flight you will be able to share out the excess baggage allowance between them, as their own luggage is not likely to take up the whole amount of each personal allowance. Talk to the airline and see if you can negotiate a good rate, and make sure that any deal you get is confirmed in writing with the name of whoever you did the deal with (attach this confirmation to the call sheet). You can pre-pay excess baggage, which is sometimes cheaper, but that leaves the crew no room to chat up the staff and get an even better rate, which they often do for you. However, if you don't pre-pay then you will either have to give the crew a float to cover it or arrange for some cash to be put in their personal bank account. It's not fair to just expect them to put this expense on their own credit card without any prior discussion. And don't forget to calculate the excess baggage *both ways*!

One small thing: remind the crew to count the number of boxes on to the aircraft and then count them off again. It sounds daft, I know, but if you have mislaid a box and travelled miles from the airport, sod's law dictates that it will be the one that you can't possibly do without.

Inoculations and medications

When setting up a foreign shoot you must determine the medical precautions for the countries your crew will be travelling in. Is it a malaria zone? What inoculations will the crew require? Get your co-ordinator to trawl embassy websites for these details and let the crew know in good time what they will need in the way of jabs. It is worth remembering that some larger countries require different jabs in different areas. The crew will want to walk into the BA clinic and get them done immediately, but if you can persuade them to visit their GP or a travel clinic these are cheaper options – inoculations can be remarkably expensive. You may need to purchase malaria tablets and there are a few to choose from, some of which can have unpleasant side-effects. I once had a team member refuse to take his malaria pills on the basis that they made him feel unwell, but the project wouldn't have been insured if he hadn't taken them so he changed his mind when faced with not being able to go on location.

If you are sending crew members to countries rife with unpleasant and exotic diseases it might be a good idea to offer them a medical check-up for tropical diseases when they get back. Be aware that there are areas in Costa Rica, for example, that have dengue fever, a very unpleasant disease for which there is no inoculation. Very strong deet-based (insect-repellant) products can help, but do some reading on deet and its side-effects and let the crew know. Lots of information on the various medical risks should be added to the call sheet: make sure they read it. Lastly (and this is very important, so tell them as well as putting it on the call sheet), remind all crew members to carry their inoculation records with them when they travel, as for some countries this is an entry requirement. And you can reiterate the easy and sensible precautions, such as wearing long-sleeved shirts, long trousers and socks at dusk. It all helps.

Visas and permits

Visas are required for some countries and you will be responsible for getting and paying for them. This is where checking the nationality of your crew is important, to make sure that any non-Brits have the same visa requirements. Contact the relevant embassy and establish what you need, then apply for the documents as early as you can. For some countries this process can be very lengthy, and the more you call up and hassle them, the longer it will take. You absolutely must keep your cool faced with such bureaucracy – it is what it is. I applied for visas for an Iranian shoot some years ago, and waited and waited and waited for them. Despite polite phone calls entreating the embassy to give me some idea of when they might come through, I had no idea and had the crew on pencils that kept getting extended. In turn this resulted in my having to make extra payments to the crew for giving up other work until the visas suddenly appeared. Another production manager I had been taking advice from on this location told me that she applied for four visas and received only three, with no explanation. The missing visa was for her director!

Some visas will require each member of your crew to be interviewed, so find this out as early as you can to avoid delaying your schedule.

Filming permits can also take for ever so, again, the longer the lead-up time the better – though I appreciate that this is easy to say and sometimes much more difficult to do (Indian visas, for instance, can take up to 10 weeks to process!). Check the embassy website carefully when arranging a shoot and apply for permits, visas and anything else that's vital as soon as you can. And if your intended location is a volatile area, get on to the Foreign and Commonwealth Office website and seek advice about where and how to travel – you may need to hire a local person to drive and also guide you through trouble spots. Check the time zones, taking into account daylight-saving countries. Check out the weather and make appropriate notes on the call sheet. And study the culture of your location. The crew I sent to Iran included a woman and we bought some appropriate light cotton clothes so that she was covered up as much as possible; this included wearing a headscarf at all times. A production manager friend always buys a Rough Guide for the country she is sending crew to and goes through it herself for tips before handing it over to the crew to take with them. You may also have to talk the crew through cultural differences to ensure that they respect these and don't stand around giggling at strange clothes or customs; this will irritate local people and can even be dangerous. Another colleague who went on lots of foreign shoots herself said she always carried a decent jacket and pair of shoes which she could wear when she had to deal with officialdom, as this was often interpreted as a sign of respect for their mores and customs. And she was unfailingly polite, even when exhausted and faced with a Jobsworth. A large gin and tonic afterwards was her reward to herself for being noble!

Floats

To calculate a float, first consider the country the crew are going to and check (in a travel guide, with a fixer or by calling up the embassy) what the cost of living is compared to the UK. Start by calculating an amount to cover breakfast, lunch and dinner for each crew member multiplied by the number of days away. Add in an amount for drinks and refreshments each day plus tips and tolls. Add in a daily fuel and parking allowance for each vehicle. Then add a hefty chunk to cover all the things that you have forgotten or that will arise, and round it up to an even number. (Don't forget to add this float figure to your cost monitor so you know it is money paid out and awaiting reconciliation.)

You may decide to issue travellers' cheques to your crew, in which case make sure that the ones you choose are large denominations and easy for them to cash. Also give them some currency that includes small notes for tips at the airport when they land. Check that your host country has the same weekends as the UK; an Iranian weekend is not Saturday and Sunday, which can make changing money a problem if the crew aren't forewarned. And find out if there are any public holidays during your shoot.

Encourage the person who is holding the float (preferably the researcher or AP) to put the bulk of the money in the hotel safe whenever possible, and make sure that the float is covered on the insurance (you may have to tweak the insurance cover if you are giving them lots of cash in countries where neither credit cards nor travellers' cheques are useful). If they run out of money then you can transfer money to a nearby bank, or through Western Union, though this can be expensive and also depends on the crew member being able to get to a bank or Western Union outlet during opening hours. If the production company will allow it you can get credit cards for researchers and raise the balance on the card for when they are away, but credit cards cost money and take time to set up, and sometimes they aren't appropriate.

Order your foreign currency and remember that the commission charges for this will need to be budgeted for. The crew will probably come back with bags full of loose change which you don't have a hope of reclaiming as banks will only take notes back. Encourage them to spend the change; they can use it for the gifts that they will doubtless be bringing back for the production team in thanks for working so hard on their perfect shoot and call sheet! Anything paid for on credit cards in a different currency will carry a high commission. These costs should be set against the appropriate schedule code in your cost monitor: hopefully there will be enough money budgeted to cover them.

Don't forget to give a small sterling float to the crew to cover cost of refreshments, parking, etc. at the airport on the way out.

Stock

When calculating the amount of stock to send with a shoot, work out how much you think they will use per day and then add a generous extra few, just in case. If they run out and ask for more (and this should alert you, are they over-shooting?), probably the quickest way is to track down on the Internet a supplier near to where they are shooting and get it couriered over to their hotel or location. This will work for somewhere like America (though the stock will be more expensive) but if it's a trickier location then you may have to courier stock to them. It's worth speaking to the researcher before they leave and telling them to give you lots of notice if the stock, or the float, looks like running short. If stock or money gets lost or stolen then you can throw money at it to get it replaced as quickly as possible; the subsequent insurance claim should cover the cost of the items stolen, but not the bank charges involved.

Filming in hostile zones and dangerous activities

Some places in the world will give you specific problems regarding the safety of your crew. I sent a crew to the Peruvian jungle on a programme about survival, and their problems included dangerous cities (they were robbed in a taxi in the middle of Lima, despite the attentions of an experienced fixer). They were uncomfortably near to the border with Colombia and thus my insurance man suggested putting in place kidnap and hostage insurance in addition to the usual cover. Some places (like Russia) might require extra insurance for possible confiscation of rushes, which also happened to a crew coming back from a shoot in Chernobyl – and that location required extra precautions because of exposure to the high levels of radiation still in existence there. A friend had to send a crew to Iraq recently and her risk assessment looked like a novel – more of that in Chapter 13 on Health & Safety. Some countries – in Africa, for example – are politically unstable and so extra care must be taken when travelling in them. It's always a good idea to consult the website of the Foreign and Commonwealth Office and be guided by them. The best advice I can give is to consult other people who have shot in your dangerous location and get the big guns of the company you are working for involved. Ultimately they must take the responsibility for sending crews to dangerous areas. You may want to consider protective clothing, special survival courses for crews, and anything else you think appropriate depending on the dangers involved. Do a very thorough risk assessment and get a Health & Safety executive to check it, perhaps even coming in to speak to crew members and talk through procedures. There is follow-up that needs to be done in case of accidents or illness on shoots, but I'll talk about that more in Health & Safety.

You must always be totally up front with the crew you are putting into potentially dangerous situations. They may want to bail if they don't feel comfortable being shot at, for example, and you should respect that and find someone else. They may also feel that a higher fee is required for added risk, which seems fair enough to me. Consider how you would feel going into the situation you are planning and take as many precautions as you can. Discuss everything in detail with the insurance company and organise a satellite phone if the area is likely to be problematic for mobile contact.

Investigate specialist climbers, divers, plane people – in other words bring in the experts and don't leave anything to chance. There are a number of companies who can help in these sorts of situations – try Global Film Solutions or Remote Trauma, for example. Speak often to your insurance contact and Health & Safety representative and make sure they both know everything about what is being filmed, and where and how.

Extreme temperatures and kit

Read Chapter 13 on Health & Safety for how to deal with people in extremes of heat and cold – but just a word here about kit in such conditions.

Cameras are sensitive to extremes of temperature, so bear this in mind when you write your call sheet. Most cameramen are sensible when it comes to care of kit, especially if it belongs to them, but I did have a cameraman once who was shooting in Dubai and took a hot camera into the air-conditioned kit vehicle to put a new tape in. The tape promptly melted and fused itself round the head of the camera – an expensive repair job and loss of camera in a location where finding a replacement (on a Sunday, of course) was a bit of a problem! And your insurance doesn't cover you if the camera fails through improper care of the kit. Consult a camera expert (someone from a kit hire company, for example) about how to treat a camera in such circumstances and add this to the call sheet.

Extreme cold will also affect your camera kit, so ditto for this situation – and find out if there is any kind of 'protective clothing' that you can buy or hire for the camera in extreme cold. It's great if you can afford to take a spare camera body with you in case your primary one goes down, but, frankly, I have never had the money for this on a small doc shoot, so maybe checking out local suppliers who can leap to the rescue might be a useful piece of preparation to get your co-ordinator on to at the planning stage. Offer advice on the call sheet for how to acclimatise to extreme temperatures and, indeed, high altitudes if you are filming in them.

Delivery paperwork

This comprises the release forms and location agreements that you need signed and brought back to you, and getting them done at the time is hugely, hugely important because trying to chase them up later will be fraught with problems. Make this clear verbally and put reminders on the call sheets. If it's absolutely impossible to get these bits of paper at the time, make sure that you know this as soon as the crew returns and get the researcher on to it immediately. Once they have left the project, you or the co-ordinator will be stuck with trying to track them down: a time-consuming pain in the arse for you both.

Stress, in writing, that without a signed release form the material they shoot is utterly useless, and remember to get your release forms and location agreements translated if you need to.

Delivery paperwork should be carefully filed, and when anyone has a few spare moments they can be photocopied if necessary for archiving purposes if you are sending the originals to the Broadcaster(s).

It's useful if the researcher or director can print the name of each contributor on their release form very clearly, so that no spelling mistakes make their way on to the straps in the completed programme (ditto for their role description on screen). It's also helpful if the back of the release is marked with brief descriptions of who is who (i.e. 'green sweater, beard and glasses') to help you and your team identify people you won't have seen in person.

Communication

Think about how you, your crew and your team are going to communicate while away. Is it worth buying a local production mobile and making sure the crew use it and not their own phones, which will undoubtedly be more expensive? Discourage them from using hotel phones for phoning home and the office by providing or instructing them to buy local telephone cards – hotels usually mark up their telephone charges enormously, all of which is wasted money. In a location where mobiles don't work, consider hiring a satellite phone and make sure they know how to use it before they depart. (This applies to any piece of additional kit that you hire in – if you don't make sure they know how to use something by arranging a training session, perhaps with the supplier, then they probably won't use it and it will be money wasted.)

Bits and bobs

A few other odd things to mention. At the beginning of your shoot, check if the location area has a local Film Office and call to get as much advice as they can offer. It's always a good idea to do the sums when you are taking crews abroad: consider the cost of sending crew and kit from the UK (with carnet) and hotelling them. It may be that, especially on a short shoot, hiring a local crew who live close and hiring locally based kit would be cheaper; if the director is happy to do this you might save money and organisational time.

Just remember that the kit needs to be reliable, so make sure they do a camera test to start with and that they run random tests of rushes to make sure there is no drop-out or other faults. (Instruct the crew to do a test tape for your insurance and keep it in case of any subsequent problems that arise.) If the director is not keen to use an unknown cameraman then perhaps using a local sound recordist would save money – and you get the added bonus of hiring someone who knows the area and can, perhaps, double as a driver. This option will reduce flight costs, excess baggage and possibly overnights, so if money is tight it can help. If, for example, you were filming a number of single days across America, you could hire a sound recordist in each location which would also save on internal travel – worth considering at least.

If you spend a significant amount of money in a European country you can claim the VAT equivalent back. It does take ages and it is a faff but it might be worth it, so you should perhaps discuss it with your head of production and the accounts department and take a view.

Here's a little reminder list to yourself when setting up shoots outside the EU and the US: weather, bugs and animals including venomous ones, crime, jabs and diseases, malaria, visas, cultural and religious differences, public holidays, filming permits, currency, communication.

Lastly, you will always be trying to save money – that's your job. But beware of false economy. A happy and safe crew is much more cost-effective.

USEFUL TEMPLATES FOR USE WITH THIS CHAPTER

Call Sheet 💻
Risk Assessment 💻
Production Check List 💻

13 Health & Safety

Following a number of fatal accidents occurring in the television industry a decade or so ago, major changes have been introduced into the industry's Health & Safety practices. For the production manager H&S is hugely important and you should take it very seriously indeed. The health and welfare of your crew is of paramount importance and, even when a budget is tight, the best precautionary measures must be afforded.

The crux of H&S management is two-fold: first identify all possible hazards on your shoot, and second, take every reasonable step you can to minimise these risks.

Risk assessments

This is a document that you and your producer should write, outlining in as much detail as possible what is going to happen on the shoot, and where, when and how. (I have included a couple of example risk assessments 🖥 for specific shoots by way of explanation.) As you can see, they begin by listing all the details of the shoot with a brief synopsis of what your programme/series is about. The template of a risk assessment usually contains a list to remind you of all the activities on your shoot which might pose a Health & Safety challenge, and you should check each one to see if it is applicable. Then you should describe the hazardous activity (and all activities are, potentially, hazardous), judge its risk level as either low, medium or high, and then make recommendations as to the practical measures which can be put in place to reduce the risk as much as possible. There is something about having to sit down and consider carefully what you are planning to do which focuses the mind to produce useful and relevant instructions. They serve their purpose when they represent a paper trail of thoughtful care and pre-planning on everyone's part, in what can be a careless and risky industry. And, of course, your insurance will not be valid until your RA is officially signed off by the producer.

Be aware that doing a risk assessment for every shoot is a *legal* requirement. As you will no doubt have seen from various high-profile accidents in the media industry, when someone is badly injured or killed at work the people who are deemed responsible end up in court, possibly in prison, and/or fined a huge amount of money.

If you are not going on the shoot you must have an honest discussion with the director or producer who will be there. They should help to draft and then sign off the risk assessment, as they will be responsible for safety on the shoot, and you must make sure that they tell you exactly what and how they intend to film. Sometimes producers/directors have risky plans for their shoot which they don't want to confess to you in case you put the block on them. However, the essence of a good risk assessment is not to prevent them from doing risky but perhaps very filmic sequences, but rather to try and make things as safe as possible for all concerned. I once planned a shoot in Africa where we were intending to demonstrate how a young ranger would overcome the various dangers that would threaten him if he were stranded in the veldt. The day before the crew departed the director told me that he wanted to shoot a sequence where the ranger would be confronted by a spitting cobra – and would that be OK? My immediate response was to shriek 'Noooo' but my series producer, sitting alongside me, coolly said that we'd do some research and get back to him. Which we did, by calling up a reptile expert at London Zoo and asking lots of questions – well, did you know that there are red and black spitting cobras, and that the saliva of one is lethal, but the other just painful if washed out quickly? To cut a long story short, see the example of that risk assessment 🖳 (one of the best aspects of being a PM is that you get to be an instant expert on all sorts of obscure things – though, just as quickly, you forget them!).

So, sit the director down and talk through their filming plans in detail, as much as possible in advance – though often it's necessarily just before they depart, as and when things get confirmed. Ask lots of questions: who is doing what? Do all the crew need to be involved? Can you find local experts to help in a specific task? Will you need to do an up-dated local risk assessment on the day? Make sure that you supply them with some easy-to-complete forms (both in hard copy and electronically) so that if any circumstances change when they arrive at the location (e.g. a field has become flooded and will need some sort of stepping boards put down) they can do a supplementary RA and send it to you – either from a local fax machine or electronically, or they can phone through the details to you so you can amend the RA. These last-minute changes can also be put on camera; in fact, it's often absolutely necessary to have specific site briefings every day if they are doing anything out of the ordinary, so that the crew are reminded of particular dangers and safety measures. These bits of filmed risk assessments can be brought back and archived. If you are filming in any non-domestic locations you should always check to see if they have an H&S policy that you can look at and perhaps incorporate in your own risk assessment. Indeed, such locations might insist on site safety briefings before filming can begin, so make sure you add this fact to the RA and the call sheet.

Sometimes the hardest risk assessments to do are those which seem, superficially, to be almost without any risk at all – for example, filming an interview in a contributor's house or garden. However, it is useful to think about access in case of fire and whether there are children or animals that need to be kept away from equipment and cables, perhaps shut up in a room away from the interview. Don't forget that there must be no smoking on set or on any film shoot, and the company will have a no-smoking policy in the offices as well. A risk assessment is largely common sense – simple instructions that spell out what seems like the obvious but can easily be forgotten in the rush to get things 'in the can'. Where there are unusual situations or hazards, seek as much advice as you can from relevant sources like experts or specialised agencies or the Health & Safety Executive.

First aid

Make sure that the crew always have a first aid kit and an Accident Book, and encourage people to take first aid courses, paying for them if necessary. (By the way, you should take a first aid course too, and remember to refresh it every two years.) Offices can be unsafe – ever tripped over a bag left lying carelessly by someone's desk? Part of your responsibility at work should be to make sure things are stowed safely under seats or desks. You can hire in paramedics or nurses for individual shoot days if you need to, and it might be well worth the money to know that they will be in attendance but hopefully not called upon. Ensure that you brief everyone before they go filming that they are to be vigilant about any accidents that may occur. That means stopping the camera and giving immediate first aid, offering further medical treatment, if necessary getting the injured person to the nearest hospital or clinic as soon as possible, letting the production manager know (who can then inform the insurance company if necessary) and then writing up a full report of the accident, including whether the victim accepted or refused medical aid. (A reminder here that the contact details of the nearest hospital and police station to each location should always go on your call sheet.)

Fire

At some point during your career you will probably be faced with someone wanting to set a fire of some kind and shoot it. I once had to re-create the Channel Tunnel fire of 1996 in a studio, and consulted a fire expert who was happy to supply a small fire crew to set, control and extinguish the fire and also act as real firemen for our drama re-creations. They attended on their day off, and came complete with lots of equipment and their own uniforms too: bonus! Probably the best way to deal with fire is to hire a package from a specialist FX company who do these sorts of things for a living. They will already have an extensive risk assessment policy covering their hazardous activities, and you can integrate this into your own risk assessment. They will also be extremely skilled at setting, controlling and extinguishing fires. If your team are thinking of planning to set a small fire of any kind, anywhere, be warned! You must alert the local fire brigade about what you are doing. If someone sees what seems to be an out-of-control fire and calls them, they will be extremely pissed off to find that they have wasted their time. In any case I think that setting a fire anywhere, even a small bonfire for a night-time shot, for example, is potentially dangerous, so ask the experts – a specialist FX fire company will give you advice on the telephone and it's always better to be safe than sorry. And if at all possible make sure that you are on location for any such risky stuff, then you can be sure that the proper precautions are being followed.

Water

If the crew are filming in, on, under or near water then you will need to pay special H&S attention. (H&S is also linked closely to insurance, so make sure you read Chapter 10 carefully in conjunction with this one.) Underwater filming is a specialist area, so it's a good idea to check out the camera operators who make this their chosen field of expertise. You will probably be able to hire a package of operator and waterproof kit; consult the relevant section of any good production guide, the Internet, or, better still, get recommendations from people who have done it before and whose advice you trust (i.e. any PMA member) and ring around to get advice and quotes. Again, be sure to ask for their safety policy to integrate into your own RA and check their insurance status with your insurance contact.

The same goes for filming on boats of any kind. The first call should be to your insurance company because they will advise you on marine insurance, and they will almost certainly need sight of the marine insurance held by the boat owners. Make sure that the crew are fully briefed about life jackets. And check if crew members will need any kind of harness for filming, as cameramen are often a bit gung-ho and will want to hang over the side with someone hanging on to the back of their jacket! Make sure that the instruction to use a harness is clearly stated in your RA, and a harness for the kit is also necessary so that the camera doesn't slip over the side. (Yes, I had someone do that once and cameras don't like being dunked, as I know to my cost.) A good waterproof cover for the camera is also a good idea, since even on dry land heavy rain can be a problem.

If you are filming at a location that has an area of stagnant water on it, be aware that Weil's disease (pronounced Vile's, medical name Leptospirosis) is caused by rat urine and can contaminate such water – so make sure you warn everyone to keep well away and, if possible, rope it off. These days I think a useful addition to any first aid kit is a large pack of those bacterial wet wipes for the crew to keep their hands clean if they aren't near a source of clean water. Encourage them to use them to clean the bottles and cans of cold drinks that you may supply. Apparently this disease can be picked up from drinking straight from cans and bottles which may become contaminated during storage, and since it can be fatal, and rapidly so, it makes sense to note it on the call sheet and, preferably, supply straws or plastic cups to drink from. Who knew!

If you ever plan to have a stunt person fall or jump into water, you will need to hire a diver or two to check out the area beforehand and make sure there are no hidden dangers under the surface like debris or old supermarket trolleys that could cause injury. The diver(s) should remain during the filming of such stunts as well. Such personnel will cost money, but even in a tight budget do not stint on safety checks and precautions (and these people can be sourced from specialist FX companies).

Extreme weather – heat

Filming in hot climates will need extra thought and preparation. If the crew are going to very hot areas you will need to supply plenty of cold drinks, preferably water and possibly salt tablets – take advice about whether this is necessary from a good travel goods supplier. You may also need to send along some water-sterilising tablets in case bottled water is hard to come by. With the Internet these sorts of precautions are much easier to research, and travel guides can be useful too. I recently discovered that the shop attached to SOAS (School of Oriental and African Studies) has a wonderfully knowledgeable staff who can advise on travel anywhere in the world and sell you the best travel guide. And the STA shops are excellent for help on the right medical stuff to take to remote parts of the world. There exist a few specialised H&S-conscious travel companies used to working in film and TV, and they are listed at the end of this chapter.

Buy plenty of high-factor sun lotion and perhaps some cheap cotton hats in case anyone forgets to bring such items, even though you have mentioned it on the call sheet. Advise light but long trousers and long-sleeved shirts so that sunburn, or worse, heat stroke doesn't strike the crew. Factor in frequent breaks for drinks and getting out of the sun wherever possible. I once sent a crew to shoot in Iran in very high temperatures, and I did a deal with the camera crew whereby they would get up very early and film until midday and then take a long break during the worst of the heat – filming again in the afternoon and early evening. But be aware that you will need to have somewhere to put them for this break time – sitting in the kit vehicle for hours in high temperatures isn't a good idea; they need to be able to get back to their hotel or somewhere they can relax, preferably a venue that is air-conditioned. It may be that this proves difficult or impossible, but if you discuss it at length with the crew they are likely to be impressed that you have, at least, tried to make their health, safety and comfort a priority.

Lastly, don't underestimate a hot, sunny day in the UK (remember those?) which can be a problem if your crew aren't suitably kitted out with hat, sun cream, plenty of water and decent breaks in the shade.

Extreme weather – cold

Filming in very cold and snowy situations also requires some forethought. Usually crews own their own cold weather gear, but it may be insufficient so you may need to buy, or more cheaply hire, down jackets and socks and boots for them. Supply several large vacuum flasks and check that their hotel will fill these for them in the early mornings. You can buy little disposable heat packs that can be slipped inside boots and pockets (and all sorts of other interesting places) to give off warmth for a period of hours and can then be replaced. Pay particular attention to the cameraman here, because while those fingerless mittens make operating the camera easier, you don't want to risk frostbite in their fingers (frostbite is when the blood freezes in extremities of the body, often leading to loss of fingers and toes). Do some reading on how to ward off such horrors and build in frequent breaks to the schedule so that people can get warm.

I once did a shoot in a cold lab here in the UK where we subjected a poor presenter to plunging temperatures and an additional wind factor to see how quickly he descended into hypothermia. There were doctors and technicians keeping him under constant surveillance and in addition I sent along a Health & Safety executive to keep an eye on things. Faced with the problem of where to site the cameraman so that he (or the camera) didn't get too cold, we had him film through a window. Filming in this lab was where I learned that the best way to warm someone who has got very cold is to gradually immerse them in a warm, not hot, bath. And once again I incorporated the laboratory's own H&S policy into my risk assessment.

Wildlife and diseases

A production manager friend of mine had to send a shoot to Iraq in 2003 to film interviews of American soldiers about their experiences in the war. A decision was made to 'embed' the crew with the army so that they would always travel around with the soldiers in their military vehicles. To cut a long story short, she did masses of research, talked constantly to the US army and the insurance company, sent the crew on a special survival course and provided all sorts of protective clothing, advice about the heat and instructions on every possible disease and infection she could think of. Her producer, drawing on his long experience as an ex-army man, put together the risk assessment himself and it resembled a small novel. They were deeply immersed in the details of war, troops, moving around safely and all the other dangers that could beset working closely with soldiers immersed in post-war security, when someone thought to say, 'What about the wildlife?' It transpired that Iraq has one of the highest levels of poisonous snakes, scorpions and other malign creatures in the world. Which all goes to prove nothing really, except that you can't forget the commonplace. Their combined risk assessment is such a brilliant example of efficiency and common sense that I have reproduced it on the website ⌨. Read it and marvel.

I have already talked about inoculations in Chapter 12 on Foreign Shoots, but just to reiterate: research carefully your intended locations and make sure that your crew have all the jabs they need for the area they are travelling to, as well as any medications that are recommended. Remember that some inoculations have a second booster jab after a period of time, so check that you have built this into the prep time. At this point it's worth saying that you can make as many recommendations and suggestions as you like, and the crew can still ignore them. They have a duty of care for their own well-being; they should take care of themselves, take appropriate precautions, and ask for breaks when they are tired and insist on a food break when they are hungry. Your responsibility is to do as much as you can in advance to point out and minimise the possible risks and hazards; if they choose to ignore your advice then they, and your producer who is on site, must take responsibility for that. You are not their mother!

Weapons and reconstructions

Never, ever, allow actors or participants in your programme to run around in public waving replica firearms or weapons of any kind. You and they are likely to be arrested and sent to prison, and it will serve you all right. Using weaponry of any kind requires planning and caution.

If you have any kind of firearms or 'projectile weapons' (like a crossbow) on your location you must have an armourer in attendance. These can be hired by the day from a specialist FX company, and they will come along to give a safety briefing, train actors on how to use a particular weapon so that it looks authentic, and take control of any weapons and keep them safely stowed when they are not in use. This reduces the possibility of people fooling around with them and causing accidents. Call the specialist company for advice about what sorts of weaponry you need and where you can hire an armourer. You must also inform your local police at least three days beforehand if you are filming in any kind of public space with any kind of fake weapon. In these security-conscious times the laws are changing rapidly and various weapons are added to the banned list almost daily, so call one of the excellent companies who deal in weaponry for the media and ask lots of questions. There are a number of companies who offer such services: Bapty and Co. is a long-established one whom I've always found incredibly helpful. (Tel) 020 8574 7700 (E) hire@bapty.demon.co.uk.

Helicopters

If a director wants to film from a helicopter, this should trigger H&S concerns as well as insurance calls (not to mention a quick scramble through the budget to see if you can afford it!). There are a number of helicopter companies who will quote you for flights during which you can film. They should have harnesses in their helicopters so that cameramen can be strapped in (rather than the old hanging-on-to-the-back-of-their-jacket routine!). There are a number of things to check out when doing such aerial filming – just call up a range of companies and ask lots of questions, possibly speaking to other PMs who have done such shoots in the past. The one piece of advice I would pass on is to ensure that only the cameraman and director travel in the helicopter. There is a tendency for everyone on the shoot to want to enjoy a bit of a jolly, but the sound recordist doesn't need to be there (too noisy to record any useable sound) and neither does anyone else. The insurance company will reiterate this and you should write it in capitals on the call sheet. Again, remember to ask for the company's safety policy for incorporating into your own RA.

Fatigue

One of the most common causes of accidents – especially in the TV industry, where long hours and crammed schedules are the norm – is tiredness. When you and your director and researcher are planning the shoot, make sure they don't try and cram too much into each day, and try to factor in some rest days where you can. (Having said that, I once gave a crew, filming for two weeks in the US, a day off in Wisconsin in the middle of a shoot, only to have the cameraman peevishly telling me he didn't need a rest day in bloody Wisconsin, 'just get me home a day early!'. You can't win them all.) Talk to your director about keeping the crew's hours within their negotiated hours; as well as being exhausting it will cost money if they keep going into overtime. Ensure that they don't break the 11-hour rule: the crew must have 11 hours off between wrap and call time the following morning, which can include their travel time but can't include work. They should stop for their meals and take time to eat, rather than grabbing sandwiches on the run (enlist the help of the researcher/AP if you think the director will get carried away on the shoot). I know this is all difficult if you are not on location, but you can always call and chat to them (at an appropriate time) to assess whether they are happy or not. Don't hesitate to get bigger guns (the series producer or an executive of the company) to speak to them if you are seriously worried. Often on shoots the crew are driving themselves around as well as working, and being tired is more likely to lead to road accidents – not something you want on your watch. If there are travel days within the shoots, try to ensure that they don't work on these days at all. They can perhaps do a quick recce when they arrive somewhere and then have a break before meeting up for dinner. You don't get the best out of people when they are on their knees with exhaustion.

Aftercare

Follow-up when someone has had an accident is crucial, so no matter how busy you are make sure you do this and keep a written record of your efforts. On a shoot in the Peruvian jungle our survival expert hacked at a branch to demonstrate how to make a fire when stranded, and instead almost took his finger off with his razor-sharp machete. He was trained in first aid so took care of the injury himself (refused medical treatment, straight into the Accident Book!) but I kept in touch for weeks after the shoot returned, checking whether his finger was scarred, whether he needed any further care and so on, all this recorded in emails so I could file the correspondence between us in case of any long-term fall-out.

And there was the researcher who scratched her eyeball with the zip of her jacket as she put it on: she needed to spend a couple of days in her dark hotel room with an eye patch on, following medical advice. I made frequent calls to her to check her progress. The rest of the crew carried on without her and as soon as she returned to the UK she went off to Moorfield's eye hospital to get it checked, making sure I got copies of her medical report for the files. Regular phone calls to see if the eye was healing properly were also documented and thankfully no permanent vision impairment occurred.

Health & Safety guidance

There is a Health & Safety Executive service which is extremely helpful (Tel) 0845 345 0055 (E) hse.infoline@connaught.plc.uk – you can phone, fax or email them your queries – so seek advice from them or from relevant experts in the area that you find yourself dealing with. I know that risk assessments tend to be the last thing to get done when you're rushing to send a shoot out, but you can use the template I have provided 💻 and fill in some details, emailing it to your director as early as possible during prep to encourage them to think about activities in advance. Once the RA has been completed, try to get it checked over by someone else – ideally an H&S adviser (if you're lucky enough to have one paid for by the independent company you are working for) or by another production manager, or your head of production. Send it to your insurance company and make sure that you attach a copy (signed off by the producer/director) to the call sheet and encourage the crew to read it. Talk to the director before they leave and demand that they contact you should any changes occur in their shoot day by day or if any accidents happen. Your RA is in part about proving that you have taken on board the responsibility to make your shoot as safe as you possibly can.

It bears repeating that you must, legally, do a risk assessment for every shoot on your project and it's a good practice to also do an RA for every recce. I have covered a number of, but not all, potentially dangerous activities and they will always depend on the sort of filming you are intending to do. Learn to trust your instincts and speak up about anything that sounds hazardous; ask questions, consult experts and use your common sense at all times.

There follow the details of three companies who are useful to consult in the area of H&S, and their websites are fascinating!

1. Expedition Media (Tel) 07900 554896 (E) info@expeditionmedia.co.uk.
2. Remote Trauma (Tel) 0844 800 9158 (E) admin@remotetrauma.com.
3. Global Film Solutions, a New Zealand company globalfilmsolutions.com (Tel) 643 442 173.

14 Interviewing and the ethics of the documentary

Some years ago, sitting at my desk at Darlow Smithson Productions, I heard a voice behind me instructing a group of young development researchers about the ethics of television and how to treat potential contributors with sensitivity and care throughout their broadcast experience. It turned out to be the renowned filmmaker of 'obs docs', Benetta Adamson, who laughed at my comment 'ethical TV – an oxymoron surely?' and went on to voice her thoughts on this crucial part of television, which is almost never directly discussed. I was lucky enough to have her as a guest speaker at some training sessions, where she spoke with passion about filming observational documentaries and showed some clips of films she had made: *Kirsty's Millions* (BBC1), a film about a Children's Hospice in Manchester, caring for children and young people with life-limiting conditions; and *Thalidomide: Life at 40* – both of which are so poignant that there wasn't a dry eye in the house. Her opinions on the contrast between the films that she makes and various examples of reality television spurred students into thinking and talking about the way that television intrudes into people's lives when it chooses them as the subject of a programme, and how this should be ethically managed. I will leave it to Benetta to discuss this in more depth, just adding that perhaps the best way for the production manager to help in this respect is to offer to step in on any discussions about possible fees to be paid to contributors, and to act as the 'bad cop' by negotiating the money transactions, thus freeing the researcher to keep the relationship between them and the contributor confined to creative discussions only.

As a production manager your relationship with the contributors might extend no further than this, although you could be their point of contact when the researcher is out of the office and they call in. And, at the end of the project when perhaps the researcher is leaving, you should make sure that someone lets the contributor know when the programme is on. Perhaps more importantly, they should be informed in good time if their contribution is, for whatever reason, missing from the final edit. There is little more embarrassing than inviting all your friends and family to watch your bit on the telly only to find it isn't there, so try never to let this happen. The last, and most important, task is to thank them: a simple thank-you note after filming is absolutely vital and should be written either by the researcher or director, but make sure it is, as these things are sometimes forgotten. And don't forget to make sure the contributor has a copy of the film once it has transmitted.

CASE STUDY WITH BENETTA ADAMSON

QUESTION: If you were training a young researcher, what advice would you offer them when they are making their initial contact with a potential contributor?

BENETTA: Firstly, don't promise anything you can't or won't deliver just to get them to agree to being filmed. You cannot promise editorial control of any kind, although virtually everyone will ask for that. You can guarantee to ensure that any factual errors are corrected, and I usually offer to show contributors the film before it's finished. However, this is very risky because if they don't like what you've done, for some reason, you will have a problem. I sometimes start by offering to put potential contributors in touch with people from previous films and this often reassures them.

You need to be honest about what taking part will involve and if necessary write a confirmatory letter/email outlining the non-negotiable elements. This is especially useful for institutions where press officers may try to impose silly restrictions, and you may need proof that you didn't agree if this happens later on in the shoot. And remember that Broadcasters may want proof that access has been granted by an institution, and may want to see a detailed contract.

QUESTION: What about paying contributors?

BENETTA: Think hard before offering a fee to contributors to take part in filming. I have practised this for years and Broadcasters don't like to pay them either. In my experience, it fundamentally affects the relationship with your contributor because they often feel as if they should be 'performing' to please you. I would always seek participants who have something they want to say and view you and your film as their soapbox. Do offer to pay legitimate expenses, though. I usually suggest that we make a payment at the end of our collaboration, which comes as a nice surprise.

Be advised that time spent recce-ing, particularly in complex institutions, can be invaluable. It gives you the opportunity to get to know key individuals and to really understand the processes you might be filming, as well as to encounter problems no one has foreseen!

QUESTION: What about gaining consent from the contributors, since sometimes they are freaked out by release forms and don't want to sign them?

BENETTA: Consent must be given freely and only after the contributor has received a full account of the production and their part in it. In some cases it's appropriate to confirm consent at a later stage (such as when someone is too distressed, tired, pissed or disturbed to give it properly). I tend to avoid getting contributors to sign a lengthy consent form on our first outing, because, I agree, they're terrifying. However, some production companies insist this is done immediately – although it's never caused a problem for me to wait a couple of days.

(Me interrupting! I worked on a project recently where we emailed or gave potential contributors a much shorter, and less frightening, release form so that they could agree, in spirit, if you like, their consent. Then the longer and more formal version didn't seem so scary when it was presented.)

BENETTA: And most Broadcasters assume that once consent is given and a signature obtained then a contribution cannot be withdrawn except in very exceptional circumstances.

QUESTION: So, let's assume that you have your contributors all lined up, what advice would you give your researcher to help them get a good interview on the day?

BENETTA: Firstly, are you going to use your questions in the final sequence? Try to make your questions as open as possible, so your contributor has to answer in whole sentences. Wait for a couple of beats at the end of an answer – that's often the time when the interviewee comes up with a jewel. Human beings generally don't like silences and will try to fill them.

For informal/actuality interviews, choose your moments carefully when answers will be intelligible and the contributor doesn't mind being distracted for a moment. If in doubt, ask. Often the best interviews are impromptu, when the contributor isn't expecting a question.

Consider doing a back-up, more formal interview so you can mix and match in the edit and also use them as voice-over, and ensure you get good clean sound. Try to avoid relying on a 'crib sheet' or list of questions. This breaks eye contact and makes the interviewee more aware of the nature of the encounter. By all means stop recording and check at the end, though.

Listen carefully and mentally edit the answers as you go. If you're not sure you have a clear, clean answer to an important question, rephrase it later in the interview. Try not to suggest to an interviewee that s/he is failing!

In very sensitive situations (such as when covering emergencies) consider leaving the interview(s) until the worst is over. Anxious people tend not to be very forthcoming or coherent.

Try to keep eye-lines consistent within a sequence. This generally isn't a problem if you're self-shooting, but if you're working with a camera operator, remember on which side of the camera you started and stick to it. I always try to keep the eye-line very close to the lens when I want an intimate feel, but a wide eye-line can be a stylistic choice as well, particularly in a formal interview.

Think about how the interview will eventually be used; how will they be cut? Varying the shot size is an old trick but can pay off. Don't change shot during an answer if you can avoid it. Try to be on a closer shot at the emotional pay-off – it's much more powerful, and try not to let interviewees tell you everything before you're ready to turn over, since it may sound stale and stilted when you're actually recording. Tell them where to look – the camera doesn't exist, and don't forget to get cutaways. Just to clarify: a cutaway is a device which allows the editor to shorten a sequence, or cut out unwanted material. In an informal interview situation for instance, where your contributor might be discussing events unfolding around him or her, filming some shots of the surroundings will illustrate the content. In a formal interview, some shots of the person's hands or something they're holding will often be really helpful.

Lastly, if you are interviewing two subjects don't worry about keeping the camera on the one who is speaking all the time, but make sure you have got listening shots (excluding the speaker) of the other participant.

QUESTION: Lots to remember, but I imagine it all becomes almost instinctive once you have done it a few times. Would you like to say a few words about filming 'actuality'?

BENETTA: Yes, consider how any actuality you film will contribute to the message you're trying to convey and the story you're telling. It's much better if the audience can see events happening for themselves than being told about them in an interview. You will need to shoot some 'wallpaper' (shots to use as a bed for commentary or voice-over), which is invaluable, but too much will make for tedious viewing. When you have finished shooting an actuality sequence, particularly if you're in a place you are not returning to, think about how it will fit in to the story and whether you need any pick-ups or establishers. This is when you can get exteriors of the buildings, CUs (close-ups) of signs or CAs (cutaways) you couldn't pick up at the time. It just might make the difference between having a usable sequence or not.

QUESTION: So much to think about. Anything else?

BENETTA: Think about cutting points; let people enter and leave the frame wherever possible, let doors and curtains close. Think about how a sequence will cut and shoot stuff – CUs of signs, walking feet, whatever – to give the editor as many options as possible. Try to stay aware of what might be happening next but don't worry if you can't cover everything; it generally doesn't matter if you can't follow every single development. Attempt to identify which events are likely to be crucial to the telling of your story and concentrate on being there for those times. There will be occasions when something unexpected happens, for instance, when getting someone to tell you what is going on will be invaluable. Imagine you're filming in a calm hospital and suddenly the red phone rings. There'll be inexplicable activity which you could explain in commentary, but sometimes grabbing someone on the periphery of the action and getting them to describe what's going on will be much more powerful. 'We've just heard there's been an accident on the motorway and we're getting ready to receive two casualties' might be much more powerful than your commentary voice saying the same thing.

If you do miss things which might be important, get someone to tell you 'on the fly' what's happened – it's much more difficult later!

QUESTION: What about anticipating events when you're filming actuality – can you talk a little bit about that, please?

BENETTA: Well, if, for example, your contributor is going to enter a room, do you need to go ahead of him or her? Is the space restricted? Can you record sound cleanly? (Perhaps you need to use radio mics for this?) Try not to stop the camera unless you're really stuck as this reminds contributors you're filming them. Be flexible and ready for the unexpected, don't try to control events and DON'T INTERFERE!

QUESTION: Any advice to pass on about the ethical side of documentary filming?

BENETTA: The BBC has always published Editorial Guidelines for production staff, even if the name varies over the years! All members of the production team are expected to be familiar with their contents whether the production is being made in-house or through an independent production company. After recent scandals I'd expect them to be even more stringently adhered to than before, so if you're working for the Beeb, in any capacity, I'd have a look at them. Remember that the BBC has a department of editorial policy who are there to offer advice if you're not sure. http://www.bbc.uk/guidelines/editorialguidelines/edguide.

Channel 4 and Channel 5 are in the process of preparing a book outlining their editorial policy, but in the meantime C4 has issued an interim document setting out their rules for maintaining viewer trust. http://www.channel4.com.corporate/4producers/ commissioning/documents/ViewerTrust Guidelines.pdf.

Most observational documentarists will have no problem complying, but for some people working on the wilder shores of factual programming there will be some surprises in this document. It's worth a read, even if you're not working on a C4/5 project, but I rarely embark on a project for those channels without knowing them inside out. Some production companies have strict compliance procedures in place: for instance, *Wife Swap* psych-test all their contributors and issue a thick tome of notes which you ignore at your peril, but most of the rules won't be a problem if you remember that your first duty (in my humble opinion anyway!) is to your contributors and their well-being.

15 Archive and copyright

A crucially important part of your job as a production manager is to ensure that all the material in your programme is cleared for the Broadcaster. Your project may include a number of elements – archive, stills, music, newspaper mastheads, posters, etc. – and if you see something 'alien' in the programme at the editing stage you must check where it comes from and whether you can use it. Heed the good advice of Barry Kim at PACT: 'If you can see it or hear it, clear it!'

You will need to examine all the elements and identify which material has not been specially shot by your team, and for any copyright-protected items you should start the process of sourcing it, getting permission to use it and negotiating a fee for use as early as possible. This permission must always be in writing and may become your final licence for the material, so it should contain details of the clearances you require, the length of use and the agreed fee.

> **USEFUL TIP**
> There are a very few exceptions to this rule which we will briefly touch on at the end of this chapter – see Fair Dealing and Public Domain and Incidental Inclusion.

It is worth saying at this stage that even if you are an experienced and senior production manager, there may be occasions when you may feel intimidated by your director or series producer, who may insist that a piece of material is OK to use for a variety of reasons. In such cases you will need to stick to your guns and perhaps seek help from senior management in the production company, as your responsibilities include not exposing the company to any threat of legal action over disputed copyright claims.

I'll leave the thorny problems of music use aside for the moment – music clearance is complex, so I have devoted Chapter 17 to it.

I have mentioned a range of visuals above which must be cleared, but we must not ignore items which can trip you up. I once managed a lovely little film about how very young children learn numeracy, and it contained a charming sequence where a six-month-old baby was being given a simple test to see if it could count. The American doctor was using Mickey Mouse dolls to demonstrate simple addition and subtraction and, after I spotted the sequence in the rough cut, I became embroiled in a major battle with Disney for use of the Mickey Mouse character. I had to send them the script, the unfinished programme and practically my blood to try and convince them that we had filmed the sequence in good faith, not realising that we had inadvertently used a copyright product of one of the largest and richest corporations in the world. I managed to gain permission to use the piece eventually, along with a very stern warning that such a thing should never happen again. All this as we were preparing to on-line and thus set the piece in stone; it was last-minute stress and anxiety we could all have done without. You will sometimes hear colleagues telling you to ignore such issues, or even to try and 'wing it', but in the case of Disney, if they had seen the Mickey Mouse doll sequence when it went out we could have been liable for copyright infringement, and any potential damages may have been worse because we had knowingly using copyrighted material. In other words, we'd have been 'screwed'. So, to reiterate, the responsibility of the production manager is to obtain licences for use of all copyright material and to protect the company you are working for from the possibility of expensive legal action. Your contract with the Broadcaster will set this out very clearly. If you feel you may have been compromised by the people you report to, then make sure you keep a paper trail itemising your concerns and the responses.

This is another argument for making brief but regular trips to the off-line edit, where you can spot copyright items of any kind that might cause you a problem in sufficient time to check them out. The editor might also have the nous to let you know that 'naughty things' are creeping in. If it is impossible to get into the edit then make sure you scroll through rough cuts and fine cuts of the project, when they are sent off to the Broadcaster. Then you can ask awkward questions in time and start the process of discovering whether a piece of copyright material is affordable, or even whether it is possible to use it. Some things, particularly music, are not clearable, no matter how much time or money you throw at them.

When you watch a screening, make notes of anything, however small or silly it seems, that you are not happy about (somehow they raise the hairs on the back of your professional neck!) and then take advice from sources appropriate to the item. Your first port of call might be a senior production manager or head of production, or a senior manager at your production company – and, ultimately, perhaps a legal consultation will need to be made. A lawyer will be expensive, but they will take a view on whether something is likely to pose a problem or not. Check whether your company has any in-house legal staff or if you have access to a Broadcaster's legal department first, as this shouldn't cost you anything and it will alert them to the potential problem early on.

Archive and stills

In respect of archive and stills copyright, if you are lucky enough to have an in-house archive producer or researcher then take advantage of their knowledge and experience! If you are not, then you may find yourself searching for and licensing archive or stills yourself. Since it's a vast area with many options to choose from, I include here some detail from an interview about the growth of film libraries and archive sources for background information. There follows a case study with Paul Gardner, in-house Archive Producer at Darlow Smithson Productions, whose passion for, and vast experience of, copyright and clearance make him an excellent person to have around.

QUESTION: Can you give us a bit of background to the business of archive research please, Paul?

PAUL: Yes, the first film emerged around 1895. We now assume that 75-80% of all the silent films ever produced have been lost to history. The first attempt at film archive in this country was post-Great War – a famous propaganda film *Battle of the Somme* was given to the then National War Museum (now known as the Imperial War Museum) who didn't really know what to do with it and their simple archive didn't even have a permanent base. The IWM was founded in 1917 and one of its functions was to be a memorial to those who had suffered and died in the First World War.

So the first real film archives emerged in the 1930s – nearly 40 years after the advent of cinema – and it was very different to what we recognise today. Being a new idea it faced suspicion from producers and anxiety about copyright issues, and it was unregulated, with no set method of funding – all a bit disorganised. In 1938 in Paris, the International Federation of Film Archive (FIAF) brought together various institutions dedicated to rescuing films both as cultural heritage and historical documents and preserving them properly. It now has 140 members in over 77 countries and these archives collect, restore and exhibit films and cinema documentation spanning the entire history of film. The members in the UK are: the British Film Institute, Scottish Screen Archive, National Library of Scotland, Imperial War Museum, and the North West Film Archive in Manchester and National Screen and Sound Archive of Wales. They share a common belief in the preservation of film as a record first, and for commercial exploitation second – commercial archives cannot join (http://www.fiafnet.org.uk/).

QUESTION: I had no idea it was all so globally organised. Any more?

PAUL: Yes, there are 12 public-sector film archives in the UK, which together form a network of regional and national moving image collections, all of which are members of the UK Film Archive Forum (www.bufvc.ac/faf/). In their collections you will find moving images in a variety of original film gauges, video formats, and digital media. They include amateur films, artists' films and animation, corporate and promotional material, documentary, fiction, educational and training material, 'local topical' films, newsreels and government films, works by public and charitable organisations, travel films and national and regional TV broadcasts.

QUESTION: And are these archives where you might find material for projects, or do you use more commercial archives?

PAUL: Yes and no. I would start there when working on specific British history programmes, but there are hundreds of film libraries now that are run solely for profit and don't necessarily contain film but more often video tape, and increasingly digital 'downloadable' formats. They might contain the collected output of, say, Granada TV or Associated Press News or outtakes from major Hollywood studios such as Universal or Warner Bros, and they currently tend to pool their resources and operate from a central office with standardised access. For example, ITN and Getty have taken over many libraries, buying up and managing their collections. ITN Source currently manages its own news output of ITN News and Channel 4 News along with Granada TV, Reuters News and the UK interests of Fox News, and the BBC Motion Gallery manages the CBS archives and NHK Japan in the UK.

Then there are also many 'Stockshot' collections set around dedicated subjects like location material, nature photography, time lapse, aerials, lifestyle, etc. which are sometimes filmed for specific commissions and then resold. These include Getty Images, Corbis Motion, and Photolibrary.

Then there any many 'specialist' and 'ephemera' collections such as Clips & Footage and the Huntley Film Archives where you can source some real gems or unusual material to really lift your film.

Finally there are also company archives which may or may not operate on a profit system, and museum collections (for example, the Midland Air Museum) and these are often not quite as well organised as the IWM and take some digging out.

QUESTION: So, if you want a bit of footage that depicts, say, a frosty river in a Scottish snow scene, you can buy it rather than having to go and shoot it?

PAUL: Exactly. You could potentially buy that 'clip' and download it into your edit for as little as £100 (rights dependent). Many non-FIAF archives belong to an organisation called FOCAL – The Federation of Commercial Audiovisual Libraries. This is a not-for-profit professional trade association providing excellent networking and marketing opportunities for content industry professionals and giving users access to over 300 members worldwide. Formed in 1985 as an international trade association to represent commercial film libraries, film researchers, producers and others related to the industry, it's a good starting point for finding appropriate sources (http://www.focalint.org/).

QUESTION: So, FOCAL is a useful starting point; any others?

PAUL: Yes, FOOTAGE.net has been, since 1994, the premier stock footage resource for news, creative, archive and royalty-free footage (www.footage.net or www.stockfootageonline.com has various indexes to specialist libraries, themed content and related websites).

Once you have established contact you will need to decide how best to research. When using a traditional archive you can, in some cases, research on site yourself. There are usually knowledgeable staff to help and card indexes and 'dope sheets', some of which may be on-line, but for best access go in person. Viewing takes time. Preserved film is usually kept in cold storage so you need to forward plan.

Increasingly libraries are investing in digitising programmes for their on-line presence but they usually have computerised 'text records' for all content. Some have on-line access to databases and there isn't likely to be any further information than that. These websites vary in user-friendliness, which might be a factor in where you find your material. You can usually either choose to receive a viewing tape within, say, 24 hours, which will cost anything between £25 and £150, or in some cases view on site for larger orders. Libraries with a large digital catalogue allow you to download low-resolution watermarked clips for free. Royalties are then paid when 'master material' is ordered at the end of production or during post production. These tend to be higher; ranging from a royalty-free clip for £99 to 'all media rights' for as much as £5,000 per minute, although everything is negotiable, especially for big orders. I'll come back to this later.

These days the Internet makes access to collections in other countries much easier and you don't have to trust someone else's research. However, all computer databases are only as good as the cataloguer, which is why some 'old-school' film researchers quite rightly get very precious about being separated from the original cataloguing system. Stock shot libraries in particular have clips available to download on-line at high resolution but you will need the appropriate technology to receive it and will have to pay royalties there and then. Traditional archives are likely to be slower to take up this technology because of the size of collections and the cost involved in digitising it all. So always ask about undigitised material, which will be logged somewhere. This is where that 'never seen before material' will evolve from and not from a clip that can be downloaded in 30 seconds by every other programme-maker in creation!

QUESTION: Fascinating and useful – now, if we can afford to hire a film researcher, what exactly will they do for their money?

PAUL: They will service your production with the best archive available within or below your budget parameters, and this entails sourcing, logging, supplying and controlling material as well as pricing it, and obtaining all the licences. Because this is their speciality they will have built up relationships with a number of archives and may well be able to negotiate deals, which may mean saving you money on your budget when you most need it: right at the end.

QUESTION: Roughly how much would I expect to pay for these paragons, and can I hire them for a small period of time only?

PAUL: Specialist archive or film researchers can be hired on a daily rate, weekly or over a whole production depending on your requirements. You can look to pay £150–£200 a day or £950 a week. There may be some movement on a long contract but not much, and they will save you money, time and be better able to protect your company against any potential legal action.

QUESTION: I have already explained what copyright is and that you need a licence to use a copyright piece of work, but what, exactly, is a licence and why do I need it?

PAUL: It's a piece of paper or contract that gives you the permission or rights to use 'third party material' owned by someone else, which can be: moving archive footage, photographs, graphics, illustrations, newspapers, headlines, movie clips or any other copyright-protected material in the body of your programme. When you are working on a programme or series you will be contracted by the Broadcaster up front for the clearances they need – territories, rights and the period you need permission to use the material for. These might be :

UK
UK (including Eire)
European
US
World excluding US
World (including US)

The last of these is the clearance that most US Broadcasters, for example, generally require, which is, of course, the most expensive.

When clearing for 'World' I would begin by asking for 'All Media' rights, but, if the supplier is reluctant to grant this or if it's just too expensive then these rights can be broken down into the ones that you need. If in doubt about what rights you need, check your production agreement:

Television: There are many different forms, but the following is a brief outline of the major recognised forms that you may have to deal with if you are asked to break down what 'All Media' means. Check with your Broadcaster:

Standard TV and Non-standard TV
Free to Air and Pay
Terrestrial and Cable and Satellite

The above can be grouped into 'ALL TV' – the rights that most US Broadcasters and co-productions generally require, and a safer option.

QUESTION: I sometimes find these different clearances confusing, but your explanations are nice and clear. Any more?

PAUL: Yes, the terms previously listed and the following terms are generally accepted by both Broadcaster and libraries. The way in which other, different uses are described can vary between different Broadcasters, but generally other uses include:

NON-THEATRIC RIGHTS – which means exhibition to non-paying audiences in educational institutions, churches, museums, prisons, ships at sea, planes, etc. excluding theatres where a fee has been paid.

THEATRIC RIGHTS – exhibiting to audiences where a charge for admission is made, including cinemas and concert halls.

HOME VIDEO including VIDEO ON DEMAND – VOD, DVD, DTO (download to own).

MERCHANDISING RIGHTS – advertising sale and distribution of goods of any description, and their promotion.

INTERACTIVE/INTERACTIVE TV AND VIDEO – interactive products coming from the programme CD ROMS.

INTERNET – streamed, non-downloadable/non-archival, IPTV (Internet Protocol TV).

TRANSMISSIONS – when clearing for 'World' it is generally understood that the licence should include unlimited transmissions (TXs), as it is impossible to predict the number of times it will be shown worldwide. This is the clearance most US Broadcasters and co-productions generally require.

Generally, BBC, ITV, Channel 4 and Channel 5 will specify 3 or 5 TXs over 5 years, but because we are clearing for World this figure becomes redundant (except on the occasions when the supplier requires clarification of the number of TXs in the UK: the BBC do this.

PERIOD – currently under the terms of trade most UK Broadcasters need 5 years' clearance. Usually American/Global Broadcasters such as Discovery, National Geographic and History Channel will contract you to deliver material 'In Perpetuity' (which means for ever), but for various reasons to do with cost and libraries not wanting to grant 'Perp' licences, in my experience the Broadcaster will allow for a 10-year licence and they will often accept a WAIVER form, which has to be submitted before the programme is delivered.

A WAIVER is a form for which most Broadcasters have templates, and is submitted when the programme-maker is unable to meet the contracted rights for the material in the programme for whatever reason. As already mentioned, stills libraries will rarely grant 'Perp' but will license for 10 years. This must be made clear to the Broadcaster and is done so on the waiver, which has to be signed off by them and is attached to the delivered licence.

QUESTION: So, what about the cost of using archive? The royalty fees?

PAUL: Each library will charge a fee based on the rights we require. There is no set fee and the way this is charged differs widely between each library. For example, you may be charged:

For a 10-second or 60-second minimum.
A clip rate (the clip could be 2 seconds or 20).
A flat fee.
A per-second charge after the minimum usage.
A minimum clip order: a 2-second clip in a programme will be charged at 5 seconds every time. BEWARE!

QUESTION: So is there any rule of thumb for estimating how much archive will cost?

PAUL: Well, as a guide, based on our standard clearance of World, All Media, In Perpetuity or for at least 10 years' clearance, the range of rates one would expect to pay would be:

£60 per second with a 20-second minimum – which equates to £3,600 per minute.
For UK, All TV, 5 years; expect to pay £10–£20 per second with a 20- or 30-second minimum, or £600–£1,200 per minute.

QUESTION: Blimey! Lotta money. Could you go on to explain what the Broadcaster needs in their deliverables, in relation to any archive footage used, please?

PAUL: Broadcasters' requirements do vary, but we usually have to supply international networks with extremely detailed logs for each second of archive and still photograph used, from each supplier, which includes the rights and costs of each sequence of archive. These are delivered with a copy of every licence from each supplier along with associated waivers. If we do not deliver a licence for every piece of third-party material – WE DO NOT GET PAID!

And just to point out – some deliverable paperwork, to Channel 4 for instance, can be delivered on-line (more on this in Chapter 19 on Deliverables).

QUESTION: Which reminds me – suppose, despite your best efforts to trace the source for a piece of archive or a still, you just can't find the owner, what do you do then?

PAUL: Much depends on how obscure the material is, but this is another area where extreme caution must be applied. Some copyright ownership may prove elusive to track down, despite all your effort and hard work. These efforts to find an owner are often referred to as 'due diligence'. In such situations you would keep copies of all your emails, faxes and other efforts to find who owns something and then set aside some money (based on a fair estimate of the value of the clip) to cover a late claim, should the copyright owner suddenly spy his material on the TV and contact you. (This is often referred to as an 'await claim'.) The company may feel that this is an acceptable business practice or they may feel that it is too dangerous and decide to remove the problematic archive or still photograph and avoid any potential legal action. So this is definitely a case where you refer the problem to a higher level of management and get them to evaluate the level of risk involved so the company can take a view.

NB 'Due diligence' or 'best efforts' does not mean a quick search on the Internet at the end of a day, but rather evidence of protracted effort from a variety of sources.

QUESTION: So to save myself all the time and effort of doing the archive research and paperwork myself, and assuming I can afford a film researcher, how do I go about hiring one?

PAUL: The best place to start is FOCAL, who have a list of all member researchers with their credits and contacts. They will also send out researcher job information to all members via email if you submit a simple on-line form. Other than that it is word of mouth, so check with other production managers to see if they have any recommendations. And good luck!

Some terms that may need explaining

Fair dealing

You may, from time to time, hear people mention something called 'fair dealing'. This is only a statutory defence in the UK for the unauthorised use of copyright-protected material; in the US it's referred to as 'fair use' and has different rules. UK fair dealing will require you to pick your way through a minefield of allowable and non-allowable uses, and you certainly should not embark on such a path without detailed legal advice from either the Broadcaster's legal department or your own legal consultant.

In my opinion, fair dealing is a term that gets bandied about from time to time by people who may erroneously think it's a cheap way of using clips from TV programmes or films without the bother and expense of clearing them. *Do not* be tempted; my advice would be to ignore fair dealing and clear everything in the usual way. In any case this decision should not be yours alone, but you should consult with the executive or production company's management and they should take the ultimate responsibility for assuming any potential risk, and always while liaising with your company's commissioner or Broadcaster.

Public domain

The commonly held perception of 'public domain' material is material that is owned by nobody and is therefore free to use with no problem at all! Clearly this is also a dangerous assumption. There isn't a recognised definition of public domain material, although if something is hundreds of years out of copyright you can probably safely say that it is in the public domain and safe to use in your programme. (But watch out for reprographic images and music.) The US has a different approach to what constitutes 'free to use' or public domain material. You may find that material shot by US federal agencies, for example NASA, appears to fall into such a category; however, this does not mean that you can gaily chuck it into your programme without any paperwork. The material may indeed be usable but will require some form of evidence (which could be an email or document from a relevant website) stating clearly that as the owner they consider the material to be in the 'public domain'.

Incidental inclusion

Lastly there is the phrase 'incidental inclusion', which most commonly refers to inadvertent shots of things – posters, works of art hanging on a wall, a programme being shown on a TV screen – the sort of thing that your cameraman may have captured as part of a panning shot establisher, for example, or some sort of actuality. There is a massive amount of guidance on what constitutes incidental inclusion, but be aware that if you have put something in a shot yourself, or have dressed any kind of set, then it is not incidental inclusion. If in doubt about anything then run it past your legal advisers.

Again, boring old me, I'd recommend talking to senior management or a legal adviser in respect of all the above terms. They are often misused, but this book is not the place to get involved in complex wrangling about their meaning. Always proceed with proper caution and be guided by people who are better qualified to define such legal terms.

USEFUL TIP

For more details on copyright, please refer to the CDPA (Copyright, Designs and Patents Act, 1988).

16 Computer Generated Imagery (CGI)

The inclusion of Computer Generated Imagery in your programme or series will take up a hefty chunk of your budget and you will need to liaise with the graphics company to schedule and plan meetings to discuss the content and delivery of the graphics. Part of the role of the production manager in this respect is to keep the flights of graphical fancy of the director and the CGI house within the budget that you have. The creation of graphic sequences can take quite a long time from conception to delivery of the finished article and this must be factored into your schedule. The completed graphics won't turn up until you are ready for your post production process and this can mean that viewing of the rough cuts and fine cuts will be an effort of will on the part of the Broadcaster, since you will probably have nothing more than a black screen with 'CGI shot here' written on it – at least at first, which sometimes makes them a bit twitchy. You will have a semi-completed shot towards the end of the off-line but the quality of this is also likely to make the Broadcaster edgy. The series producer or exec will probably have to do some explaining and reassuring here.

However, proceeding down the CGI route does not necessarily have to break the bank as there are modest varieties of graphics that can make your programme look effective. So don't curb the enthusiasm of the graphic designers too much because they may come up with cheap and very cheerful options for all sorts of creative problems that may present themselves. It might help here to examine exactly what is meant by the term CGI.

CGI or VFX are umbrella (catch-all) terms. CGI can refer to everything from simple-looking graphics (maps, explainers, etc.) right through to photo-realistic CGI elements composited into live action backplates. There is a spectrum of different types of CGI available to you with a very wide range of budgets attached, and this is why extensive discussions with your CGI company will be useful to you, as well as to the creative members of the team. They should be able to offer you a wide range of options that get the most out of what might be a low budget.

At the lower end of the CGI budget are the basic, didactic, explainer graphics with a simple finish (costing as little as £5K per minute), and at the higher end of the CGI budget are the photo-realistic creature shots composited into live action backgrounds (up to £20K per minute). Put another way, there are graphics that are used to explain complex ideas simply, such as weather fronts moving over an area or how fuel is pumped to an aeroplane engine (events a camera could never capture), and then there are drama-enhancing, seamless, photo-realistic shots such as digital storm clouds added to a plate shot on a sunny day and a plane falling out of the sky – mundane or extraordinary events made to appear as if shot with a real camera.

I can explain this more easily via an example. I once managed a drama/documentary in which we explored the conundrum of where the Romans might first have entered Britain in 43 AD, or thereabouts! There is a field in Kent which contains what is presumed to be the ruined foundations of the first Roman gateway, an enormous marble and brass structure built to celebrate this invasion. We spent a large part of our budget re-creating this from a 'backplate' and helicopter footage of these foundations to show a magical graphic sequence where the archway 'grew' from nothing into what it might have once looked like. We also had some sequences throughout the programme where we wanted, for example, to make the shots of a few Roman centurions (a group of enthusiastic re-enactor chaps in their historical finery) look like a battalion of centurions – something which CGI does easily, reasonably cheaply and very effectively. The modest CGI budget was apportioned over these two contrasting styles and added substance to the enhanced passages of the film as well as a visually stunning culmination to the programme, where it was repeated, with swelling composed music, for maximum effect. It proved very good value for money.

Once your team is on board and discussion of what is going into the programme or series is under way, you will need to start thinking about the CGI content and which company you are going to use to produce it. The director or executive may have some idea of whom they want to use, and there is a short list of some graphics producers included at the end of this chapter to start your search. Get some showreels and then invite a shortlist of companies to chat about the project and quote for it. It's not always about whether they have content on their showreels that is appropriate to your project (though that's a good place to start); it's also about whether they are 'hungry' and have a talented, versatile team. It might be that they just haven't had an opportunity to create CGI dinosaurs or digital crowds of people, but they'll give you real value for money and super-enthusiasm throughout for the chance to add that material to their showreel.

Once you have made a decision and accepted a quote, arrange some more detailed meetings about the actual content and form of what they are going to create. This is a meeting you need to be at, gently reminding everyone about the limitations of the budget if plans get too grandiose. The graphics designers will then go away and start to produce storyboards (possibly) or more details about what you can have for your money. They might also produce mood boards/concept art or do full 3D test shots for you, depending on the requirements of the Broadcaster – even more likely if there is a development budget, though this is a rare luxury!

You should certainly have some guarantee that your chosen company can deliver to the required standard before committing your project to them. So a word here about the contract that you will draw up. The production company you are working for will probably have a template for this, and you should get a draft ready early so that any negotiations which follow with the CGI company don't hold up the process. This contract will probably pay a percentage of the fee upon signature and then stipulate some subsequent payments which will be tied in to the delivery and approval of portions of the graphics. This contract will probably include a delivery schedule that will need to be agreed by all parties.

Copyright is a slightly grey area. In the main, Broadcasters retain copyright of the final shot as it appears in the film. But either the CGI house or production company could own the 3D models/elements/backplates, etc. that are composited together to make up the VFX shot. As more and more production companies have in-house graphics capabilities I would advise that the contract stipulates that the production company own all 3D assets. To give an example, if the CGI company buy a 3D bi-plane 'off the shelf' and add detail to use it in a First World War aerial battle, the purchase cost of this small 3D model will most likely be charged to the production company. Therefore this should become the property of the production company as a digital asset (just like a physical model) for possible use in future productions. This may make good economic sense if the company you are working for has an ongoing use for graphics and can reuse and alter basic 'models' on future projects.

Once the graphics studio has been chosen and you know what they will create for the money you have, then it's a good idea to draft a list of what graphics you will have in each programme. It can be useful, on series particularly, to ask the CGI studio for a menu with approximate costs for different type of shots, from the simple (maps) to the very complex (photo-realistic plane crashes). It's then easy to see how many and what type of shots you might get for your budget and how they can be balanced over the series.

Next time you watch a film, especially something 'epic', see if you can spot the join where actual footage has been upgraded by a clever use of graphics. Vistas and horizons may well be enhanced 'in post', digital matte paintings extending streets, adding mountain ranges, or removing TV aerials for period accuracy. Backgrounds can be replaced or treated by filming characters or objects against blue- or greenscreen, and breathtaking stunts made believable by painting out wires, harnesses or crash mats.

Returning to the list of graphics which has been agreed by your director(s) and the graphics studio, you will need to create a schedule of delivery where items will be viewed and approved by the director/series producer and Broadcaster, and the dates when this will happen. It's probably best that you base it on the delivery of certain stages, rather than the actual graphics shots (i.e. all shots as block outs by the rough cut stage, and all shots as previs by fine cut – see the end of this chapter for an explanation of terms used). Finally, perhaps, all final shots to be delivered by picture lock. This document should be regularly up-dated, in case dates slip, and circulated to everybody who has an interest in it. It may also form the basis of your payment schedule: each delivery, agreed and approved, will trigger a payment.

One thing to be aware of when commissioning CGI is that you need to make firm decisions about style and content of graphics as early as possible to give the designers as much time as you can to work on them. As things progress on the research and contributor front, there may well be quite major treatment changes as various content ideas evolve and change. This is when you should ensure that tweaks are communicated to the CGI house so that they can adapt their models to the changing requirements. This sounds simple enough, but it often gets overlooked in the rapid changes that may take place through development to filming. And if changes are too many and too drastic it may seriously compromise the CGI house's ability to produce what you want, when you want it – so be aware that too many changes will destabilise the delivery process and there will be a deadline beyond which you can't continue to alter the graphics.

Shooting for CGI

You will need to get your head around the CGI process in order to run it properly. Again, if you don't know, you should ask. It might be possible to visit the CGI house and get your contact there to show you around and explain some of the jargon and/or processes for you. (I can't say this often enough – have you ever met anyone who doesn't want to talk about what they are passionate about?)

The graphic designers will require some backplates or elements for some of their graphic shots, and they may want either to send a VFX supervisor on your shoot or to give you a specific list of images they want shot or details recorded, along with possible copies of particular rushes tapes. These backplates are used as the basis for some graphics work. For example, if the camera is moving and a 2D or 3D object needs to be composited into the footage, the shot will need to be motion tracked with specific software and a certain number of fixed points need to be visible in the frame for this to work. Similarly, green- or bluescreens need to be lit correctly; sometimes camera data, including height, angle, lens, distance to object, etc. need to be recorded; and digital stills of the environment may be required to convincingly light and composite the element that will be added. This is all quite specialised filming work and needs to be carried out correctly to avoid additional costs further down the line. For example, if the greenscreen is not properly lit, or does not cover the area that needs to be separated/replaced, this can involve many more days of keying or rotoscoping (cutting the object out frame by frame). This impacts on your budget when you consider that the average cost of a designer is (at the time of writing) up to £500 per day.

You will need to agree at a very early stage who pays for this. If they want to send an operative along they will probably expect you to pick up the tab, but you might argue that it should be part of the CGI budget if your budget hasn't allowed for it. Their flights, travel, accommodation and living allowance will need to be covered. And if you are providing copy rushes to them, again, who pays for this? Make sure this is all sorted and agreed before anyone goes anywhere, though it will probably be easier for your co-ordinator to book the whole thing while they are doing the rest of the crew's arrangements. You should keep a tally of all the costs and then you can deduct it from the final CGI invoice, but make sure this doesn't come as a last-minute surprise!

I have asked an in-house producer of CGI at Darlow Smithson Productions, Mike Davis, to explain some of the CGI terminology which may baffle you in early meetings with the graphics house. It is unusual to have someone in-house to supervise the CGI process; this is usually something which falls within the production manager's remit, so calling on his experience and knowledge may help you to pick your way through the terminology to start with.

GLOSSARY OF TERMS FOR CGI

VFX
Visual or Digital Effects. An all-encompassing term for any 2D or 3D (CGI) effects content.

MOTION TRACKING (or match moving)
The use of specialised software that allows the insertion of virtual objects into real footage with the correct position, scale,

orientation and motion in relation to the photographed objects within the scene.

BLUE or GREEN SCREEN

Literally a blue or green screen or large piece of fabric against which you can shoot to achieve a colour or chroma key, allowing a compositor to separate or lift the foreground element and combine with separately shot elements or backgrounds. For example, if you shoot the set of a room interior in a studio and you want an active sky/exterior through the window, you could fill the window with lit blue- or greenscreen (as opposed to a painted cyc) and then anything that passes in front of this can be keyed and a background shot to fill the view in post production.

You can hire blue- and greenscreens from kit companies in varying sizes for your shoot.

MO-CAP

Motion Capture is a method of recording the performance of an actor or puppet and translating those animation data on to a 3D model. For example, both Gollum in *Lord of the Rings* and the ape in *King Kong* were played by actor Andy Serkis, covered in tracking points, whose performance was mapped on to the CGI character.

MOTION CONTROL

A rig that allows separate elements to be shot in one precisely repeated camera move and composited together. For example, in *Lord of the Rings*, big-scale differences between characters were achieved by running the camera along the track in precisely the same move/timing, with different actors sitting in each pass, so that a hobbit, for example, could be scaled down in frame but still accurately and believably exist within the frame beside the other actors.

MODIFICATION REPORTS

These are fairly industry-standard report forms used to feed back comments to external CGI suppliers at key stages of the animation schedule. A director may be required to comment or sign off at each stage. The steps towards final delivery of a CGI shot are as follows:

STORYBOARD

First stage to establish what needs to be conveyed editorially and what content/assets exist within the frame. Storyboard frames can be thrown into assembly cuts to determine pacing, etc. With this storyboard a costing can be estimated, and when a budget is agreed this advances to:

BLOCKOUT/PRE-VISUALISATION

The first, simple, and wire-frame/grey-scale stage that gets dropped into rough cuts to determine timings, key animation, etc. Pre-visualisation is often shortened to 'previs'. Once the basic shot requirements are established and signed off the animation moves on to:

SECOND STAGE

More detailed models and animation for fine cut stage to give a greater sense of final shot composition but with none of the render heavy/expensive final textures or lighting passes applied. Only when final sign-off on timings and animation is approved does it go to:

FINAL RENDER

Final CGI shot (now usually HD) submitted to on-line fully rendered. Rendering is where computers process all the information/layers in a 3D scene, frame by frame, to produce the final image. The more complex and detailed the image (and size of the image), the longer this can take.

Though CGI may seem at first to represent a scarily expensive component of your programme – certainly on a comparative cost-per-minute basis – it can also introduce huge savings if it is used cleverly and efficiently.

For example, a Gulf War drama/doc budget had assumed and allowed for traditional methods of shooting a wide shot of tens of armoured personnel carriers/jeeps, etc. in convoy through a desert, without considering the possibility and cost saving of shooting one or a few trucks and multiplying them in 2D or with CGI, or entirely with CGI. Obviously other requirements for the scene would have to be taken into account, but if this establishing shot is the only time you see the whole convoy, then shooting for real would not represent good value on screen: archive or VFX may well present a better solution. Similarly huge decisions about where to shoot – which have a massive overall impact on the budget – could be resolved by shooting in a more cost-effective environment but factoring in digital extensions or removals. For example, shooting in the UK but digitally adding a distinctive US landmark in a background might be a much smarter solution than actually filming in the US!

At the smaller end of the scale, and using a very different but real example, costly and tricky macro natural history footage of a mosquito on a particular skin type could be avoided by using existing archive and quickly applying a key off the mosquito and grading the skin separately and controllably in post production. This could save half a day of specialised filming that still might not capture the rushes you require.

Visual effects are now a crucial consideration for any production and are often a big USP (Unique Selling Point) for commissioners. So, as a production manager, you should be fully aware of the major advantages of being able to use visual effects to enhance your programme at a cost which might well be affordable, even on a skinny budget.

Some UK-based CGI studios

The Mill (www.the-mill.com)

Red Vision (www.redvision.co.uk)

Jellyfish (www.jellyfishpictures.co.uk)

Fluid Pictures (www.fluid-pictures.com)

Prime Focus (www.primefocuslondon.com)

Lola (www.lola-post.co.uk)

17 Music: a brief guide

Copyright

The term 'copyright' encompasses several separate rights which automatically belong to the creator of a piece of music once it is set down in a fixed form (usually a recording or written on manuscript paper). This includes the right:

- To produce and sell copies of the work (referred to as mechanical rights, print rights and distribution rights)
- To import or export the work
- To make arrangements of the work
- To perform the work in public (including broadcasting rights)
- To sell or assign these rights to others

Additionally there are moral rights, which include the right of attribution (you have to be credited as the author/composer), and also the right not to have your work treated in a derogatory fashion (i.e. parodies).

This is the clearest description of copyright you could hope to find, and you do need to pay attention to music copyright as it can be one of the worst nightmares if you get it wrong.

In most countries copyright in music now lasts for 70 years after the death of the composer, or in the case of co-composers, 70 years after the death of the last one to die. After that the work moves into what is known as 'public domain', which means you can use it without permission or fees. However, a new arrangement of a public domain piece of music also has a 70-year copyright, so if you think you have no problems using Beethoven's Fifth you will be right, providing you check that the arrangement of this piece is also out of copyright (i.e. 70 years after the death of the arranger). If it isn't, then the music version you plan to use is not public domain and will require the standard clearances.

Music licence

This is the vital piece of paper that you get when you have cleared all the copyright on your music. It gives you permission to use the music in the project you have named and for the clearances you have listed. In television, licences are usually obtained either by a music consultant you have employed for this purpose or, quite possibly, by the production manager. They are vital because they will form part of your deliverables which will need to be returned to the Broadcaster, and they may also form part of your E&O paperwork (see Chapter 10 on Insurance). You *must* get licences for all the material in your programme that you have not shot specially, and you must keep them all safely in your production file. In some cases your licence may double as an invoice for the cost of the copyright material – whether music, archive, stills, whatever!

Music cue sheet

This is a (mandatory) record of precisely what music you have used in your programme: the CD title and number, the track number and title, the composer and publisher of the track, the recording artist and record company, and all the timings for each separate segment used. You shouldn't aggregate the music use – that means you have to report each separate music clip (even if it is only a few seconds) and not add the uses up to a payable total. You can download a template for this from the Broadcaster's website; failing this Audio Network also have a template on their website (see the end of this chapter for a list of useful websites). This music cue sheet will be delivered to the Performing Right Society (now known as the PRS for Music) by the Broadcaster, and they will make the correct payments to the various bodies who have produced the music you have used. You should also keep a copy of the music cue sheet both for the E&O certificate if you have one, and for your files. In many cases the music publisher issuing your licence will also require a copy of the music cue sheet.

Music – which route to choose?

Most TV programmes contain background music which underscores the narration, accompanies the action and fills in the gaps; they may also boast a piece of title music. When you make your music choices the route you take will fall into one of three major options:

1.   Commercial music.
2.   Composed music.
3.   Library or 'mood' music.

Commercial music

Commercial music will need two clearances – publishing rights and recording rights. Simply put, the person(s) who wrote the music and the artist(s) who recorded it will need to give their permission for use. *Do not* assume that everything is clearable for TV use, even if you have a huge budget and shed-loads of time.

When you are trying to clear a piece of music you want to include in your programme I'd suggest that you write an email, fax or letter listing the details and giving a brief but honest account of the nature of the programme you are making – in other words, the context of the use. Add a note about the clearance you require (i.e. World in Perpetuity, 2 x UK, etc.). Send it to the owners of both sets of copyright (composer and artist – search for their details via the PRS and the PPL if you need to) and await their reply. You can, of course, do this by telephone to begin with, but all these details should at some point be put in writing and filed away.

If you are making a project for the BBC, they have what is known as a 'blanket agreement' with a huge number of music producers and your music clearances might well be covered by this. If so, they will confirm whether or not the use is OK under their blanket. Anything excluded from a blanket agreement will have to be individually licensed.

Channel 4 and Channel 5 both have smaller blanket agreements, so you can deal with them in a similar fashion. Remember, though, that if you wish to subsequently exploit your programme with sales abroad or DVD retail, etc. this will require separate clearances for all tracks.

I have made the point about the context of music use because some years ago I managed a documentary about Irish women who come to London for terminations, abortion being illegal in Ireland. It was in the days of faxes, and the programme was for a documentary strand on the BBC. The director wanted to use a piece of typically 'Irish-sounding' music and I faxed the BBC music department giving them all the details of the piece plus an outline of what the programme was about. The music was covered under their 'blanket' and they returned my original fax to me with their handwritten permission, which I filed in my production folder. When the programme was transmitted, the composer of the music – a staunch pro-lifer – contacted us through the Broadcaster and threatened to sue because his music had been used in a programme that, he felt, advocated abortion and he objected to this context in the strongest possible terms. I was able to demonstrate (thank goodness) that I had checked the music use with the BBC so they then had to deal with his subsequent legal threat, which eventually, I think, came to nothing. But the moral of the story is: always be up front with *how* you are going to use your choice of commercial music. This also has implications for musical parody, which should be handled very carefully, if at all.

If you ever find that you are using a piece of archive or a feature film clip which has music on it, you will have to clear the music separately from the clip. This means that you have a number of clearances to obtain: the copyright for the visual piece of material, and the two copyrights – publisher and recording artist – for the music. It goes without saying that this will require more time, effort and cash to do.

USING AMERICAN COMMERCIAL MUSIC

Clearing American commercial music can potentially be more problematic. For a start, instead of the one music organisation that we have in the UK to handle music clearance (PRS for Music) there are three in the US. Their copyright laws are different (the details of which are too long a story to go into here). And music companies have often been bought and sold repeatedly, so nobody really knows who owns what!

Clearing music in the US is often a very long and arduous process, and since you may not know what music is desired until the post period, you may not have long to get the required permissions – so that by the time one is refused you'll have to expensively rip that track out and replace it. *Never* try and wing it and hope it won't be noticed, because, by sod's law, it will be!

There are a number of curious examples, to pass on to the uninitiated in regard to music use. The little ditty 'Happy Birthday to You' is a favourite one. Two sisters in the US were teachers – Patty and Mildred Hill. Patty wrote a tune called 'Good Morning to All', which was sung by pupils at the beginning of class each day. It had the tune we now know as 'Happy Birthday to You' and the following lyrics:

Good morning to all, good morning to all
Good morning, dear teacher, good morning to all.

Patty Hill died in 1916, and so this tune was well and truly out of copyright. Patty's sister Mildred made a small change to the melody and rewrote it with the words 'Happy Birthday to You'. The work was first published in the US in 1935. Mildred died in 1946, and because of this the work is protected in the EU for 70 years after this date. So, to save you doing the sums, the copyright does not expire in the EU until the end of 2016 and in the US (due to different terms of protection) possibly not until 2030. So you will have to clear it with their publishers, and pay quite a lot of money for it, and then you can laugh loudly at anyone who tells you it's public domain or 'traditional' and can be used freely. Some nursery rhymes are still in copyright – like 'I'm a Little Teapot' – though others are OK to use, but you should still check them (PRS for Music again) and they will, of course, need to be added to the music cue sheet.

Some music is anonymous so it may be all right to use, but my firm advice is to check *everything* to make sure you don't come a cropper. Mistakes could be very expensive to rectify.

I was once employed to finish the post production on a *Dispatches* about domestic violence, and one of the films included a moody and beautiful sequence showing a mother who was living in a 'safe' house. She was putting her children to bed and then pouring herself a glass of wine and listening, over and over again, to 'Everybody Hurts' by REM – a wonderfully apposite lyric which brought comfort to this woman living in fear of an abusive partner. The only problem was that we were told it couldn't be used for a television programme when we applied for copyright clearance. Faced with what seemed like an insurmountable problem the woman herself wrote an emotional appeal to the lead singer of REM, explaining how she had found the strength to carry on with the help of this particular song, and he replied with permission to use it in this particular situation and wishing her good luck in the future. I claim no credit for this at all because it all came about before I joined the team, but it demonstrates how particular circumstances might sway a decision. We still had to pay for it, though.

By contrast I once tried very hard to secure permission to use Celine Dion's recording of 'My Heart Will Go On' in a small, educational documentary about the raising of the wreck of the *Titanic*. My pleading fax to the publishing house came back with the single word NO! written across it. When I telephoned to ask did this mean no, you can't afford it or no for some other reason, they replied 'it just means no' and that was the end of that.

INCIDENTAL INCLUSION AND FAIR DEALING

You might find that the rushes come back from a shoot with an interview or GV (general view) in a location where incidental music happens to be playing in the background, like a disco scene or radio broadcast. This is usually described as 'incidental inclusion' but it still needs to be cleared. If you can't do this because it's too expensive or hard to track down then you should suggest that it is stripped out and replaced with something similar from a sound library, preferably before the final sound mix is completed. Your director may say that it can be included under the term 'fair dealing'. This is where you can be allowed a small amount of copyright work to be used where its inclusion is 'incidental' or for educational purposes, without obtaining permission or paying a fee. However, because different countries have different interpretations of what actually constitutes fair dealing, it's safer to ignore the concept altogether and ensure that every single second of audible music in your film is cleared for the uses you require.

If one of your contributors sings or plays something themselves you will, of course, only have to clear the publishing/composer rights for it, and I would perhaps include a note on their release form covering the use of their voice or instrument. And, yes, it goes on the music cue sheet – have I mentioned that enough yet?

FAVOURED NATIONS

If you have a number of commercial tracks in your programme or series and are dealing with lots of different publishers and artists, one or more of them may insist you offer them all the same rates for their music under the Favoured Nations rule. To clarify, each representative can insist that nobody else gets offered more money than they have been offered, and if you can't negotiate a price down to the same level that you have agreed with everyone else, then they will all have to be paid the higher rate.

PROBLEMS OF COMMERCIAL MUSIC USE

So, commercial music is likely to be expensive, problematic to clear, and may not be clearable at all. But if your director insists on using commercial music then my advice would be to enlist the help of a music consultant who offers assistance in these sorts of situations. It will cost you, of course, but it may save you money and time further down the line. Call a few, ask lots of questions and see if you can negotiate a deal with them that will include their securing the proper licences for you. Or check out the PMA website and see if you can find a production manager who specialises in music programmes and call them to pick their brains. (See also the recommended websites at the end of this chapter.)

Composed music

This is a very controllable option for the production manager. You find a willing composer and agree a fee. Get them familiar with the project, by sending a treatment followed by rough and fine cut, for example, and set up a schedule of when you want pieces by and pay them as per contract. There are two music composer contracts on the PACT website – one gives the composer copyright and the other assigns copyright to the Broadcaster. Find out which one your composer is happy to sign and make sure this will be acceptable to your Broadcaster. Often these days an American Broadcaster will want total copyright of everything that is in the programme and the composer will not agree to this, so you may have to negotiate between the two. For this I'd recommend taking advice from PACT or an independent legal adviser.

Almost certainly, the first time the music is heard the director won't like it! Be prepared for this and for it to grow on them. It has been suggested that the music brain requires six listens for something new to become familiar.

The advantages of composed music are that you get exactly what you want and for the budget you have. It's hard to say what a reasonable fee will be for, say, an hour programme, and you may have to find someone who is hungry for the work if you don't have much dosh.

And, yes, you still need to do a music cue sheet which you should also copy to the composer at the end of the process.

PROBLEMS OF COMPOSED MUSIC

Time may be a factor. Your composer will almost certainly be doing other work so that getting pieces delivered on time may be problematic. So unless you know that your composer is reliable in this respect then you might want to build in some failsafe time in your post schedule so you aren't wasting expensive sound time waiting for your music to arrive. And please bear in mind that composers often shut themselves off from answering telephones or emails when they are in a studio composing, so they may be hard to contact when you want urgent replies to your queries.

Library music

A real benefit of library music is that both the publishing and sound recording are owned by the same company, so you need only one clearance. There are a number of music libraries (such as De Wolfe Music and KPM – and something like 150 others in the UK) who will send you endless CDs, or you can download tunes from their websites. The rates of pay for these will be standardised for each 30 seconds (or part thereof) used according to the clearances you need.

Indeed, you may also be able to negotiate a fixed rate for each programme based on an estimate of use. As of 1 October 2008 there are new TV programming rates for independent production companies who have signed up to the IPC Licence. These new rates provide a simpler and more affordable way for you to obtain additional rights such as Worldwide Broadcast, DVD and on-line. If you are producing a series or number of productions then it might be a good idea to call up the IPC team at PRS for Music (Tel) 020 7306 4101 to discuss how these rates and discounts can benefit your production. They can also send you a rate card of the various costs for each clearance, which is too extensive for inclusion here.

You must always calculate the music used throughout your programme by individual clip, and you may not aggregate it. This means that you can't simply add up the total number of seconds of music used and pay for it, but instead must record each individual clip on your music cue sheet.

> **USEFUL TIP**
>
> If a music clip is, say, 32 seconds you will pay for two 30-second clips under the old '30 seconds or part thereof' rule. You can submit your application on-line through the PRS for Music and they will send you an invoice and a licence. Done.

PROBLEMS

Library music traditionally has a reputation for being a bit 'bland', though recently it has upped its game considerably. You may well have heard it before, as anybody can buy exclusive use of a library track. Finding the track you need can involve trawling through library after library and ease of search can vary enormously.

USEFUL TIP

When I started this chapter I said that there were three options for music, but I lied – there is a fourth option. Traditionally, music libraries are all members of the MCPS (Mechanical Copyright Protection Society), and their music must be licensed through the MCPS using their rate card. Recently some libraries have been set up outside of the MCPS model, allowing them to set their own, more competitive, sync licence rates.

Audio Network

This company, which was started in 2001, is a music library which has streamlined the clearance process in various ways, by operating outside of the MCPS model. An independent production company or Broadcaster can either pay for unlimited Audio Network music used per production, or by an annual fee whereby all the music used in every project that the company makes is paid for within that fee and all the music is pre-cleared for World in Perpetuity. And there is no catch! An annual fee for a standard TV production company (at the time of writing) is £4,000 including unlimited retail. The advantages of this are obvious. Anything that the director finds on their website, or on the CDs/hard drives that they will send you if you prefer, can be used for any clearance that you may have; the only thing you, the production manager, will have to do is complete a music cue sheet and submit it to Audio Network and your Broadcaster.

Their library contains some 25,000 tracks and is updated by approximately three CDs per week of new music. They also offer an excellent service of help and assistance if you call them up about your project. Their website is friendly – have a look at it and remember that your life will be so much easier if this is the chosen route for music. And the company is staffed by very experienced people who all know their musical onions!

Problems

Sometimes the music may sound familiar because so many companies, especially in these tight economic times, are using Audio Network's facility and the best bits of music are the bits that get used the most. To avoid this you can ask Audio Network for some specially composed music and, for a bit more money, this may well be possible – just call and ask.

And one last story. If you ever listen to the longest-running radio soap on Radio 4 you may be interested to know that the composer of that iconic title tune emigrated shortly after he composed it (in the 1940s) with no idea that his music was being used, as he lost contact with his publisher. On a visit to London several years later he called in at the publisher's by chance and mentioned his name at reception. Knowing full well that this man was sitting on a royalty goldmine (every time it plays he gets paid!) the receptionist rushed off to get the copyright manager, who told him the good news: his PRS royalties had been stacking up happily over the years and he was now a very rich man. Rumpty tum ti tumpty tum indeed!

Sound effects

Finally, a word here about sound effects (SFX). Audio Network (see above) have a library of 50,000 sound effects which currently cost between £2 and £6 each for the usual World in Perpetuity clearance. Generally, if you buy a sound-effects CD you will find that the price you pay for it covers the use of any of its contents for the total clearance buy-out. There is no regulating body for sound effects, but I would still include them on your music cue sheet in the interests of being super-efficient! As most SFX contain no music, there is no additional fee to pay – and most SFX libraries operate on a buy-out licence structure.

Audio Network produce a little booklet called *Know Your Rights*, which is a useful and concise guide to music clearance to keep on your desk – call them up and ask for one!

And to return to Barry Kim's concise advice: 'If you can see it or hear it, clear it.' I would add that if you are in any way concerned about anything to do with music copyright in your project – check it. This is best done with either the PRS or MCPS, who both have very helpful staff to point you in the right direction.

MUSIC ACRONYMS

MCPS　Mechanical Copyright Protection Society (Tel) 020 8769 4400

MU　Musicians' Union (Tel) 020 7582 5566

PRS　Performing Right Society (Tel) 020 7580 5544 (now known as PRS for Music)

BPI　British Phonographic Industry Ltd (Tel) 01787 477277

PPL　Phonographic Performance Ltd (Tel) 020 7534 1000

USEFUL WEBSITES

http://en.wikipedia.org/wiki/Copyright for massive amounts of further information on copyright.

http://en.wikipedia.org/wiki/Fair dealing in the United Kingdom for more information on this concept.

Music supervisors/clearance companies: try www.musicalities.co.uk or find more on http://en.wikipedia.org/wiki/music supervisor.

Audio Network's website address: www.audionetwork.com (Tel) 01787 477277

Soundmouse: www.soundmouse.com (Tel) 020 7420 2120 are the company who accept the music cue sheets for projects made for Channel 4 and ITV. They also offer a range of other services – check out their website.

18 Post production and editorial staff

I'll try to explain here the process of post production as simply as I can, and translate some of the common terms that are used. But please be aware that this is an area where technology changes incredibly fast – cameras and shooting formats are developing all the time and the process of editing can be very technical, so don't panic if you don't understand something when you are working on your project. As ever, find someone who does know and pick their brains unashamedly.

The edit process

The process of off-lining a programme is the initial period of editing where rushes, archive and any kind of 'other' material is edited or cut by an editor, supervised by the director or edit producer. The edit suite and the editor will probably be 'dry-hired' (hired separately from each other) or you might hire an editor who will supply his or her own edit equipment, for an extra charge on top of their daily or weekly fee.

The editing equipment will probably be either Final Cut Pro or Avid. Final Cut Pro (or FCP) is the system which has become very popular recently.

Editing during the off-line is often done on a reduced resolution – i.e. the source tapes will be digitised into the edit machine at a low resolution ('res') so as to take up less space on the machine.

At the time of writing this would be followed by the conform – the process that returns the project back to full resolution. The higher the quality, or resolution, the more disc space the material takes up. To reduce disc space a clever technique called compression is used, but this can result in a lower visual quality. Technology is making disc space less of an issue, allowing you to ingest at higher resolutions.

The first stage of the off-line edit may be a rough assembly. This is exactly what it says: a loose, probably too long and very quickly put together approximation of the finished programme. Usually the first useful version of the programme is a rough cut, which is produced about halfway through the off-line edit period and is viewed by the Broadcaster(s) following a viewing by the executive or series producer. A DVD or tape of the rough cut could be sent to them for viewing, or, more usually because it saves time, it will be put up on some sort of viewing platform for them to see and comment on (i.e. an FTP site – File Transfer Protocol – and there are other platforms available). The edit may stop during this process or the editor may use this time to do twiddly bits (technical term).

The next few weeks will be spent working to absorb the Broadcaster's feedback to produce a fine cut which, again, will be viewed and comments returned and accommodated. By this time the programme should be roughly to length and looking pretty much like a finished programme, though it may not have final archive material or finished CGI in it. This will usually happen fairly near the end of the edit, and once the programme has been tweaked we end up with a picture lock (sometimes shortened to pix lock) which is a finished off-line where the pictures are fixed, though the narration can still be changed. One of the reasons the pictures should be locked (and stay locked) at this stage is that there will be a temptation to finesse visuals during the very much more expensive and time-consuming on-line, and this should be discouraged. Ideally, all CGI, archive, stills and music elements should be fitted at the picture-lock stage, though anything that is late arriving can usually be accommodated.

Post production process

When the off-line has been completed you will have a finished programme which is of the right duration (you should check what leeway the Broadcaster will give you; usually no more than 15 seconds either way, so if the programme is more or less than this you will have a problem) but it will not yet be up to broadcast standard for transmission (TX). Thus follows the post production period where the visuals and the sound will be upgraded and this will probably happen in a specialist facilities house.

At a late stage in the off-line process the editor will have produced an edit decision list (EDL). This is simply a list of all the edits or cuts within your programme which shows exactly what source tape the edited piece of material comes from and precisely how long each edited segment is. This EDL is used to reproduce your off-line cut at high resolution. This process is known as the conform and incorporates your original rushes, plus any CGI and archive material. The EDL is a useful list for the post production co-ordinator (or whoever is making sure that all the source tapes are in the on-line when they are needed) and this will include, of course, all the archive, rostrum and CGI tapes which have been used in the project, as well as the rushes tapes. (Rushes is the name given to specially shot material that your camera crew has filmed during your production period.) At this point an OMF export (Open Media File) will also be produced which contains all the sound information required for the dub. You will also need a digi cut of the final locked tape, which is a low resolution guide.

There may follow a 'pre grade online' where processes such as sync, aspect ratio conversion and technical alignment are carried out to bring the programme up to Broadcast standard.

A grade may follow, which is a process where the colours within the material will be adjusted – i.e. rushes may have been shot at different times of the day and thus will vary fractionally in colour tone. They might also have been shot on a variety of different formats so these irregularities can be ironed out. This process will be paid for by the hour and the operator may be a favourite the director wants because they have an exalted reputation for grading well. It's an expensive process but can make the programme look infinitely more sumptuous if done well.

After this comes the final on-line which is also booked by the hour and will include an operator. The director and/or the editor will attend this process. Some editors want to be there to nurture their project through; others may prefer to move on to their next edit.

Their attendance also depends on whether you can afford to pay them for this time. During the on-line you will add straps or lower frame supers (those captions that tell you who an interviewee is and what they do. The UK brand name for these is Aston and the American brand name is Chyron, just in case they get referred to by these descriptions), the title sequence and the credit roller or cards (the final list of acknowledgements and staff who contributed to the making of the programme). If you are making a programme which is part of a 'strand' then you will need to obtain from the Broadcaster a tape of the strand titles to add to the beginning of your programme in advance of this process. The text elements of a programme are added by an online editor and I would advise you, or your trusted co-ordinator, to attend this to check there are no spelling errors or typos sneaking through on to the screen to cause you embarrassment at TX.

You may stumble across a number of acronyms during the edit process, some of which are explained above. In addition you might be asked to 'ARC' some material. This translates as Aspect Ratio Conversion, which is where a piece of archive, for example, may arrive in your edit suite as 4x3 ratio instead of the required 16x9 ratio. If you edit this material into your 16x9 format you will end up with people looking very short and fat, so you will need to pass the archive through a machine that alters its ratio to the desired one; 16x9 is the common format for today's widescreen TV screens.

Sound post production

If your programme has a narrator you will need to book some time for the voice-over record – again booked by the hour. This includes a sound operator, and is probably run by the director or series producer. I usually book V/O sessions in the morning when the narrator's voice is likely to be better rested, and allow around 4 hours for an hour-long documentary, though many experienced narrators will take much less. Make sure that you send a copy of the V/O script to the narrator before the record so they can spend some time prepping their lines. You could also send a phonetic list of any pronunciation problems (for example, foreign names or technical terms) so they can prep these, or at least make sure that the person in attendance at the V/O record knows the correct pronunciations.

If you have any contributors speaking a foreign language or heavily accented English in your programme, you will either have to dub their words using another voice-over artist over the original sync, or subtitle the words on screen. Often Broadcasters prefer dubbed voices to subtitles, but check with them and remember that you will have to pay for another artist (unless you can find a volunteer on the team to do it) and extend the V/O record to accommodate this extra process.

There will follow a process of sound prep where the sound engineer will import the OMF and ingest the digi cut pictures and enhance and clean up all the tracks that have already been laid in the off-line. This process is called track laying.

Once the voice-over has been recorded it will be fitted into your project as part of the track laying process. The music, FX and sync dialogue are brought together as part of the pre-mix to create an M&E (which contains music, FX and sync dialogue).

Now you are ready for your final mix – the master transmission sound with commentary. It is normal to supply a full mix and an M&E (music and effects) version so that the M&E can form the basis of any international versions required. These tracks are then laid back to the master tape that has been created in the on-line.

You now have a master tape or DVD of your project – hurrah!

Broadcasters run a quality control (QC) on every programme that is delivered to them for TX. You may want to run your own QC, in which case you can get the facilities company that you have used, or another one, to run a quality test on the project which will pick up problems like poor quality in picture or sound. Your master will probably also be analysed for PSE (photosensitive epilepsy); flashing or strobing images can induce epilepsy in some viewers. Usually you will be asked to get rid of them but if they are unavoidable then you will probably be asked to issue a 'disclaimer' at the beginning of the programme, or even the beginning of each segment if they are repeated throughout.

The machine that used to check this was once a Flash Gordon – but is now more usually a Harding machine!

Once the QC has given the programme a clean bill of health it is a master and ready to be delivered, with the appropriate paperwork, to your Broadcaster. Congratulations!

The last job for your facilities house is to produce safety copies of the master. Most American Broadcasters will be sent their copy around two weeks after the first master has been delivered and approved. A copy is also made for your production company to keep in their archives and run other copies from, which may be sent out as press and publicity samples. I would also advise a DVD copy with 'burnt in time code' (BITC – see below for explanation) so that you and/or your co-ordinator can use it to time all the elements within the programme and produce the post production script for it. This last item is a document that minutely records everything within the programme and will be explained in more detail in Chapter 19 on Deliverables.

OTHER JARGON EXPLANATIONS

BITC – BURNT IN TIME CODE – a graphical representation of hours:minutes:seconds:frames eg 10:28:13:08.

VITC – VERTICAL INTERVAL TIME CODE – time code that is recorded as part of the video signal but not visible on the picture.

LTC – LONGITUDINAL TIME CODE – time code recorded as an analogue audio signal normally to a dedicated time code track.

Production manager's responsibilities to the editor

Once you have hired the editor your director prefers then you will need to keep them in the loop with any information that will help them in the edit. Having sent them a treatment you can then send them the relevant call sheet(s) so they know what is happening during shooting and what to expect back in the way of rushes. You should also make sure they have an up-dated contact list so they don't have to ask you for contact numbers. Send them a clear indication of what the technical specifications are for the programme they are working on at the beginning of the off-line. (This normally forms part of the contract from the Broadcaster, and should also be sent to your post house so that their sound engineers and graders know what is required.)

You can just send the tech specs as they appear on the contract, but I usually take a bit of extra trouble and compile a chart of dated deliverables that I will expect from the edit. If you're making your project for an American Broadcaster they will want a number of deliverables from the edit during the course of the off-line and at the end, and this is explained in more detail in Chapter 19.

At the beginning of the edit you should also give the editor a file of transcriptions of all the interviews relevant to their programme plus a few pens and paper pads, and maybe a ring binder for keeping papers in one place. It is easy to forget about edits, especially when they are taking place away from the office, but a bit of time spent visiting them is always a good idea – and here's why.

If you make friends with your editors they are likely to tell you when there may be problems – e.g. the director has slipped some commercial music into a cut even though you are using composed or library. (We can take this out later, the director assures you, but if the commissioning editor sees the cut and says 'love the music, guys' then s/he may start arguing to leave it in.) You can also check with them that the edit is running to schedule and the programme is not wildly over-long, or, conversely, short. In which case will they need some extra pick-up days of filming? You can also check to make sure that they are not doing impossibly long hours and the editor is not getting exhausted early on in the edit. Sometimes when I visit an edit I am greeted coolly by the director with a 'what are you doing here, we're very busy' sort of comment, to which I normally smile and reply jauntily 'just carry on as if I weren't here, chaps'. Sometimes though they are keen to show you something that has just been finessed, so your feedback as a 'fresh eye' can be useful – keep it positive! Often edits take place in tiny, windowless rooms and a visitor from outside can provide a welcome break and some enthusiasm. Don't outstay your welcome but don't ignore them either. It's just a question of judgement.

And a word here about edit suites when you are booking them – a six-week editing stint of long, intense hours in a room without a window is enough to drive anyone crackers, so do try to find them somewhere decent with reasonable kitchen facilities. Often edit houses offer plenty of snack and fancy coffee options, so make sure that if your director and editor use the in-house runners to fetch lunchtime sandwiches they don't end up on your invoice at the end of the edit. Unless they are working late and you have agreed to pay for their dinner and possibly a taxi home, you should not be paying for their food and any drinks other than the standard being provided by the edit house. I always make a point of sorting this out with my edit manager at the facility at the start of the project to avoid any embarrassment later on.

Which brings me on to:

Relationship with the post production house

Since your post production is often a buyer's market you should be able to do a good deal with the post house you want to use. Check with your series producer and directors to see if there is a facility they prefer, and start the negotiations as early as you can, so you can get the people you want and the dates you need to fit your delivery schedule. It's easier to pencil dates and then tweak them as things slip than to have to book from scratch. You may want to use different post facilities for the visuals and the sound – some post houses specialise in either visual or sound post, or you can do the 'one-stop shop' option (i.e. both processes under one roof). The advantage of this latter option is that you may be able to do a better deal, or even a 'buy-out', and you have one fewer place to lose tapes in! A buy-out in this regard is a set price to post produce each of your programmes based on a reasonable estimate of the time required for each process.

Do bear in mind that you get what you pay for in post production as well as in everything else. You may be able to negotiate hard and get a cheap deal on post with a company that you have not used before. Try to get some independent feedback from previous clients, and if you're nervous about their expertise it may be worth paying for a slightly more expensive but experienced facilities house with good technical support and a proven track record who are likely to respond quickly and efficiently when machinery goes down or problems occur.

Remember to always pencil dates and don't confirm them until as late as possible in case edits overrun. Some of the post production processes can happen in a different order from the one spelt out here, and some of the processes can happen at the same time; just talk to the facilities manager about the route they will follow. A diagram of how things will progress can be very helpful to you, and to other members of your team – you can do this yourself and distribute it.

One last thing: if you use a post house that has off-line suites in-house as well as all your post production facilities, you will probably get a better deal if you book everything there (i.e. the off-line edit cost will be cheaper if you stay in-house for all your post needs). Expect to pay a bit more if you separate your off-line and post facilities.

Co-productions and re-versioning

If you are running a co-production project which requires one or more re-versioned masters, then obviously this will take more time to post produce and will be more costly. It might be that the length of the final programme will vary, with more breaks which may occur at different points, or, indeed, a 'seamless' version (no breaks at all) may be required for one of your Broadcasters. There may also be a requirement for different material in each version. For example, if one of your co-funders is British and the other American, each may require more UK or US stories respectively. The UK version will have a UK voice-over but the US version may well be narrated by an American voice-over. There are plenty of American-accented V/O artists in this country, so be prepared to run a selection of them past the US Broadcaster and they can choose a preferred option. As soon as you have a potential artist, pencil the V/O dates with their agent and check that they are available for all your sessions and not busy on other projects.

If the versions are significantly different, involving re-cuts of the project, then you will need to book extra off-line time to cover this and extend your editor and director's contracts accordingly. My advice would be to first be very clear about what each version requires; a chart demonstrating these requirements will clarify it for all concerned. Then speak to the post production house about how best to achieve a route for these different versions to be post produced. Again, pictorial explanations of the route the post production will follow are useful to circulate to everyone and you should make sure that you understand these requirements and have costed them accordingly. Post production is an area that can go spectacularly over-budget in the twinkling of an eye, so be aware of any late changes that a Broadcaster might try and make to the demands – they will have to expect to pay extra for anything that wasn't stated clearly in the original contract specifications. Send a list to the facilities house of exactly what copies are required and for whom, and put in writing exactly what you want printed on the labels of these different tapes before sending this to the post production house in good time. It will help keep the different versions clear and ensure that you don't send them to the wrong Broadcasters.

Re-versioning should be discussed with the whole team as early in the prep period as possible as it may impact on all sorts of things like choice of contributors, locations, stories – anything in fact that goes to make up your programme or series.

So, keep in close contact with your post production facility, and – at the risk of being boring – I'll say again: don't ever be afraid to ask questions if you don't understand something.

See Chapter 19 on Deliverables for details of the paperwork that must accompany the masters.

19 Deliverables

I have mentioned these crucial documents at various points in previous chapters – now we need to look at them in more detail.

It used to be that when you delivered master tapes to a Broadcaster you also had to send them a raft of paperwork, but this seems to have dwindled to a mere trickle for UK Broadcasters. And, of course, the actual physical paperwork is more often replaced with its electronic equivalent. Let's deal with UK deliverables first.

UK deliverables

Whether you are working on a UK or an international project the principle is the same: you should obtain your deliverables list, which is usually part of the contractual documentation, as early in the process as you can. Read through it carefully and raise any technical queries that you have with your editor or post production facility.

When you deliver a master to a UK Broadcaster, you will also send along with it some sort of form or letter which lists its technical specifications, which should comply with the Broadcaster's requirements and which, hopefully, the post production house should have compiled for you. Forward this on to the Broadcaster and keep a copy in your production file.

When you deliver a master you will also be required to submit a post production script (PPS) which is a verbatim transcription of exactly what is in your programme. This is usually presented in a particular format, with two columns – the one on the right containing all the sound content (voice-over, music, sound effects, etc.), and the left one representing precisely what is on the screen at any given moment (for example pieces to camera, captions, archive, stills, etc.). Somewhere in the page will be a third column which will contain the timings of what is on the screen, although this may be included in each of the other two columns (see the example page of a post production script on the website 🖥). These scripts can be done by your co-ordinator, if they have the time, or you can send them out to a specialist company, in which case they will cost you a bit but will be done, efficiently and quickly, by someone very experienced in producing such documents.

British Broadcasters used to require a 'programme as completed' form (PAC) as part of their deliverables. This was a fairly long and detailed document that contained, for example, a source list for archive and stills, a music cue sheet, plus a synopsis of the programme(s) you were delivering. A BBC PAC, for example, began with details of the actual programme, whether it formed part of a strand, what its TX time and date were, and then went on to request a programme synopsis which would often form the basis for a description in a TV listings magazine. There was a section where you listed all the contributors in the programme and whether they belonged to any union – for example if the actors were Equity members. There followed a number of sections for listing information on the copyright of any material within the programme which had not been specially shot, and also a music cue sheet itemising, sourcing and timing all the music used within the programme. Once you completed this PAC and submitted it, it was kept on file by the Broadcaster and referred to if the programme was sold internationally. These requirements are changing all the time, so it's best to be clear about exactly what your particular Broadcaster needs at the start of your project.

Whereas all release forms and location agreements used to be delivered in hard copy for all UK Broadcasters, there is now an on-line platform called Silvermouse which electronically accepts all these items, and other deliverables, on behalf of Channel 4 and ITV for example. Soundmouse is the sound arm of this organisation and is where you upload your music cue sheets using their software and creating it from the 'ground up'. All this information is stored and can be accessed by the Broadcasters and other production companies, making the paperless office a present-day reality.

Check out www.silvermouse.com to gain insight into the world of deliverables, or call them on 020 7420 2120 to chat or email: info@silvermouse.com.

Even if your co-ordinator actually plods their way through the deliverables, you need to check them yourself before they are sent out – errors could be costly for the Broadcaster and, by extension, your company. For example, if you know that one piece of archive can be cleared for World except for use in the US, then you need to flag this clearly so that it can be replaced by the Broadcaster if there are sales to America. Completing deliverables requirements is a laborious but not particularly difficult task, so you should make sure you make time for it at the end of your contract. If this isn't possible and you have to leave it for someone else to do, make sure you pass on information about any unresolved problems in your handover notes when you leave.

You will also be required to keep, on file, copies of all the freelance contracts on your project: the music composer if there is one and the CGI house, the narrator plus all your freelance personnel along with, of course, all the licences you have gathered for archive, stills and any other copyright material. I'd recommend producing a log of all the archive and stills, itemising all the timings, sources and fees for this material. I would always send deliverables with a covering document which lists precisely all the items you are sending so that you know what you have completed and what might still be outstanding. When late items come in you can deliver them with a further covering note. It's useful to have this confirmation of your actions, especially when you are delivering multiple pro-grammes, not just as an *aide mémoire* but also as proof of sending so that you can then invoice for your final portion of production fee when everything is finally delivered. I once had an almighty bust-up with a UK Broadcaster who lost every last deliverable and swore I'd never sent them until I produced the copy of the accompanying letter. Which wouldn't now happen, of course, because you could just send the lost documents again electronically.

And a mention here that even if you haven't been sending regular cost reports to your Broadcaster, they will almost certainly want to see a copy of the final cost report as part of your deliverables. When you begin a project, a new trust account will generally be set up in the specific name of that project and all your money transactions will go through that account. The Broadcaster, under the terms of their contract with your company, will have the right to see all the relevant bank statements and though they may not exercise that right they will need to feel confident that everything is pukka on the accountancy front.

On each new project make sure you check carefully the deliverables required by the Broadcaster, as they may change each time. I can't say this often enough: never assume that the deliverables will be the same on your next project as they were on the last one. And remember that if you are doing a co-production with two or more different Broadcasters, then your deliverables lists may vary considerably and you'll need to keep on top of who wants what. Again, logging everything required early in your project will help you collect the required items throughout the project, rather than having to chase after things at the end when it will all be much more difficult to pin down.

Now let's just look at the US Broadcasters' deliverables, because they do tend to want more of everything.

US deliverables

Broadcasters like National Geographic and Discovery Channel usually require more information, along with various logs of what you are sending. Some US Broadcasters want their deliverables uploaded electronically, but some still require hard copies so you'll need to check with your Broadcaster what they want. If they do require hard copies I'd advise you to try and start the process of photocopying everything as early as you can, in 'down' moments throughout your project, so you aren't left with rain forests' worth of photo-copying to do at the end. And you need to clone your US deliverables and keep this clone in the office as archive. I would advise you that if this is on paper you should organise it well with labelled dividers to separate out items and with as much attention to detail as you can muster. A neat, carefully produced file of paperwork is likely to impress its recipient who will, be assured, check everything down to the last detail.

As with UK Broadcasters you will need a post production script; check to see if they have a particular template they want you to use. And National Geographic will also want a fully annotated script. This is a hefty document, a script with added information, which takes considerable time to produce; indeed the researcher should be working on it during the edit period. Every single fact within your script will need to have two sources that have been verified and listed in footnotes by your researcher. The researcher will liaise with National Geographic's Standards and Practices Department (S&P) and the facts must all be verified in time for the script to be signed off well before the narration record. Nat. Geo. require this high level of scrupulousness, in line with all the material they produce – for example their magazine, which can be quoted as a source in academic dissertations.

Firstly you will need to deliver, or scan, every release and location agreement to the US Broadcaster – but you must also use your time coded master to list when each contributor makes their first appearance in the programme (time code it) and also when each location first crops up. This forms a log that gets sent with the originals. And if any contributors are filmed but don't actually make it into the final programme they must be listed as well and their absence duly noted.

All your freelance contracts, along with a log of who is who on the team, will also be required and this should include personnel who are staff (paid on the payroll), which fact should be noted against their names, although you won't have a contract for them. And of course they will need the licences for all the archive and stills and a log of all their source details plus what sort of licences you have, timings, and the cost of each use (see template ▣). You will have to do this yourself unless you have been able to afford a film researcher to draw up a log before they leave the project – and even then you will have to add in the precise timings yourself, once you have the BITC DVD master to help you.

Make sure you send a full contact list at the beginning of the project which should be regularly updated, and keep a copy too – always handy to take on to future projects to remind you of the contact details for good people. The Broadcaster will also want a log of all the CGI shots and their timings, plus a full caption list and, of course, the credit roller or cards in their final form.

If I haven't covered it already, once your edit is nearing its end you should be compiling a list of people and companies for the credits, and you should obtain the appropriate template from the Broadcaster to see what order they want this list to follow, and also how long it should run. Draft it and send it around to the series producer, the executive, the director, the head of production, the film researcher, the AP – in short, anyone who may have names to add – and check and double-check that you have spelled every name correctly (I speak from bitter experience). The list should also be sent to the Broadcaster so they can add their in-house credits. Run it past someone else for a further typo check because sometimes it needs a fresh pair of eyes to pick up errors. Once your credit list has been completed, get it signed off by the Broadcaster (it may form part of a payment Milestone) and it's ready to send to the post production facility along with the caption list in time for the on-line, when these bits of text will be added to the body of the programme. Eventually it will, of course, form part of the deliverables as well.

American projects usually demand a number of deliverable items throughout your project and not just at the end. For example, the US Broadcaster will require a shooting script and a call sheet a given number of days prior to your shoot period. And you will be expected to deliver a number of stills, taken during principal photography, in a preferred format and accompanied by a log which details what is in each still. And since these should not be 'screen grabs' (stills taken from actual rushes) you will need to arrange this in advance with your crew and provide a digital camera for this purpose, along with written instructions on the call sheet outlining exactly what is required. It might be best to discuss this in advance and deputise someone to take these photographs and return them to you after the shoot for logging.

Once your edit begins, a selects promo reel will probably be required at the rough cut stage. Usually this is a Milestone requirement and is a 20-minute selection of footage chosen by the director and editor of 'action oriented' and similar footage for use in making trails for the programme or series. There is usually a very prescriptive description of what this footage should consist of from your Broadcaster. In addition, at the rough cut stage, you could also be required to send: behind-the-scenes footage (material depicting the crew at work), a brief synopsis of each programme and the series, spokesperson contact details (people who could be approached for their contributions to possible PR opportunities), talent biographies (a CV and written biography of any major actors or presenters from your project), a host biog (self-explanatory), and a GPS description of each shoot location. Check for any or all of these.

At fine-cut you might also be expected to deliver: a paragraph and one-page description for each programme and the series, some web facts, blogs – and I won't go into any more detail because these items get more and more complex and exhaustive (and exhausting!). I mention them to reiterate how carefully you need to examine these specifications when they land on your desk. You would be well advised to draft a log of all the items required, which indicates what was required and when. I'd then have a brief meeting with your editor(s) at the start of each off-line to go through these demands and set up a system where they are reminded, in good time, of what is about to fall due. Some of these deliverables take time and effort to produce – time taken out of your precious off-line edit – but it has to be done, and done on time, because usually they are tied in to cash payments from the Broadcaster and failure to send them will mean a cash flow problem for your company. These payments are known as Milestones and they occur throughout the project period as dates when the next cash flow payment can be 'drawn down' (but only if the relevant delivery items have been received). The selects promo reel, for example, will require an accompanying document that lists timings and details about what is contained within it, and most of the other items will also require some sort of covering paperwork which you or your co-ordinator will be preparing in advance wherever possible. These fragments of the programme are generally used for trails which are put together by the Broadcaster, so it might be better to send material that is specially shot as any archive will need to be cleared for promotional purposes. One last thing: check and double-check what sort of format your physical deliverables need to be done on and what technical specs are required (NTSC or PAL and clean tapes or DVDs rather than with BITC). There may also be material to be delivered at picture lock and all this will be listed in those pesky deliverables requirements!

At the time of writing my example of a Channel 4 deliverable document is two pages long. The US channel document runs to 19 pages!

Delivery of masters to the US is usually done twice - one master couriered and a second one sent two weeks later, upon confirmation and acceptance of the master. Depending on the contractual terms of your project you may have to deliver the rushes to the Broadcaster as well, and since this is usually done using a courier company like Fedex it could prove expensive, so try and keep some money back in your travel budget (schedule 31) to cover it. It wouldn't hurt to deliver everything by courier when you are working with the US and, for safety's sake I would deliver anything in the UK either by courier, Special Delivery or Registered mail; keep the paperwork from these courier or post office transactions as proof of sending. If you are delivering electronically there isn't such a problem, though it might be helpful to draw attention to each delivery with your Broadcast contact by email or telephone, just to remind them that they can pay you your next cash flow payment.

20 The other side of production management

This final chapter, in some respects, contains the most important elements of production management. I can bang on endlessly about compliance, budgets, cost reports, schedules and the like, but the real heart of production management is not so easy to teach because it's about people skills. Human beings are a strange lot and can behave in all sorts of unfathomable ways; your job is to try and work out roughly why and how you can get the best out of your team (and stop them from killing each other!). In the long working hours and stressful atmosphere of modern-day television, people can lose both their sense of perspective and their sense of humour, and part of your remit is to defuse potential discord before it threatens to explode. I don't mean to paint a black picture of the typical production office; it's often full of comedic moments and people rubbing along with each other in an agreeable way. But there may be times when you will have to head off or confront discord, antipathy or aggression. And of course, it helps if you can remain calm and reasonable in such disputes. Screaming matches in the middle of the office are unpleasant and don't do anything for the team's morale.

To help maintain your sanity in a crisis of any kind, try to concentrate on being professional. By this I mean not taking things personally and employing courtesy at all times, even when you're actually furious. Speak in a quiet but firm voice and try to maintain an unruffled demeanour, at least superficially.

A sense of humour has often been my most useful tool so don't forget the value of a bout of silliness or the odd joke in a tense situation. Sometimes teasing a colleague – not in an unkind way, but with a twinkling eye – can make a point with grace and humour. You are not laughing *at* them but encouraging them to see the funny side of the situation you all find yourselves in. And if they tease you too, that's good – it shows that they feel comfortable around you.

I had the good luck to work with a chap on several projects who is a rare example of a brilliant people manager. He never (well, rarely!) lost his temper, was calm, funny, thoughtful and he listened to people, to what they meant as well as what they said. I recall running a voice-over session with him once where the narrator was a nightmare of fluffed lines, pronunciation errors and sheer bad temper. My colleague kept his cool and when we broke for lunch quietly told me that he thought the narrator was screwing it up partly because he hadn't done any prep, but also because he hadn't eaten any breakfast! At the time I thought this hysterical, but he was probably right: indeed, the narrator's whole demeanour changed after he had eaten lunch (and also, probably, sunk a couple of pints) and his performance improved from then on. That particular narrator was always, thereafter, hired in the afternoons for the voice-over recording sessions.

So it helps to be empathetic. This entails careful listening and working out the possible cause of anger or irritability. Can you help to alleviate the negative feelings? It might be a good idea to keep a supply of sweeties or fruit on your desk so that people can help themselves when they feel peckish (assuming the budget can stand this small outlay). Often irritability can spring from anxiety. A director who is being difficult might be extremely worried about an upcoming shoot or Broadcast screening, so try and cut them some slack even if you feel like smacking them. A word or two of reassurance about their superior abilities might help too.

The lesson here is that as you get to know the people on your team, you should play to their strengths and not their weaknesses. This seems obvious, but all too often people are put into situations for which they are ill-suited and this will predispose them to fail, which is a humiliating and pointless waste of time for everyone concerned.

My favourite co-worker also had a nice habit of spotting when anyone around him had put an extra bit of effort into something. A much put-upon office manager, faced with yet another desk move and demand for computer and telephone, still managed to smile and do the impossible with grace. She was rewarded with an email from him, copied to all the upper management in the company, thanking her for her efforts and goodwill, and she almost cried with gratitude. I learned a valuable lesson there – praise people as often as you can about the things they have done right. And a useful by-product is that they may be more willing to listen if and when you ever have to chastise them.

It goes without saying that you should always try to behave with integrity and honesty. As a production manager you will be responsible for someone else's money, sometimes a very large amount of it. Your whole reputation rests on being honest and transparent in all your dealings. I would never, for example, borrow cash from the petty cash tin without putting in an IOU, and even then I would borrow only in an emergency. I always discourage members of the team from treating petty cash as a useful substitute when they've forgotten to go to the hole in the wall. That isn't what it's there for, and when you come to ask for it back people can be remarkably forgetful that they borrowed it in the first place.

Behaving with integrity towards the people you work with should always be a priority, even when you don't actually like them very much. You will always like some colleagues more than others, but try to prevent it affecting your fair dealings with everyone on your team.

I think it's also part of your job to bring a little fun into the office. Even on a tight budget you should be able to provide the odd treat: a bottle of wine at the end of a hard week, a team lunch, a slap-up afternoon tea, or a picnic in a nearby green space. Some of the team may grumble that they haven't got time for such silliness, but you will know better and will see that after such a break everyone will feel energised and work more enthusiastically than before. The projects that will stay in your mind at the end of a long and successful career will be the ones that were the most fun. Honestly. Even if they also contained the most nightmares …

Which brings me to the egos that you will come across in your professional life. When you consider the competitiveness of the industry, to succeed in it one needs to have a strong sense of one's own worth coupled with driving ambition to get to the top of one's chosen field. Inevitably, this often results in egotistical behaviour. The people on the creative side of a project are more likely to get demanding and intractable, and less likely to listen to budget concerns. I am often asked how to deal with difficult people, and the answer is that I don't really know – you just have to try and keep calm, work out why they are behaving as they are, and then consider how best to deal with them. You could try and take them away from the office, for a quiet coffee or lunch somewhere, and discuss what is making them hard to handle. I did this once with a series producer who was a bit of a bully, and he was gobsmacked to have this pointed out to him; he just hadn't seen it in himself, and his behaviour began to change immediately. This kind of thing is hard to do but can get a really positive result (and if you meet in a public place they are less likely to become loud and aggressive). And don't hesitate to call on upper management to help make your points. Sometimes a stroppy male director will listen only to another stroppy male!

In television it is curious how the various roles tend to end up as male or female jobs. Production managers, for example, are more often female. In the 210-plus members of the PMA a very small percentage are men, though these chaps are often the ones who run high-end dramas and feature films. Production co-ordinators, secretaries and production staff in general are females, as are heads of production, probably because they work their way up the production ladder, honing their people skills on the way. Directors, series producers, camera operators, sound recordists and editors tend to be male – with exceptions of course, but female DOPs are still rare. The common excuse is that camera and sound equipment is often too heavy for them to carry around, but many mothers carry heavy children around for hours on end, so how can that be?

There also exists a very clear hierarchy, and sometimes the people higher up the ladder take out their bad temper on the less powerful simply because they can. You should always protect your production team from such spleen-venting by requesting that if a director or series producer, for example, has a problem with a team member they should come to you and you will deal with it, quietly and privately.

Knowing yourself

Before you embark on the career path of production management, think carefully about whether you are suited for it. You should be organised to the point of being anal, have an eye for detail and be meticulous about doing critical things like issuing contracts on time and getting deliverables back. You should also have a natural affinity for figures and money. That's harder to learn, but you can't avoid it; much of your job will be staring at columns of figures and trying to make the cash stretch to cover what you need. So if numbers scare you – do something else. I think you also need to be reasonably punctual and able to remember things. My memory is poor so I write everything down and keep endless lists. And you mustn't be afraid to ask questions. There are occasions where people in the know will bandy jargon about, and if you don't know what something means – just ask.

You need to be fit and healthy with the stamina for working long hours with a lot of stress, and this isn't everyone's cup of tea. If you are the sort of person who takes more than the odd 'sickie', that doesn't sit well with the job, and neither do you want people like that in your team. Your co-ordinator, for example, needs to be punctual, reliable and hard-working and, almost more importantly, they need to be cheerful. I work closely with my co-ordinator and don't want someone sitting opposite me with face like a smacked bottom. Part of their remit is to be chipper. You and they will need to treat the rest of the team with courtesy and good humour, and to have a pleasant and helpful attitude, even when the going gets tough. You should give your co-ordinator lots of praise when you can, and the odd box of chocolates or bunch of flowers, or an early departure or day off when things quieten down a bit. Co-ordinators, production assistants and secretaries often work harder than anyone else for longer hours and get paid less, so nurture them and they will blossom. It's useful to give them a bit of training when you have time – teaching a good co-ordinator to study the budget and use a cost monitor in down-time will be good for everyone. How else do people advance up the ladder when training in the industry has virtually disappeared?

In order to maintain your health during a gruelling career you must also make sure that you take regular holidays and time off when you can. Try always to have a good break between freelance projects and spend some of that hard-earned cash on relaxing – if you can't take a long holiday, can you manage a weekend away? Or a few days at a spa for a bit of pampering? A long and luxurious massage followed by a facial or pedicure? Or a week off at home sleeping in and catching up with your friends – remember them?

When you are working all the hours that god sends, a few minutes to yourself and a change of scene can help. I always leave the office at lunchtime, for instance. Going to collect a sandwich (could you eat it in a café rather than at your desk while gazing at 57 unanswered emails?) and taking a walk round the block will revive your energy and set you up for the long afternoon. Try not to skip meals, because your blood sugar levels will plummet and you'll feel tired and dispirited. I wouldn't call meetings over the lunch period unless I was providing food because I can't think straight when my stomach is grumbling and I assume nobody else can either.

Keeping fit needs a bit of work too. Yoga, swimming, kick boxing – whatever your favoured form of exercise, make sure you keep it up. Try to maintain your outside interests even when working like a dog – I know how hard it can be, but there is more to life than work. And a hobby needs to be attended to so you can have another topic other than telly to witter on about to friends, some of whom may not work in TV and will tire of your endless anecdotes of broken cameras in Dubai.

Pay attention to your diet. There will be a tendency to eat fast food and junk, so try to ensure that you eat healthily with plenty of fruit in your desk drawer. Personally I regard chips as medicinal when I'm feeling fed-up but I try to offset this with green vegetables and fruit whenever I can. I suppose what I'm saying is pay attention to yourself and don't expect your body to respond well to constant bad treatment – it's a machine and will need care, fuel, exercise and rest in between the stress and hard work. Life is not a rehearsal and good health is precious, more precious than the TV programme that you have just invested a year of your life in only to have your best friend say, 'Oh, was it on last night? Sorry, I missed it!' Lecture over.

A few other bits and pieces require a mention.

Learning to delegate can be a hard lesson. If you pass on chores to your co-ordinator, let them get on with it and be prepared for them to make mistakes. Try to keep an eye on their progress but they must have the time and space to learn and get it wrong sometimes. We *all* make mistakes and most of them can be put right somehow. If you can't trust other people to work without interfering every five minutes you will be in the office until midnight every day checking their efforts. And if you spot that someone has a skill at something, try to give them the opportunity to exploit it.

Conversely, there may be occasions when team members are set on a career path (like being a director, which is what most youngsters seem to want to do when they come into the industry) for which you feel they are not suited. In such a case you might gently suggest that they consider pursuing a different goal that might be more suited to their amazing talents. It's all in the telling, so you start that sort of conversation by outlining their terrific aptitude for whatever it is and encouraging them to think clearly about their ambitions.

Being a cheeky young girlie can sometimes work wonders when your own brand of sober responsibility might not … so if you have production staff who can get things done just by being persuasive on the telephone, for example – exploit it! Speaking of cheek, I recall making a lovely little programme once about a chap who could teach people to speak a foreign language very quickly and had actually taught Woody Allen to speak French in a weekend. The director sat at his desk one day musing about how nice it would be to have an interview with Mr Allen about this experience and, just like that, he called up Woody Allen's company and asked if he could grab a quick interview on his next shoot. Much to my amazement an interview was granted and it made a lovely little piece in the programme. The lesson here is – risk it. They can only say no.

A word about firing people. If you manage to get through your career without having to do this you will be very lucky. Sometimes you hire someone and they just don't work out, for whatever reason, and you will have to get rid of them. Be aware that there are very clear guidelines about how you go about this and take advice from your legal representative, PACT or ACAS (see Appendix) about what to do – it's usually verbal warnings followed by written notification, but make sure you follow all the procedures. Being fired is one of the most humiliating things that can ever happen to you, so while it will never be painless, try to be as kind as possible. Be clear, firm, don't confuse the issue and do think beforehand about what you want to say – and always, always have someone else with you in the room.

If you find yourself being fired and you don't think it has been a fair process, then take advice from ACAS. Ring them up, explain your situation and see if you have grounds for any kind of appeal or claim. They are extremely helpful and the service is free. If your claim progresses into a Tribunal situation they will mediate between you and your ex-employer completely neutrally and try to arrange settlement before anything goes to court.

Finally, do consider the subject of a dress code for the office. We all know that TV is very relaxed about such things and jeans and tee-shirts are fine in the office. However, if you are going to see someone about a job I would always advise something a bit smarter. I think – old-fashioned thing that I am – that if you are going to be responsible for a lot of somebody else's money then you should look as if you will take it seriously. The same is true if you have to meet a Broadcaster. The creative members of the team may get away with looking grubby and dishevelled, but first impressions count, and wearing something on the smart side when discussing budgets and cost control tends to reassure management as well as Broadcasters. And if you are sending your crew to film in any kind of smart or very formal occasion you should check with the location beforehand whether they will be required to wear something other than grimy tracksuit bottoms and a baggy fleece. It is a rare joy to see a cameraman shooting at a swanky event wearing a suit and tie.

And when you have some down-time between projects, try reading *The Devil's Candy* by Julie Salamon or *Final Cut: The Film That Sank United Artists* by Stephen Bach. They are both books about profligate and out-of-control filmmakers – the former about the film *The Bonfire of the Vanities* and the latter about what happened during the making of

Heaven's Gate. Both movies caused mayhem and financial meltdown for their various backers and funders. It's somehow reassuring that other people, in a huge and spectacular fashion, can make a complete hash of completing a project on budget.

Good luck in your future career ... and have fun!

Appendix: help agencies, trade unions, industry jargon and other useful references

Help agencies

There follows a number of help agencies who can assist you with specific questions you may have. I have also listed a couple of training organisations followed by a small selection of other groups you might want to check out. For a much more comprehensive list of media-related organisations and contact details, please see the Production Managers Association website, which lists contact details for most of them; alternatively just enter their name in your search engine and follow the directions on the websites.

ACAS: Advisory, Conciliation and Arbitration Service
www.acas.org.uk
Acas helpline (Tel) 08457 47 47 47
ACAS aims to improve organisations and working life through better employment relations. They help with employment relations by supplying up-to-date information, independent advice and high-quality training, and working with employers and employees to solve problems and improve performance.

British Council
www.britishcouncil.org/arts-film.htm
(Tel) 020 7389 3194
The British Council Film Department promotes contemporary and innovative UK film to audiences around the world, working in both lead and supporting roles on showcases, workshops, festivals, conferences, tours, residencies and virtual projects. It also collaborates with artists and other cultural organisations, building skills, capacity and cultural awareness, creating access to audiences and markets, and promoting international partnership and creative exchange.

PACT: Producers Alliance for Film and Television

www.pact.co.uk

(Tel) 0207 380 8230

PACT is the UK trade association that represents the commercial interests of independent feature film, television, children's, animation and interactive media companies. PACT offers a range of business services to its members, actively lobbies government organisations at local, regional, national and European level, and negotiates minimum terms with the major UK broadcasters and other content buyers.

PMA: Production Managers Association

www.pma.org.uk

(Tel) 0208 758 8699

Email: pma@pma.org.uk

Situated at Ealing Studios – the office is run by the hugely helpful and knowledgeable Caroline Fleming. The current cost of full annual membership is around £190 and worth every penny!

Some of the benefits of membership are: an employment register – when you are looking for work, you add your name and contact details to a list that prospective employers can consult and then contact you about up-coming projects; and a jobs noticeboard just for members if you miss the global emails about employment opportunities advertised through the PMA.

PMA members are eligible for a variety of industry discounts and have access to a list of recommended production co-ordinators and accountants. 'The Forum' is a private email newsgroup where members share useful information and support each other professionally; it has proved an enormous success and has built up an archive of information which can be searched by the members. There is also a quarterly newsletter entitled 'The Bottom Line', and a really useful legal service – you can call for excellent legal advice on a range of problems, all free. PMA has over 200 members at the time of writing and the organisation has a number of sponsors who run regular social and training evenings for the members. At these evenings you can find out what services are on offer and they will give you a discount if you mention you are a PMA member when you call. You can also network with other PMA members and find out what's going on – as well as having a nice glass of pink wine and a vol-au-vent.

Training organisations

Documentary Filmmakers Group (DFG)

www.dfgdocs.com/training

(Tel) 020 7249 6600

Email: info@dfgdocs.com

A national organisation working to promote documentary filmmaking talent and innovation in the UK. DFG is a centre for documentary-specific training for established and aspiring filmmakers, and a member of the Skillset Media Academy Network. They provide a wide range of consultancy services, long and short courses, corporate training and bespoke training, covering every aspect of documentary filmmaking, and all their tutors are practising broadcast professionals. Unusually for a training provider, DFG is directly linked to a production company, Mosaic Films.

DFG is committed to encouraging, stimulating, promoting and supporting the growth of a strong community of documentary filmmakers and film audiences, and runs a range of networking, information and advice events for documentary filmmakers at different stages in their careers, as well as providing a number of resources via the website, www.dfgdocs.com, and the DFG Community, a growing online community of documentary filmmakers who share insider news and a range of practical resources.

Indie Training Fund

www.indietrainingfund.com

The Indie Training Fund is a charity that funds and delivers training for the UK independent TV and digital media production sectors. Established, funded and run by member companies (big and small from around the UK), ITF provides members with in-house training and consultancy, plus a range of short courses. For more information see www.indietrainingfund.com.

National Film & TV School (NFTS)

www.nfts.co.uk

(Tel) 01494 677903

The National Film & Television school offers the only year-long Diploma in Production Management, with industry-recognised workshops including Health & Safety, First Aid, 1st AD-ing and EP Scheduling and Budgeting. Students work alongside award-winning MA filmmakers and get experience on a vast range of projects including drama, animation, documentary and television entertainment. Application deadline in June for September start. For information go to www.nfts.co.uk and look under Diploma courses.

ShortCourses@NFTS also offers one-week courses for Production Management (both in Drama and Factual) for people already in the industry. These courses are offered at various times throughout the year. Check out the ShortCourses section on the NFTS website for details: www.nfts.co.uk or ring 01494 677903.

TV and Film Organisations

BAFTA

www.bafta.org

The British Academy of Film and Television Arts exists to support, develop and promote the art forms of the moving image, by identifying and rewarding excellence, inspiring practitioners and benefiting the public.

As a charitable organisation, one of its key activities is to give members, the industry and the public the opportunity to learn first-hand from leading practitioners in the film, television and video games industries, via its year-round Learning & Events programme.

Among BAFTA's other activities are its annual Awards ceremonies, held in the UK, which set the gold standard for industry practitioners everywhere.

BFI
bfi.org.uk
(Tel) 0207 928 3232
The BFI (British Film Institute) promotes understanding and appreciation of Britain's rich film and television heritage and culture. Established in 1933, the BFI is custodian of the BFI National Archive, the largest archive of moving image material in the world, and also runs a range of activities and services, including venues BFI Southbank and BFI IMAX, the BFI National Library, film magazine *Sight and Sound*, nationwide theatrical and DVD releases, educational programmes for all ages and the internationally renowned London Film Festival and London Lesbian and Gay Film Festival.

Women in Film & Television (WFTV)
www.wftv.org.uk
Women in Film & Television is the premier membership organisation for women working in creative media in the UK, and part of an international body consisting of more than 10,000 women. They host a variety of events throughout the year, present a glamorous awards ceremony every December, and run a mentoring programme for their members. They also organise networking evenings, collaborate with industry bodies on research projects, and lobby for women's interests.

Trade Unions

BECTU: Broadcasting Entertainment Cinematograph & Theatre Union
www.bectu.org.uk
As a trade union with extensive responsibilities in the media and entertainment sectors UK-wide, BECTU represents the interests of staff and freelancers on issues as broad as pay, Health & Safety, training and equality. The union's membership reflects all industry occupations (with the exception of actors and musicians, who are looked after by their respective unions); the background artist is the only performance occupation organised by BECTU. Students working towards a career in the industry are invited to sign up to the Student Register, www.bectu.org.uk/student-register, the union's contact scheme, for relevant up-dates on the union's work and for invites to special events. New entrants are offered a discounted rate on their first year's membership. More information about the union's activities, benefits and services is at www.bectu.org.uk. Queries can be raised via info@bectu.org.uk.

Equity
www.equity.org.uk
(Tel) 020 7379 6000
Email: info@equity.org.uk
Equity is the UK trade union representing professional performers and other creative workers from across the spectrum of the entertainment, creative and cultural industries.

MU
info@musiciansunion.org.uk
(Tel) 0207 840 5504
Musicians Union – exactly what it says!

British Chamber of Commerce
The BCC provides the media with British Chambers of Commerce surveys, reports and high-level comment/reaction to news that relates to and impacts on business. They also pass on the views of the Chamber of Commerce Network, which is spread across the UK. Using the media is a part of their lobbying strategy.

Film London
www.filmlondon.org.uk
(Tel) 020 7613 7676
The organisation that can help you find locations and guide you through the shooting process of filming anywhere in London, from parking to permits. Don't be afraid to call them even if you don't have much money – they deal equally helpfully with feature films and tiny budget TV programmes.

Film Offices
All London brozoughs and most areas throughout the UK have some sort of film office – call them and see what they offer. They also exist in many major towns abroad.

Global Film Solutions, Expedition Media and Remote Trauma
Three organisations who advise on anything to do with Health & Safety on a shoot, including hostile and unstable environments and adventure TV. (See also Chapter 13 on Health & Safety.)

HM Revenue and Customs
For advice regarding tax issues, self-employment, VAT, pensions and a host of other related issues.

The Independent Producer Handbook

This can be obtained from either Channels 4 or 5 and is a useful guide to programme-making. It contains, among other things, help on media law, compliance procedures and the OFCOM Broadcasting Code.

The Knowledge

www.theknowledgeonline.com
Email: knowledge@wilmington.co.uk
(Tel) 020 7549 8666
(Fax) 020 7549 8668

The Knowledge, available in printed and web formats, is regarded as a 'bible' for the UK film, television, video and commercial production industries. It is packed full of all the contacts and services you will need at any stage in the production process. The database contains over 19,000 entries, including more than 10,500 freelance crew and technicians spanning over 1,000 classifications. Included with this essential guide is The Know How, containing practical information, articles, maps – all useful information at any stage in the production process.

There are also a number of other media 'bibles' such as The Production Guide www.theproductionguide.co.uk.

London Underground Film Office

Email: filmoffice@tube.tfl.gov.uk
(Tel) 020 7918 0003

Filming in the tube or on the tube trains has become much easier than it used to be – if you have a crew of no more than five, for example, you can get a two-hour permit for £300 plus VAT (at the time of writing) for a location. If you have more than five crew then the rates are higher per hour. They will offer student and non-professional permits for a five-piece crew or less using lightweight handheld equipment for £30 plus VAT (at the time of writing) and you can negotiate rates for filming in a driver's cab – for more information email: filmoffice@tube.tfl.gov.uk.

Spotlight

www.spotlight.com
(Tel) 020 7437 7631

Very useful for casting directories and for finding out who an actor's agent is.

Jargon and industry terminology

Carnet – put simply, a passport for the film and sound kit which is stamped in and out of every country by Customs and Excise officers where it is required (i.e. anywhere outside the EU). Issued by the Chamber of Commerce, a carnet must be returned to them at the end of the shoot. It was put in place, I think, to ensure that people don't take items of kit abroad to sell.

Clapper board – that piece of equipment that you sometimes see on films; two pieces of wood or plastic clapped together with the slate and scene numbers written underneath. Its purpose is to synchronise the exact timing of the visual and sound elements of the film (which are being recorded separately) so that they can be perfectly matched in the edit. We have all seen amusing examples of mouth movements and words being 'out of sync'.

Disclaimer – the verbal warning at the beginning of CSI, for example, which tells the viewer that there are gory and bloody images to follow. Or that distressing sequences are contained in a news story. Or that there are flashing images in a programme – these can sometimes trigger epileptic fits in some viewers. Or a warning about bad language or 'scenes of a sexual nature' – anything, in short, that is the responsibility of the programme-maker to warn the viewer about so that they can turn off if they don't like it.

Honey wagon – mobile toilets for use on locations. They are driven there and supervised by a driver and hired by the day. Apparently they are called honey wagons because that's the colour of the dirty water when they are emptied. Yuk!

In the can – the process of having captured a shot or material on film (or tape). The expression is a relic of the days when film stock was kept rolled up in one of those big, circular tin cans.

Noddies – the shot of the person running an interview that the editor will use to illustrate that the interviewer is listening! They will often be almost imperceptibly nodding in agreement.

Pencil – what you do when you are booking but not confirming dates with crew members or your post production house. It means that you are not confirming the dates you are asking for until much later down the line. It has variations, too: a light pencil (very tentative booking), a heavy pencil (much more likely), and a second pencil – perhaps where you are asking for dates that already have a pencil on them but you're second in the queue. It carries with it an agreement that should someone else start asking for the same dates, you will have another conversation. When a pencil becomes a booking then you will be liable for part or full payment if you cancel.

Principal photography – the main period of filming on your project. This will also include any pick-up days during the edit, and you will need to extend this period in your insurance if your schedule gets extended.

Scratch narration or **guide narration** – the draft narration which is added to a programme during the off-line stage, usually recorded by the editor or director and which is replaced in the voice-over record at the end of the editing process.

Title search – you may be asked to check that your intended programme or series title has not been used before. There are companies who do this for you for a fee, and they will send you a full report on what they find.

Wildtrack or **Atmos** – the invaluable sounds that your sound recordist should record on the shoot. Even what sounds like silence will have bird song, traffic hum or a ticking clock in it. If the S/R doesn't do this automatically, remind the director to ask for it – valuable time will be saved in the edit searching through CDs of sound effects.

TV is stuffed with **acronyms** – here are some of them, but by no means a comprehensive list. Pay attention, there will be a quiz at the end!

ARC – Aspect Ratio Conversion – when a piece of material needs to be converted from one format to another (i.e. from 4x3 to 16x9).

BITC, VITC, LTC – all timing codes shown on tapes – see full description in Chapter 18 on Post Production.

CGI – Computer Generated Imagery or graphics.

C/U – a close-up. Just what it says: up close and personal. As opposed to a mid shot or a wide – all fairly self-explanatory. See Chapter 14 on Interviewing for advice on when to change shots during an interview.

GVs – general views, moving wallpaper for covering up the thin bits in your film, or the picures that accompany narration.

I/V – interview or piece to camera.

MIC – microphone.

RECCE – stems from the word reconnoitre, and refers to the visit to location (and possibly contributors) that is done prior to filming. Now sometimes known as a 'scout'.

SYNC – synchronisation is the root of this word and it usually refers to the dialogue that has been spoken by an interviewee. Thus the director will 'pull sync' when he decides which pieces of an interview he wants to include on screen. Sometimes this process is called a paper edit.

TECH RECCE – the recce where the various crew members go to locations to check power sources, etc. (See Chapter 12 on Recces.)

TECH SPEC – the technical specifications that apply to your programme, issued by the Broadcaster. You should ensure that both the editor and the post production house have copies for producing the master.

TX – transmission.

VAT – Value Added Tax, which is currently set at 17.5%. You need to know roughly how this works, but production managers ignore it because all budgets and costs are calculated 'net' or excluding the VAT element. However, you must ensure that all receipts and invoices which contain an element of VAT have a VAT number on them so that you can claim back the tax. These receipts must be secured: if they are missing, then the VAT element will have to be absorbed into your costs.

WRAP – refers to the end of the filming day and actually springs from the old days, standing for 'windback reel and print'. When the day's rushes were finished, the camera assistant would write this on the end of the film.

My favourite bit of industry jargon is 'kick, bollock and scramble', which means exactly what you'd imagine – the situation you're in when the going gets very stressed indeed.

And I once contracted a cameraman for a tiny interview that I was arranging for a friend making a corporate programme in the States. He asked me did I want 'arty', or just 'pan, tilt and invoice'?

Index

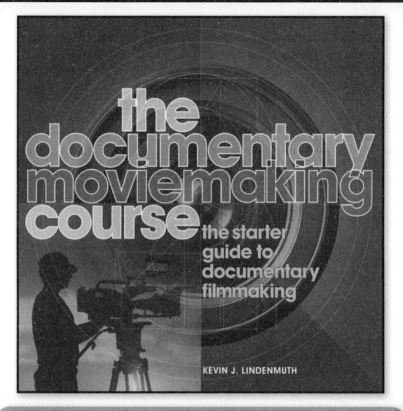